BERTOLUCCI'S DREAM LOOM

BERTOLUCCI'S

DREAM LOOM

A Psychoanalytic Study of Cinema

T. JEFFERSON KLINE

The University of Massachusetts Press

Amherst, 1987

Copyright © 1987 by The University of Massachusetts Press
All rights reserved
Printed in the United States of America
Set in Linoterm Aldus at The University of Massachusetts Press
Printed by Cushing-Malloy and bound by John Dekker & Sons

Kline, T. Jefferson (Thomas Jefferson), 1942–
 Bertolucci's dream loom.

 Bibliography: p.
 Includes index.
  1. Bertolucci, Bernardo—Criticism and interpretation.
 2. Moving-pictures—Psychological aspects.   I. Title.
 PN1998.A3B466357   1987   791.43'0233'0924   86–25038
 ISBN 0–87023–569–9 (alk. paper)

British Library Cataloguing in Publication Data are available.

Lovingly dedicated to
Julie, Ethan and Chloe

a friend may well
be reckoned the masterpiece
of nature.

RALPH WALDO EMERSON

CONTENTS

PREFACE

My interest in Bertolucci's work grew out of an initial encounter with *Last Tango in Paris*, which I found so disturbing that my unconscious "went to work" on the film. Upon waking the morning after first viewing the film, the word "Orpheus!" came to mind as some sort of talisman, which I could, at that moment, neither explain nor exorcise. This "disturbance" led me back to the film and ultimately to an essay on *Last Tango*, which was originally published in the *International Review of Psychoanalysis* in 1976 and formed the first threads of this book. From it and because of it, many other encounters with Bertolucci's work and with Bertolucci himself followed, moving forward to each new film that appeared, and backward toward *Prima della rivoluzione*, the last chapter to be written. Each film demanded an unusually complex and individual response, so fine was its architecture; yet from the entire set emerged a consistency of concern that demanded an overview. Given the implications of the Orpheus myth for *Last Tango* and the director's own tendency to speak of his work in relation to his own analysis, a psychoanalytic approach virtually imposed itself on this critical undertaking. There is, of course, a danger in imposing any methodology, coherence, or unity on a body of work so rich, complex, and, at times, anarchic. Most critical studies, however, attempt such coherence even when they disclaim it. Such is the fate of a careful reading: It offers a particular interpretation as somehow legitimized by the work under scrutiny.

I do not claim that the coherence I shall describe in Bertolucci's work is exclusive of other coherences. As Roland Barthes noted, coherence is the result of system, and it is up to each reader to acknowledge how his particular system manages to engender coherence. The ideology implicit and explicit in my approach I shall attempt to expose here in ways that both define it as a "legitimate" approach to the subject and relate it as an approach to Bertolucci's work.

I am indebted to many friends and colleagues for their encouragement, readings, and suggestions. I am especially beholden to Murray M. Schwartz, who first directed me to psychoanalysis as a tool of literary and cinematic analysis and without whose steadfast support the publication of this study simply would not have been possible. I am deeply grateful to Katy Kline for her early conviction that I should undertake this project. Charles Bernheimer, Tom Conley, and Rachel Jacoff provided extraordinarily perceptive readings of my manuscript and excellent suggestions for revision. Caroline Hemans provided much secretarial and bibliographical support. My thanks as well to Jerry Oremland, Marsha Kinder, Virginia Wright Wexman, Gerry Fitzgerald, and Bruce Sklarew for their interest in my work. Finally, to Julie Anderson, my constant inspiration for the last three years, I owe unlimited gratitude for her love, encouragement, and patience. I also owe special thanks to Boston University's Humanities Foundation for a grant that partially funded the publication of this book.

Several of the chapters in this book appeared in earlier versions in article form, and I would like to thank the following for their generous permission to reprint sections of those articles: excerpts from "The Absent Presence: Stendhal in Bertolucci's *Prima della revoluzione*," reprinted by permission of *Cinema Journal*; excerpts from "Endymion's Wake: Oneiric Projection and Protection in Bertolucci's Cinema," reprinted by permission of *Dreamworks*; excerpts from "Father as Mirror: Bertolucci's Oedipal Quest and the Collapse of Paternity," reprinted by permission of *Psychocultural Review*; excerpts from "Doubling *The Double*" in *Fearful Symmetry: Doubles and Doubling in Literature and Film*, reprinted by permission of The University Presses of Florida; excerpts from "Orpheus Transcending: Bertolucci's *Last Tango in Paris*," reprinted by permission of the *International Review of Psychoanalysis*; and excerpts from "The Unconformist" in *Modern European Filmmakers and the Art of Adaptation*, reprinted by permission of Frederick Ungar Publishing Company.

BERTOLUCCI'S DREAM LOOM

> It would be fine for me if films became a way of life. . . . Unfortunately
> there is still a kind of barrier of glass to break. . . . I said glass because
> behind it everything moves as in another world.
> BERNARDO BERTOLUCCI

1 BERTOLUCCI AND THE SPECIFICITIES OF CINEMA

"Where's love fit in?" shouts the middle-aged duenna of the dance hall in *Last Tango in Paris*, "Go to the movies to see love!" And so we did, for reviewers of the film proclaimed it "the most powerfully erotic movie ever made." [1] Response to *Tango*'s eroticism created an overnight box-office success in the United States, and suddenly Bernardo Bertolucci had become as familiar a name to American filmgoers as Fellini, Visconti, Antonioni, and Pasolini. In 1972, Americans were discovering a filmmaker who had already made his mark in Europe with *Before the Revolution* (1963), *Partner* (1968), *The Spider's Stratagem* (1970), and *The Conformist* (1970), none of which had been accorded more than scant attention in America. *The Conformist* was rediscovered following the success of *Last Tango*, and the future looked bright for the young Italian filmmaker. But American audiences have never again responded to Bertolucci's work as they did to those two films. *1900*, which appeared in 1976 after a protracted court battle over distribution and editing, was generally panned for its overly ambitious scale, its overt violence, and its exaggerated presentation of fascism. Not even Jill Clayburgh, fresh from her success in *An Unmarried Woman*, could save Bertolucci's next film, *Luna*. Although Bertolucci touted it as a new kind of melodrama, it failed to generate much critical or box-office interest. *Tragedy of a Ridiculous Man* emerged and disappeared with such rapidity that Bertolucci watchers began to wonder what had gone wrong.

Figure 1. Bernardo Bertolucci on the set of *Luna*. Courtesy The Museum
of Modern Art/Film Stills Archive.

The question implies, of course, that Bertolucci "lost his touch," that he was unable to sustain the intensity of his creative genius as displayed in *Last Tango* and *The Conformist*. It is the thesis of this book, however, that Bertolucci's work has not been adequately understood in the United States and that the films preceding and following *Last Tango* can be best appreciated when seen as integral parts of a larger project. Bertolucci implicitly endorsed such a thesis when he said of his work:

> The cinema is not an exceptional moment of life. I would like the cinema to parallel life. I am making always just one film. . . . It's one film even if it has many titles or chapters. It's the same film and it walks along with me. To make a film is a way of life. If we take out the title of the film and "The End" and put the films all together, we will have the figure of one man, of an auteur, transferred in many different characters naturally. But the film is one film.[2]

One might even say "one poem." The son of a major Italian poet, Atilio Bertolucci, Bernardo's artistic emergence was as a poet. His collection of poetry, *In ricerca del mistero* [In search of mystery] (1962), introduced many of the same themes, images, and concerns that were to characterize his later cinematic work. The fifth poem in the collection reads almost as an unconscious invocation of his future work in film:

> Che voglia di scapare via
> da Roma, senza dir niente
> in familia e alla gente
> che mi saluta per via,
> se scopro che cosa muta
> sulle gote e nelle pupilla
> di una madre—come brilla
> e arde la figura seduta
> felice ed obbediente della bruna
> giovane in una fotographia !
>
> Perdonami se sai amare la viltà
> di tuo figlio, intento a soffrire
> a voce alta, per farsi sentire.

(How I wanted to escape far
from Rome, without saying anything
to my family or to the people
who greeted me along my way,
something can be seen moving
on the cheeks and in the eyes
of a mother—how the seated figure
of a happy and dark haired youth
shines and glows
in a photograph !

Forgive me if you know how to love the unworthiness
of your son, I intend to suffer
out loud, to make myself heard.)[3]

The mother's tearful look at the photograph of her wayward son in this poem encapsulates much of Bertolucci's cinematic creativity, for to see and to be seen by the mother are opposite sides of a single issue: the quest for identity.[4] The way the poem projects this maternal glance into photography—and, with the phrase "se scopro che cosa muta," extends this projection into the realm of the cinematic—suggests that the cinema is a matrix of creative looking. The poet's intent to "suffer out loud" to make himself heard further emphasizes the degree to which the maternal look is related to poetic expression. Twenty years later, Bertolucci was to agree that the general title of all of his films could indeed be "Scena madri": the scene of the Mother.[5] At the anecdotal level of his films, Bertolucci's concern with maternal figures grows gradually from the presentation of surrogate mothers in the early films to the frankly incestuous mother in *Luna*. At a less explicit level, Bertolucci will conduct an extraordinarily rich meditation on the relationship of the cinematic act to the maternal figure.

But "Scena anti-padre" might also be an appropriate, if uncolloquial, general title of Bertolucci's cinematic opus, for struggles with father figures pervade his work. Having begun writing poetry in imitation of his father, he nevertheless felt "a competitive need to find my cinematographic identity." From the moment he began to make films, Bertolucci says, he stopped writing poetry, clearly rejecting his father's chosen way.[6]

Another, "more sensual" language beckoned, and Bertolucci launched into this new expression. In a sense, both languages were learned from his father: Not only was Atilio the avowed major influence on his son's poetry, but "My father taught me to look at cinema, to understand cinema, to love cinema. My love for films thus depends to a great extent on his love for films." But this indebtedness immediately gives way to a competitive reaction, for the younger Bertolucci adds, "I had the good fortune to be able to observe a cinema which preexisted me and to have roots, in order, I hope, to be able to liberate myself from them."[7]

At one level, Bertolucci's entire oeuvre can be understood as a long and intensely ambivalent battle of liberation from two paternal figures: his father and Pier Paolo Pasolini, to whom one of his most intimate poems is dedicated. "Vicino a te, timida come una sposa / era la mia emozione," wrote the young Bertolucci ("Near you my emotions were as timid as a bride"). Pasolini was to give Bernardo Bertolucci his start in film and was to continue to be a major influence in his early work. This paternal complex will be figuralized and thematized in many different ways in Bertolucci's films, and it never ceases evolving. Its most obvious representation occurs in *The Spider's Stratagem*, where the main character is an exact double of his dead father, but it may take other, more subtle or unconscious forms.

Indeed, given the conflict between poetic language and cinematic language that thematizes Bertolucci's liberation from the authority of his father, the relationship between text and film can be shown to be central to the young filmmaker's early work. If Bernardo Bertolucci describes *La commare secca* as "not really my film" it is precisely because both the text and the cinematic idea were already appropriated by Pasolini. In the following series of films created as adaptations of literary models (*Before the Revolution, Partner,* and *The Conformist*), however, Bertolucci was able to give free rein to his struggle against the less present but no less symbolic authority of a paternal logos, with all the ambivalence and anguish that this implies. Although this theme resonates throughout Bertolucci's entire work, its particular expression in these three films represents Bertolucci's most intricate and creative solution to the problem of discovering his own poetic voice or, more properly speaking, "image." In this latter term are united the dual problematics that were to inform his cinematic enterprise most deeply from 1963 to 1968: personal identity and cinematic expression. The focus of the first three chapters of this study will be, then, the weaving of these two interrelated issues onto the "dream loom" of Bertolucci's cinema.

Whether *scena madri* or *scena padre*, the films as a whole present a

"frenetic search for identity."[8] Together they suggest that the title of Bertolucci's collection of poems might itself be the best résumé of his work: In
search of mystery. Identity and the specificity of cinematic language are not
easy to discover. "I have many stories," said Bertolucci of his work, "and it
would be fine for me if films became a way of life. . . . Unfortunately there
is still a kind of barrier of glass to break. . . . I said glass because behind it
everything moves as in another world, one passes into it and then turns back
out, it is always like this."[9] "For now we see through a glass darkly," says
the text of Corinthians 2 : 13, "but then, face to face; now I know in part, but
then shall I know even as also I am known." Paul might have been describing
both the process of psychoanalysis and Bertolucci's cinematic enterprise, for
in each the barrier (be it the unconscious or the "glass" of Bertolucci's
search) is to be "translated" by an interpersonal dynamic of self-expression
and analysis. Bertolucci's project can thus be termed an effort to see
"through a glass brightly." Just as the celluloid image must be projected by
a strong light through a lens in order to be seen, so will his search for knowledge and identity be translated into the medium of cinema.

So, as well, must the explicit and implicit imagery of his films be projected
through the lens of analysis to be fully appreciated. Bertolucci himself said:
"All my films have been very much worked out in the framework of analysis
which is based to a great extent on oneiric material—and, after all, aren't
films themselves constructed of oneiric material? Aren't films made of the
same stuff as dreams are?"[10]

As I shall demonstrate in the pages that follow, Bertolucci's particular
genius is to have created a set of optics for his viewers that bring them ever
closer to an understanding of the particular language of the cinema as it
stands in opposition to the language of the text.

As Bertolucci worked out his own imaging of Stendhal's, Dostoevsky's,
and Moravia's texts, he adopted a particularly psychoanalytic "lens": "Psychoanalysis is like another lens on my camera, or an instrument that was
simultaneously a lens, a dolly, a traveling mechanism, something that constitutes an additional working tool with all of these capabilities mixed
together."[11]

This particular metaphor derives, of course, from Bertolucci's own experience of analysis over the period in which he created his first five films.
But the language of psychoanalysis imposed itself for another, equally profound reason. If Bertolucci were to develop a new cinematic language against

the "author-ity" of his models, he had to do so in terms that were, as Christian Metz would say, "specific" to the medium of cinema and that account for what is essential in the spectator's relation to the film act. As if following Bertolucci's lead, recent film theory has privileged the following set of specificities of cinematic presentation: the display of moving images to a passive spectator immobilized in a darkened space; the projection of these images onto a screen; the spectator's essentially private relation to those images;[12] the inevitable absence of what is represented as authentically present, and the relationship between that absent presence and the dynamics of desire.

Jean-Louis Baudry has suggested that, as early as Plato's discourse on the cave, man sought the ability to reproduce images that would correspond to an impression of reality—an attempt at repetition, at a return to former states: that is, "the enforced immobility of the child at birth, deprived of the resources of mobility," and "that of the dreamer—also necessarily immobile—who repeats both the postnatal state and intrauterine life."[13] So convinced was Baudry of the resemblances among infant, dreamer, and moviegoer that he theorized that a psychic need for cinema actually preceded and presided over the technical invention of the movies.[14] The cinema, as a mental process, Baudry argued, was always already in our psychic apparatus!

Roland Barthes saw in the film spectator's very predisposition to cinema a prehypnotic state, which invites the viewer to "plunge into a darkened, anonymous, and indifferent cube which allows this festival of affects we call a film . . . an erotization of the space."[15] This erotization and the prehypnotic tendencies of the spectator's attitude point emphatically to cinema's remarkably extensive parallels with dreams and dreaming. Freud's *Interpretation of Dreams* proposed the theory that all dreams are expressions of unconscious wishes that, unacceptable to our conscious mind, emerge when conscious processes censoring them are relaxed in sleep. He further postulated that this relaxation of censorship was not complete and that the unconscious mind was forced into disguising its wishes in order not to disturb the sleeping consciousness. These disguises Freud termed "dream censorship," and he called the images that we retain from dreams the manifest content of the dream. The wishes disguised in the manifest content Freud named the "latent" content of the dream, and the process by which the mind translates wishes into the dream's imagery he called the "dreamwork."

According to Freudian and most post-Freudian theory, dreamwork is accomplished by means of a variety of mechanisms: principally condensation, doubling, and displacement. These are termed by Freud "primary processes," and their translation into words (the telling of the dream and its interpretation) he terms "secondary processes," or secondary elaboration. The primary processes, Freud contended, were responsible for the peculiarly oneiric nature of dreams—principally their "overdetermination" or ability to hold several different meanings at once, and even to hold conflicting meanings simultaneously.[16] As if theorizing the relationship between dreams and cinema in the very theory of dreams itself, J.-B. Pontalis defined the dreamwork as "An ensemble of operations which transform very diverse material—'provided' by the body, by thought, by the 'remains' of the day—in order to work it into a product: a sequence of images which tends toward the form of a narrative and in which there intersect at nodal points almost indefinite chains of representations."[17]

Given recent developments in film theory, the question has become not so much whether cinema is analogous to dream but exactly how and to what degree. Bertolucci is extremely conscious of the interrelationships between films and dreams and once said: "In dreams as in the cinema, or in cinema as in dreams, one has the great liberty of using free association. Cinema is really a language which uses signs drawn from real life. . . . Cinema is made from raw material woven on a dream-loom."[18]

Both dreams and films "weave" (to use Bertolucci's own term) sequences of images which approximate the form of a narration composed of "chains of representations."[19] Although there is (and will undoubtedly always be) disagreement on this point,[20] many theorists believe that, to misparaphrase the Bible, in the beginning was the image.[21] Writing and language themselves, as Susan Sontag has noted, would then always already be an interpretation.[22] Thus cinema, with its predominance of the image, would have a particular affinity with unconscious processes that are likewise primarily imagistic and, in particular, with dreams.

As for the latent content of dreams and primary process thinking, there seem to be many further affinities with cinema. Peter Wollen writes:

> Any film . . . is a network of different statements, crossing and contradicting each other, elaborated into a final "coherent" version. Like a dream, the film the spectator sees is, so to speak, the "film facade," the end product of "secondary revision" which hides and

masks the process which remains latent in the film "unconscious." Sometimes this "facade" is so worked over, so smoothed out, or else so clotted with disparate elements, that it is impossible to see beyond it, or rather to see anything in it except the characters, the dialogue, the plot and so on. But in other cases, by a process of comparison with other films, it is possible to decipher, not a coherent message or world-view, but a structure which underlies the film and shapes it, gives it a certain pattern of energy cathexis.[23]

Elsewhere Wollen adds, "The film is not a communication, but an artifact which is unconsciously structured in a certain way."[24]

Just as in a dream, in cinema this structure and the unconscious processes that form the latent content are not wholly hidden. The beauty of the dream's censorship is that it hides unacceptable wishes well enough to permit the dream to appear but not so well that we are unable to see the censorship at work! It both masks and reveals itself. Cinema reveals its latent work in many ways, most importantly through the rapidity with which it is able to move from one shot to another, creating an effect of condensation.[25]

Eisenstein's theory of montage (the most celebrated example of which is the sequencing of a shot of a crowd of people followed by a shot of a flock of sheep) articulated a highly self-conscious technique for metaphorical expression.[26] But film need not operate with that degree of self-consciousness to produce the effect of condensation: Indeed, a single powerful image in an appropriately charged context may condense into one moment many disparate and even self-contradictory or illogical connections.

That cinema proceeds, like a dream, with a continuous flow of such images enormously heightens its tendency toward condensation. Bertolucci notes of his own work, "It is very difficult to imagine that something in my films signifies only itself; one thing always means many other things and often its opposite."[27] In any case, inasmuch as condensation and displacement as primary processes "refuse enclosure within the limitations of the word as unit," they are essentially properties of cinematic "language."[28] As operations, they are more unconscious than conscious and "would be the very contrary of all thought; veritable operations of anti-thought."[29] As such, in film, they might remain indecipherable were it not that film tends to combine both primary *and* secondary processes; that is, it contains both images and dialogue as well as other textual materials.[30]

Inasmuch as cinematic images are representations of fantasy and function as displaced desires (either of the director as author or of the spectator as participant in the fantasies), it is arguable that displacement is also an essential aspect of cinema. "The screen," corroborates Stanley Cavell, "makes displacement appear as our natural condition."[31] Cavell's comment neatly ties the production of cinema (as the conscious/unconscious expression of the director's desire) to the consumption of cinema (as the viewer's conscious/unconscious identification with that representation). Not only is displacement a factor for the filmmaker (in displacing emotions from objects in his/her own life onto representations), but it functions for the viewer via a strong identificatory tendency with the projected images themselves qua images.[32]

In this triad of projection/identification/screen occurs yet another parallel between cinema and dream. Projection, Leo Bersani argues, may be common to many forms of artistic expression in that it is "a frantic defense against the return of dangerous images and sensations to the surface of consciousness; therefore, the individual urgently needs to maintain that certain representations or affects belong to the world and not to the self."[33]

Thus the filmmaker and the film viewer may conspire in locating in the projected image fantasies that they prefer to believe exist "out there" independently of themselves.[34] It is noteworthy that this tendency toward projection may not be limited to a single character. Inasmuch as the film is like a dream, the film *as a whole* may represent the viewer's projection just as the dream as a whole represents the dreamer.[35]

There is, furthermore, some evidence that for both film spectator and dreamer the locus of their identificatory projections is a screen. Bertrand Lewin's theory of the "dream screen" proposed an oneiric process so close to the cinematic one that one may surmise that film may have been meant on the unconscious level to reproduce this dream process as closely as possible.[36] Although neither dreamer nor moviegoer is hyperconscious of the screen per se, its existence as a blank surface onto which fantasies are projected suggests analogies with the mother's breast for the infant, locus of a potentially profound ambivalence. Joyce McDougall wrote of the

> love-hate visions projected on the breast of the mother—this
> breast which the infant devours with its mouth and eyes. This
> condensation of primordial experience in each of us makes of the
> breast a fantasy of a loving and destructive exchange between the two
> partners. Undoubtedly it is the artist's function to render

communicable and tolerable that which isn't: i.e. the immanent
violence of the infantile experience which continues in the
unconscious of every human being.[37]

If indeed cinema is enough like dreaming to elicit such archaic and antithetical complexes, then it may be that our desire to see films derives from
some of the "perverse" desires that activate our dreams: regressive primal
scene fantasies, sadomasochistic tendencies, and fetishism in general. Just as
Freud called dreaming "a normal hallucinatory psychosis,"[38] we might, by
analogy, call cinema a "normal perverse fantasy." To do so is in no way to
point an accusing finger at filmmaker or film spectator but rather to explore
the ways in which what is normally considered perverse is in fact perversely
normal. Bertolucci's express purpose was to make films that would, in some
way, constitute an "analysis" while at the same time creating "a cinema that
looks at itself, a cinema that speaks about cinema . . . in confronting the
language that has been chosen."[39] If Bertolucci's films appear to contain
more than the "normal" amount of "perverse" elements (e.g., incest,
fetishism, masturbation, sodomy, bestiality, pederasty, etc.), it is, as I shall
argue in this book, because of a deep interest in exploring, come what may,
the seventh art's unconscious dynamics between the cinematic act and the
film spectator's position.

Although I have concentrated my analogy thus far on film viewer and
dreamer, in order to deepen our understanding of those dynamics, it is
necessary to extend that analogy to the desires that activate the dream.
I compared the status of dreamer to that of spectator, passively seated in
a darkened space, viewing a single source of light as though through a
window or keyhole, whose fascination resides primarily in the representation of motion, as if it were real. It should come as no surprise that the film
spectator's place be analogous to that of the voyeur—anonymously watching through a keyhole—participating in yet absent from the action.[40] But
I would go further in arguing that the scene viewed is always potentially or
symbolically a primal scene, reevoking "the child's total store of unconscious
knowledge and personal mythology concerning the human sexual relation,
particularly that of his parents."[41] It is this voyeuristic attempt at the re-
creation of a primal scene that leads Susan Sontag to call photography itself
a voyeurism[42] and Stanley Cavell to assert that "the ontological conditions
of the film reveal it to be inherently pornographic."[43]

The relation between the act of cinematic viewing and the primal scene goes well beyond a merely pornographic tendency, toward ontological considerations; and if I insist on this affinity it is because it is rich in implications for Bertolucci's entire work as well as for cinema in general. Guy Rosolato argues that

> the primal scene constitutes, among all the unconscious fantasies, a nucleus where origins are especially marked: first of all as an originating fantasy—genetic vis-à-vis the individual and even phylogenetic; secondly, as the nexus of curiosity about origins, birth, procreation, identity, filiation, and parenthood—in this sense paternity can be included in this fantasy (for the male child). The primal scene can thus be considered as the most general yet concentrated of fantasies.[44]

Among the fantasies and directions taken by the primal scene fantasy are included fantasies of castration (considered by many French psychoanalytic theorists to be at the center of meaning itself),[45] incest (of course), sadism and violence, the mirror and the double.[46] Each of these themes will assume a particular importance for Bertolucci inasmuch as his works function doubly as reflections on the dynamics of both the individual psyche and cinema itself.

A further essential aspect of those dynamics links cinema to the phenomenon of desire itself: Cinema, more than any other art form, functions simultaneously as presence and absence. In no other art form is the impression of reality potentially so strong, nor do the representations we observe seem so present.[47] Christian Metz describes this duality in these terms:

> The (possible) doubling which is the nature of the fictional status of the work is always preceded, in the cinema, by a primary doubling, always already accomplished, which is the nature of the signifier. The imaginary by definition combines a certain presence and a certain absence. . . . The act of perception is real (the cinema is not a fantasm), but the perceived is not really the object, it is its shadow, its phantom, its double, its reflection in a new sort of mirror. . . . To understand the film I must perceive the photographed object as *absent*, its photograph as *present*, and the *presence* in this *absence* as signifier. Cinematic fiction is experienced rather as the quasi-real presence of this irreality itself.[48]

In encountering this presence–absence duality, we find ourselves at the heart of the metaphysics of desire itself, which is always based on a lack or (temporary) absence.[49] If we are drawn to film, then, it may be at some unconscious level because the absent presence of the film's object recapitulates the nature of desire itself, which is always an effort to resurrect a lost pleasure.

Redirection of desire from its original object is often the source of perversion, and yet it is also, paradoxically, the foundation of the ego itself and its only possibility of cohesion. Without such a redirection, the infant would be forever locked in a dependency upon the maternal object. Perversion as a *structure*, then, can be understood to be generalized in early human experience and subsequently incorporated into "normal" forms of behavior.[50]

It is precisely in the awareness of this set of dynamics that the possibility lies of transforming the perverse structure into a creative state. And it is exactly at this juncture that my own meditation on cinema meets Bertolucci's self-consciousness about cinema. To see a perverse structure in the film viewer's relation to the projected image is in no way an attempt to condemn cinema. On the contrary, failure to appreciate such a structure allows filmmaker and spectator to continue a fetishistic complicity that tends endlessly to repeat an obsessive, primarily voyeuristic scenario whose latent message may forever remain repressed. To reveal that obsession as an integral part of the cinematic experience has the potential not only of understanding the special language of cinema but also of redirecting cinema toward a new, less fetishistic relationship with its spectator.

In this sense, the film may come to function as what Winnicott termed a "transitional space," a space in which, on the one hand, primary drives may be completely satisfied, yet, on the other, the primary object is totally unobtainable.[51] Despite its structural resemblance to the perverse scenario in which a set scene is repeated tirelessly without progression, the transitional space allows the possibility of growth and development through a balance between internal and external demands. In this potential space, illusion is no longer a form of withdrawal and/or a symptom of alienation but a medium of potential creativity. Film is likely to remain a potentially destructive fetishism as long as it hides from itself and its anonymous spectator its own latent configurations. By laying bare its "perverse" nature, it opens the possibility for an intersubjective creativity, for development, for analysis. By its very essence as *absence*, film cannot hope to "see face to face," but it may aspire, under certain conditions, to see more clearly through the glass that so often distorts, filters, or obscures our vision of reality. In this sense Bertolucci's work unites an analysis of the language of film with an exploration of the psychic structures of the individual.

Poet and son of a poet, Bernardo Bertolucci's movement from his own written poetry to film can be understood to be both a revolt against the paternal word and, paradoxically, through the analytical work of these films, a long effort of recovery of both father and mother and the discovery of a new and full language. It is a revolutionary process that to date has spanned twenty years and eight major films. Throughout, Bertolucci seems never to have lost sight of the interrelationships between, on the one hand, the analytical concept of desire in its avatars of perversion, voyeurism, doubling, death, and transcendence and, on the other hand, the purely cinematic properties that correspond to those issues. It is Bertolucci's particular genius to have known how to translate those issues into a cinematic *style*—which, as Rosolato has noted, "is also the unconscious speaking between the lines and which we enjoy listening to."[52] Indeed, as I shall show in the following chapters, the "translation" of traditional forms of literary discourse takes on the uncanny "double" of a revolt against the "authority" of that tradition and the creation of a new, admittedly self-conscious language of cinema out of film's specific properties. The conscious and unconscious revolution of Bertolucci's style was to begin, paradoxically, in the "sweetness of life before the revolution" in *Prima della rivoluzione*.

> The essence of the image is to be more inaccessible and mysterious than
> the thought of the innermost being; unrevealed yet manifest, having that
> absence as presence which constitutes the lure and fascination of the
> Sirens.
>
> MAURICE BLANCHOT

2 THE ABSENT PRESENCE

Stendhal in *Prima della rivoluzione*

In an unusual sequence early in Bertolucci's *Prima della rivoluzione*,
Fabrizio (Francesco Barilli) meets his friend Agostino (Allen Midgette) on
the road in front of Cesare's house. As Fabrizio approaches the camera,
we hear an insistent circuslike music and the sound of a bike. For a few
moments, Fabrizio passes out of range of the camera, which has not yet
located Agostino on his bike. Once Agostino appears, he begins a dance,
a sort of *sarabande à bicyclette*, moving around Fabrizio *in a circle* and
passing in and out of view. After he passes out of sight, we hear a crash and
Agostino's words, "Don't come near me! That is for my father."[1]

The sound of a second crash, off, elicits, "And that's for my mother!"
Bertolucci's camera reveals an extraordinarily frustrating inability to catch
the exact sequence of Agostino's falls from his bike. In each of the five
crashes, Agostino is variously lost from the camera's range, *edited* out or
hidden by Fabrizio's body. The viewer never once sees a complete sequence.
The final crash, hidden once more by Fabrizio's body, evokes, "And that's
for me!" Fabrizio's only response is, "Hey, let's go to the movies together.
Let's go see *Red River*."

Up to this point in the film, Bertolucci's camera has demonstrated an
exceptionally high degree of mobility. The film opens with a hand-held shot
of Fabrizio running and mixes close-ups, long shots, aerial traveling views
of Parma, and an automotive traveling shot through Garibaldi Square in

Parma. This initial activity of the camera is an almost vertiginous conceit, and yet in the Fabrizio–Agostino sequence, the camera demonstrates a curious inability or unwillingness to follow an action once initiated to its immediate conclusion. Five times the dénouement of Agostino's "spectacle" is accomplished "blind." In his introduction to the film's published scenario, Bertolucci had written, "As for the soundtrack, I would begin by saying, 'Let's go listen to the images in *Weekend'* and 'Let's go *watch* the soundtrack of Straub's film on Bach.' "[2]

Clearly, the Agostino bike sequence invites us to "see" the sound of the bike falling and generally to reexamine our usual relationship to film grammar and film aesthetics. This otherwise somewhat ambiguous scene, then, can be understood to occupy the focal point of an extremely complex meditation on film aesthetics proposed by Bertolucci's film as a whole.

While the scene's dialogue enunciates some of the explicit themes of the film (a masochistic relation to the father, mother, and self, coupled with a reference to *Red River* as another important version of an Oedipal conflict),[3] Agostino on the bike attempts to complete a series of revolutions around the film's protagonist, which Fabrizio is unable (or unwilling) to imitate and whose failures we are unable to see. In this single moment, Bertolucci's cinematic style alone has evoked the status of the film spectator and his ability to see, standards of film grammar, the theme of absence, and the problematics of revolution. Each of these themes was to become central to Bertolucci's subsequent cinematic development, and each plays a crucial role in this film.

La commare secca, written and directed by Bertolucci two years before *Prima,* was, by the young filmmaker's own admission, "not really my own," and of *Prima della rivoluzione* he said simply, "I wanted to do a film of my own."[4] The value of *Commare* for the young director lay in the chance to begin to develop his own style, and of that film he says, "The major effort was stylistic, that is, to render the film *mine* through the style." In the same interview, Bertolucci went on to assert:

> A film director must begin to take a position not only in
> confronting the world that he describes, and the society that he
> describes, but also, in confronting the art he creates. It would be good
> to see films becoming conscious of what they are as music has done,
> as literature has done, that is that there might be a cinema that looks

at itself, a cinema that speaks about cinema. . . . The story is only important to a certain point, because in a film the relation between shots is independent of the needs of the story. . . . Every angle has its own particular value.[5]

Bertolucci is certainly not the first director to stress the importance of style over content, yet the insistence on the primacy of self-consciousness over imitation does run counter to the then prevailing trend of European film theory, as articulated by André Bazin. For Bazin, the ontology, the very teleology, of film was realism, and the French theorist felt that every cinematic element should be subordinated to this effect.[6] Bazin's belief in the ontological status of the real led him to condemn montage and short sequences as anticinematic. His preference was for the long, in-depth take, which, he thought, maximized the effect of realism. Bazin's particular hero was the documentarist Flaherty. "The camera cannot see everything at once," Bazin wrote of Flaherty's work, "but at least *it tries not to miss anything of what it has chosen to see.*" Elsewhere he praised Welles for his "reluctance to break up an event or analyze its dramatic reverberations within time as a positive technique which produces better results than a classical breakdown of shots could ever have done."[7]

It is precisely Bertolucci's camera's failure to see "what it has chosen to see" and his decision to "break up an event in time" that casts him in direct revolt against what was still considered, despite Godard's and Pasolini's growing opposition, the prevailing aesthetic of film.

Godard had published a series of articles that constituted frontal assaults on Bazin's theories.[8] The most succinct statement of that criticism occurs in *La Chinoise*: "Art is not the reflection of reality; it is the reality of that reflection."[9] In his *Critique of Film Theory*, Brian Henderson argues that Godard used references to the French eighteenth century (i.e., to a period before the revolution) as an "extended metaphor" for the aesthetic battle being waged. Allusions to Diderot, especially, suggest a preference for a natural order of the heart and mind over any a priori application of a fixed standard to art, for example, Bazin's ontology of the real. Indeed, argues Henderson, in terms that are particularly resonant with our own analysis,

The autonomy of the work, its status as a *rival* totality to the real, is to Bazin literally unthinkable. Hence he downgrades any kind of

form except that subservient to the form of the real. Bazin's
emphasis on the art, the sequence, serves to keep the cinema in a kind
of *infancy or adolescence* always *dependent* on the real, that is,
on another order than itself.[10]

Against this enforced "adolescence" of film, Pasolini had also revolted. In
his contributions to *Officina*, the journal he had cofounded with Gian Carlo
Ferretti, Pasolini offered "the first critical revision of a rationalist kind of
neo-realism . . . which, although it had Marxist origins . . . tended to give
in too much to a certain sentimentalism."[11] Like *Prima della rivoluzione*
itself, Pasolini "describes the crisis of the bourgeois intellectual trapped
by certain historical forces."[12] Gian Carlo Ferretti describes their effort
as a "socio-politico-linguistic analysis concerning the link between the problems of style and language and the history of the intellectuals and social
classes, an analysis clearly distinct from both the branch of stylistic of
hermetic-modernist criticism and from the content oriented critics of
Marxist inspiration."[13]

Pasolini denounced the tendency in neorealism to resort to the very language developed in the neofascist period, yet he suffered from an inability to
envisage a new literature. Naomi Greene's description of Pasolini indicates
how closely his aesthetic and political dilemmas resembled Bertolucci's: "A
Janus-like creature, Pasolini was torn between his nostalgia for the culture of
the past he sought to renounce (however deeply rooted within him as an
individual, it was still a *class* culture) and his longing for a new society, and
a new culture not yet in existence."[14]

Prima della rivoluzione appeared in the midst of this crisis of poetic language, to add Bertolucci's "voice" to the paradoxical struggle of a group of
Marxists against the domination of neorealism.

The invisible bicycle crashes that open the film are hardly the only examples of Bertolucci's nascent revolt against this dominant film language.
The other major fall of Agostino is also missed by the camera. Indeed,
Agostino is never seen again after his dance on the bike, for, three sequences
later, Fabrizio watches as police take away Agostino's clothes from the bank
of the Enza River, where he has drowned. Too late to "catch" this scene, the
camera now displays its ability to execute precisely the movement that would
have been needed to "see" Agostino in the earlier scene of the bicycle:
A panoramic view of Fabrizio in a close shot is followed by a *circular* dolly

shot of him as he looks at the water, the locus of Agostino's *absence*. What Bertolucci has effected here is a stylistic enactment of an absent presence: first in space, then in time—insisting on the camera's refusal of realism by its present but immobile status in the first scene followed by its "absent" but mobile status in the drowning scene. Fabrizio is reduced in the following sequence to describing Agostino verbally: "Agostino was blond, with hair . . . that resembled canary feathers" (*Prima*, 16). This portrait immediately insists on the metaphorical nature of linguistic description. Clearly the revolution envisaged here operates within the larger framework of realism, yet against the unthinking subservience to the dominant traditional forms of that aesthetic.

Agostino's stylized absent presence in *Prima* thematizes another major level of the film. The situation of this film, in Parma, the names and relationships of the major characters, Fabrizio, Gina, and Clelia, suggest that Bertolucci has based his film on Stendhal's *Charterhouse of Parma*. Yet aside from the coincidence of locale and names of characters—and a glib allusion to the French author's birthplace (Grenoble) on Agostino's funeral wreath—the novel seems to have no substantive role in the film. Not only does there seem to be an absence of anecdotal reference to Stendhal, the very tone of the novel is completely missing. "An unadulterated pleasure," writes one critic of the novel, "*The Charterhouse of Parma* is, for the reader a great joy to read, which corresponds precisely to the joy that Stendhal experienced in writing. . . . It is a nearly ecstatic happiness of a perfectly liberating odyssey."[15]

The tone of *Prima*, however, resembles Flaubert more than Stendhal and evokes the ennui of Baudelaire's poetry rather than the sublime of Stendhal's prose.[16]

One may legitimately question why Bertolucci bothered to allude to Stendhal at all if there is so little development of that allusion. The answer must lie in unraveling an extraordinarily complex meditation on the relationship between literature and film, begun in *Prima* and developed elsewhere in Bertolucci's work. Stendhal's novel and Bertolucci's film occupy a curiously symmetrical relationship to a Franco-Italian dialectic. Stendhal, disgusted and alienated by the vanity and stupidity of the bourgeois French society of the 1830s, chose to locate his novel in a highly romanticized Italy, which bore more resemblance to the Renaissance Italy of the *Italian Chronicles* than to Stendhal's contemporary neighbor. For Stendhal, Italians seemed potentially free of the *vanité* which characterized French social life, love, and politics. "Italian hearts," wrote Stendhal, "are, far more than ours in France, tormented by the suspicious and wild ideas which a burning imagination presents to them, but on the other hand their joys are far more intense and long lasting."[17]

Looking at *Prima*, one cannot fail to appreciate the irony of Bertolucci's reference to Stendhal, for if the French author found in Italy his source of "burning imagination," the Italian cinematographer, faced with the cultural impasse of mid-twentieth-century Italian society, gleans his inspiration from a French source. A transalpine nostalgia pervades both works, one explicitly, the other implicitly, each running counter to the other. At the level of character, other important oppositions emerge. If Stendhal's Fabrice becomes and remains a social renegade, even when cloaked in his archdiocesan mantle, prefers the solitude of his prison to the social crowd, and is literally consumed by his passion for the unobtainable Clelia Conti, Bertolucci's Fabrizio bemoans his inability to engage in a similar revolt: "I had the feeling that for us children of the bourgeoisie there was no solution." His teacher Cesare (Morando Morandini) accuses him of speaking "like a book," and he aborts his affair with Gina in order to accept marriage with a bourgeois woman (ironically named Clelia) who excites no passion in him (*Prima*, 40, 29). If Bertolucci's Fabrizio ends up realizing the failure of his ideals, it is precisely because, as he says, "I speak like a book because I have to speak like a book to be convincing" (*Prima*, 29). It is ironic that one of the reviewers of *Prima* accused Bertolucci of the same problem,[18] for it is in Bertolucci's refusal to allow his film to "speak like a book" that the film articulates its deeper message. What he has succeeded in doing, contrary to his own protagonist, is to translate Stendhal's literary thematics into the language of cinema. In so doing, Bertolucci takes his first major step in creating "a cinema that looks at itself, a cinema that speaks about cinema . . . *in confronting the language that has been chosen.*"[19]

The clearest explicit rejection of cinematic "literariness" comes following a somewhat Brechtian announcement of the subject of cinema.[20] The camera frames one half of a movie poster "*La Donna* . . ." while the soundtrack reintroduces the theme of "Ricordati" ("Remember"), a musical theme we have already heard in a previous scene, this time played on a harpsichord without libretto. The poster is blocked by a pan of Fabrizio, and then its second half is revealed: "*e donna.*" An identical sequence of Fabrizio passing a smiling woman in the street *repeats* the message, this time framing the poster as a whole: *"La Donna e donna."* Bertolucci has achieved here a purely stylistic allusion to Godard's cinema by breaking down the usual (Bazinian) cinematic sequence into two temporally ambiguous, discontinuous, and overdetermined parts. (The camera play on a woman while the half-poster signals *". . . e donna"* gives another dimension to the sign it would not have had qua movie poster.) By the time the film's spectator is able to read *"La donna e donna"* as a completed graphic or textual allusion to Godard, Bertolucci has already completed a stylistic and purely cinematic rendering of that allusion. Moreover, soundtrack and visuals do not function as parallel systems of a realistic effect (as they do when music is used to heighten the emotional effect of a sequence) but are used to comment on each other. While the sequence splits the first half of the poster from the second, the song's *absent* lyrics ("Remember . . . the film we saw. . . ," sung in an earlier scene) urge the spectators to remember what they have seen in order to make sense of the whole. Here Bertolucci has avoided the use of montage-as-metaphor (remaining faithful to Bazin's larger principle of the long take), yet "broken up an event to analyse its dramatic reverberations within time" (in direct violation of Bazin's theory of realism).[21]

The ensuing dialogue between Fabrizio and his friend as they emerge from the Supercinema Orfeo reinforces the preceding stylistic statement. Gianni Amico, who plays the *amico*, was one of Bertolucci's collaborators on *Prima*, and his presence in this sequence lends a particular weight to his words.[22] Bertolucci says of this scene: "We made this sequence almost as a joke, because I felt the need for a space [*vide*] at this point."[23] But like all jokes,[24] this one signals a deeper intent—even the word *vide* is a charged pun signifying both "empty" and "look!" The friend repeats nearly word for word many of Bertolucci's own ideas on film:

> Can you live without Hitchcock and Rossellini ? . . . You claim
> that Resnais and Godard are making escapist films . . . but
> ultimately *Une Femme est une femme* is more politically engaged
> than all the films of Lizzani and DeSantis and in a sense than the films
> of Franco Rosi. . . . Cinema is a matter of style . . . and style is
> a moral fact. [*Prima*, 35, 26]

In the midst of this verbal theorizing, Bertolucci has inserted another purely cinematic allusion. In mentioning his love for Hitchcock, the friend articulates Bertolucci's own theories on film: "An angle, a shot in a film has its own moral. A tracking shot for example may be moral or not moral. . . . There is an ethic in the style of many directors, for example for Godard the style is already a way of seeing the world. For Rossellini as well."[25] The friend next pointedly hands Fabrizio his scarf. Theories and scarf as Bertolucci's own personal "trademarks" themselves become a subtle visual allusion to Hitchcock, inasmuch as they constitute a pseudo cameo appearance by the director in his own film.

Another side of this "joke" lies in its allusion to *The Charterhouse of Parma*, to literature and the relationship between literature and film. Throughout this sequence, Fabrizio plays the typical filmgoer who has paid but scant attention to the film he has just seen, preoccupied as he is with his own love affair. When his friend asks him why he is not paying attention, Fabrizio responds, "I am in love, that's all." And, in direct allusion to his counterpart in Stendhal's novel, he adds, "I realize that had never happened to me before, I didn't know what it meant."[26] The friend's reply is capital:

> Ah, well then, the problem becomes a matter of *content*. . . . it's no longer a question of style. You thought love was a superstructure, right? But in fact, a woman is a woman. . . . *Things happen in life whose deeper meaning doesn't at first appear, but these things are important and they can even change you.* A dolly shot, for example, is also just a matter of style, but style is a moral fact. . . . Three hundred sixty degrees of dolly shot, three hundred sixty degrees of morality. [*Prima*, 35; italics mine]

The beauty of this "bookish" address is that its message (and Bertolucci's camerawork) constantly undercuts its literary quality. The camera is unusually active during this scene but for the most part avoids the friend, who presents most of his discourse *off*. Thus, although discourse is not banished from the soundtrack, Bertolucci uses the images of this sequence in counterpoint rather than in a mere reinforcement or doubling of the narrative progression. As the friend continues (again, off) "Cinema is a question of style," the camera moves from a close-up of Fabrizio to a shot of the two men sitting face to face, and then the friend finishes his sentence, "but style is a moral fact." As in the breakup of Godard's title, Bertolucci subverts the shot–countershot rule of dialogue. Shot selection and style are among "those things that happen whose deeper meaning does not appear immediately," to paraphrase the friend, but which are important.

To Fabrizio's "I'm in love," the friend responds in terms of a dialectic that opposes Stendhal's content and the superstructure of love—Stendhal's *On Love*—to Godard's stylistic and moral (i.e., politically engaged) *Une Femme est une femme*. The entire sequence serves, among other things, to reorient the allusion to Stendhal's novel from *content* to *style*. The question thus becomes: In what way does Bertolucci's style become, imitate, or respond to Stendhal's content? The answer is already adumbrated in the style of the sequence itself, for it is only through the particularly *cinematic* style, selection of shots, angles, and so on, that the question can be properly perceived and framed.

Stendhal's Fabrice does not arrive at love as easily as Bertolucci's counterpart. He exhausts over one half of the novel wondering if what he feels for women is really love. Several times he concludes that his nature was not meant to know love. He is finally ready to proclaim "Je suis amoureux!" at precisely that moment at which two conditions have rendered that love doubly impossible: (1) He is in view of but physically separated from the object of his love, and (2) she is for social and family reasons unobtainable. A massive work complicated by several subplots and political intrigues, *The Charterhouse of Parma* subordinates all other events and characters to Fabrice's discovery of Clelia and to the recognition of the impossibility of their union. Stendhal belabors this point almost compulsively, for he effects Fabrice's escape from the Farnese Tower only to reiterate and emphasize the young hero's desire to be reimprisoned *near but not with* the object of his desire. The particulars of Fabrice's imprisonment are worth noting, for the entire arrangement is remarkable for its regressive configuration. The Farnese Tower is dubbed "the queen, governing by fear, of the whole of that plain" (*CP*, 117), and Stendhal invents gratuitously the story that the tower was "built in honor of a Crown Prince who, unlike Hippolytus the son of Theseus, had by no means repelled the advances of a young stepmother. The Princess died in a few hours; the Prince's son regained his liberty only seventeen years later when he ascended the throne on the death of his father" (*CP*, 373). The cell in which Fabrice is placed is so constructed as to be elevated from the stone floor and separated from the stone walls of the tower—that is, it is a space apart, somehow exempt from ordinary spatial constraints. Indeed, Fabrice wonders as he enters his cell, "But is this really a prison?" (*CP*, 376) and repeats the question, "Is it possible that this is a prison?" as he stands "gazing at that vast horizon . . . the stars . . . in this airy solitude where one is a thousand leagues above the pettinesses and wickednesses which occupy us down there" (*CP*, 378). In this space removed from the world, Fabrice quickly loses all sense of the passing of time,[27] a period we later learn to have been exactly nine months (*CP*, 481). It is, in other words, a womb with a view. But that view is repeatedly obstructed by the construction and reconstruction of a blind, and Fabrice must use his rosary cross as a saw to pierce a small hole, through which he can perceive Clelia with her birds.[28] Stendhal insists on the incestuous origins of this tower because they so subtly underscore the maternal function of Clelia: Reduced to a totally passive infantile state in which he voyeuristically re-creates a primal scene activity, Fabrice is fed and protected by Clelia. When eventually freed, he desires only to return to this original egocentric and maternal containment. The real locus of incest in the novel, then, is not the apparent (Fabrice–Gina) one but rather the symbolic (Fabrice–Clelia) one. Stendhal's Fabrice is happy only when reduced to the state of voyeur, in which he can see but cannot be connected with his love object. Clelia's *absent presence* becomes the *condition of pleasure*. Moreover, it is clear that the novel (fiction) can continue only through the maintenance of this tension between absence and presence. With the union of two presences in the real, literature ceases (the novel ends abruptly when Fabrice and Clelia become lovers in full view of each other). Voyeurism is, of course, a form of perversion but one that is not limited to the sexually aberrant personality. It is an activity that each of us pursues unconsciously in the act of dreaming. J.-B. Pontalis's analysis of dreams indicates a remarkable degree of congruence with the situation Stendhal has described in the Farnese Tower:

> Dreams have a special relationship with the visible, but they are a reworking of the visible, they allow us to see only because they re-present what is impossible and forbidden: "the infant's scene can never be reattained" (Freud). One of the functions of dreams is a particular type of object: they make present a certain absence, they double the visible with the invisible, they are complete being only partial; to dream is to have at a distance. . . . It is as if, ultimately, the originating model of perception were dreams; originating perception were oneiric. We could, following this line of thought, argue that every dream is a figuration of the mother or that the mother is a dream.[29]

For Fabrice, the infantile scene desired can be played only in this space outside of space and time, where absence is rendered as if present, where partialness is perceived as completion, and where he succeeds in having at a distance this figure of the mother—a dream. It is significant, moreover, that for Clelia possession is conceivable only as an invisible and therefore unreal event. Because, *out of fidelity to her father*, she has vowed never to look at Fabrice again, she agrees to receive him only in the dark of night (like a dream!). The exchange of looks in the light of day eradicates this dream and, as with Orpheus and Eurydice, leads to the loss of love.[30] Unlike Fabrice but like the dream, she attempts to double the visible with the invisible.

The symbolic content of Stendhal's novel thus focuses on an enactment of a dream space as the major creative matrix of the story. Theirs is a regressive play space of childhood, what Winnicott was to name a transitional space:

> a reality which has no other quality than to be there or to become confused with the *projected surface* of an internal reality, of a closed fantasmic system . . . The self finds itself in an intermediate space between outside and inside, between I and not-I, between child and mother, between the body and the word . . . a play space. From play to I [*du jeu au je*]: such is the ceaseless movement, constantly reinvented, without any linearity in its passage. Something takes place which has no place. . . . In its presence-absence, a witness to something never experienced . . . It takes on meaning in order not to be embodied in the flesh.[31]

As readers of Stendhal, we hold the printed page up to our eyes, invoking presences that can never materialize. Clelia's absent presence recapitulates our own "transitional" dynamics with the book[32]—and her own version of this game of distance, blind possession, introduces but a variation of the process of partial possession. The sequence in the tower bears an uncanny resemblance to the dynamics of cinema itself. If it is true that "the presence of words is the proof of the absence of everything else,"[33] the photograph, like Clelia in her *volière*, constitutes specifically an image that cannot be possessed. Maurice Blanchot notes that "the essence of the image is to be altogether outside, without intimacy, and yet more inaccessible and mysterious than the thought of the innermost being; without signification yet summoning up the depth of any possible meaning; unrevealed yet manifest, having that absence-as-presence which constitutes the lure and the fascination of the Sirens."[34] Stanley Cavell terms this type of desire the wish for "that specific simultaneity of presence and absence which only the cinema will satisfy."[35] And, as if she were discussing Fabrice's initial desire to peek at Clelia through the small hole he has effected in his shutter, Susan Sontag notes:

> Having a camera transforms one into a voyeur. . . . Taking photographs has set up a chronic voyeuristic relation to the world. Essentially an act of non-intervention . . . the act of photographing is more than passive observing. . . . Like sexual voyeurism, it is a way of at least tacitly, often explicitly, encouraging what is going on to keep happening . . . to have an interest in things as they are . . . unchanged. . . . Between photographer and subject there has to be distance.[36]

It should be evident, then, that consciously or unconsciously Stendhal introduces a long symbolic meditation on fantasy and dream and, by an anticipatory extension, on their relation to cinema. Like the movie spectator, Stendhal's Fabrice prefers the darkened enclosure of his private space, from which he can view voyeuristically, through the tiny aperture (reeffected when closed) in his shutter, an erotic but unattainable image. Over his freedom to possess Fabrice prefers a return to this confining/liberating space to reenact his voyeurism. Like the film spectator, he prefers, we might say, the reel to the real.

Bertolucci would thus appear to have chosen *La Chartreuse de Parme* as a model for the metapoetic meditation that occupies its central episodes and dénouement. Rather than merely repeat this meditation on Clelia as absent presence, Bertolucci chose to appropriate and deepen it through a visual dialectics opposing Clelia and Gina as representatives of two attitudes toward cinematic style. Linda Williams was entirely justified in perceiving an opposition between the static style that opposes Clelia "and everything that is associated with that part of the city Fabrizio has denounced" to "the nervous probing camera" that Bertolucci trains on Gina.[37]

Clelia, in fact, stands somehow outside the moment of Fabrizio's investigation and experience of political engagement. The film opens with Fabrizio running toward the immense doors of a church, reciting, as he goes, Pasolini's "La Religione del mio tempo," which contends

> . . . this Christian faith
> Is bourgeois in the sign
> Of every privilege of every repetition . . .

As Fabrizio concludes this invocation of Pasolini, he looks at the burghers of Parma about him and says:

> They don't want to *know*. . . . Their consciousness doesn't want to understand, even though they have reality right before their eyes, and they, as actors, refuse the reality of their characters, of their scene. . . . I see them as characters outside of history. . . . I wonder if they were ever born, if the present resonates obsessively in them as it resonates and cannot be consumed in me. [*Prima*, 8]

When asked what he was trying to do in his films, Bertolucci answered, "To know, I want to know,"[38] and added, "The public does not know what films are; it is necessary to teach them. This is the thing that interests me most."[39] Like the burghers of Parma (and like Fabrizio himself emerging from *Une Femma est une femme* later in the film), the film's spectator does not know, wants only to emote outside of history. "From the moment poets speak about reality they are also moral. . . . I pose myself moral problems in the style," said Bertolucci.[40]

The reality that bourgeois and moviegoer alike "don't want to know" is the resonance of the present. It is the dynamic of the filmic situation as it relates to social consciousness and conscience.

Fabrizio's opening invocation concludes with a repetition of the words, "I wonder if the present resonates in them as it does in me without consummation." His next word is "Clelia!" (*Prima*, 9). The absent presence who resonates without consummation is, of course, the Clelia of Stendhal's tower prison, that is, the cinematic image itself when appreciated solely as the external appearance of reality. "Clelia is that part of the city I have refused," says Fabrizio. "She is the kind of purity," the scenario indicates, "that one wants to disturb" (*Prima*, 9). She is the unexamined and unexamining relationship to image naively held by a romantic vision (of cinema) that a more self-conscious vision (Bertolucci's moral style) seeks to disturb. It is partly for this reason, moreover, that as Linda Williams noted, "Clelia and everything that is associated with that part of the city . . . [are] presented in predominantly static compositions . . . in perfect harmony, by a steadily held camera that contrasts with Fabrizio's own agitated movement recorded by an unsteady camera.''[41]

Significantly, Bertolucci's camera never misses anything of what it was meant to see of Clelia. Filmed initially and finally in a church, Clelia remains a pure image shot with a static camera and is never heard to speak a single word in the film. In his presentation of her, Bertolucci uses a classical and almost trite montage of religious statues to emphasize the relationships among social caste, religion, and pure image. Style, classical montage, and pure, external, rather static image are all united here to express a bourgeois religious ethic.

Clelia then disappears from the film until the final sequences in the opera in which Fabrizio is separated from Gina and becomes totally accepting of the bourgeois world. In these scenes, Clelia is again perceived as a mute but classically beautiful image and is compared verbally to a portrait by Parmigianino. More significantly, however, Fabrizio's reentry into her darkened loggia at the opera constitutes a reentry into this static world of purely external images. Just as in Stendhal's novel, Clelia's own interdiction is exercised, and *we never see his face again*. Several times in the marriage scene, the camera focuses on the back of his head, but not once does it succeed in "seeing" him face on. Like Stendhal's characters, Fabrizio has returned to the status of an absent presence, but this time through a purely cinematic stylistic device.

If Clelia is "this sweetness of life that I cannot accept," the cinematic style that frames her corresponds to a moment in cinema that lies, to continue the paraphrase of the Talleyrand quotation that opens the film, "before the Revolution"—notably a French revolution begun by Godard and carried on in Italy by Bertolucci. This introduction of Clelia merely sets the stage (in the sense of establishing a problematics) for the mise-en-scène of Gina. Fabrizio's aunt (Adriana Asti) is initially presented in the dissolve that confuses her image with his mother's, the two women intertwined, then walking away from the camera arm in arm, almost as one body. This melding of mother and aunt emphasizes, of course, the incestuous relationship that will emerge between Fabrizio and Gina but also introduces a long series of *self-reflective* meditations.[42]

To emphasize the extremely self-conscious or metacinematic nature of his examination of Gina, Bertolucci presents her in a sequence in which he plays the cinematic presence of Gina against her photographic absence. In the

center of a large bed, Gina sits nearly motionless, clothed in white, which has
the effect of making her body appear to dissolve into pure light. She spreads
a group of photographs of herself in a circle around her, almost as though
engaged in a game of clock solitaire. A series of inserts of these stills shows
Gina as a young girl with her father, then as an adolescent with different
men, then, in a current photo, as a mature woman. Each of these interspersed pictures contrasts with the "real" Gina on the bed.[43] Once again,
Bertolucci's camera encourages a meditation on the absent presence that is
photography and, consequently, cinema.[44] Gina's photographs force us to
realize that she too is merely a photographic image and that we must search
in this cinematic self-consciousness for what it means to look at (or make)
cinema beyond the illusion of reality that is there.

Gina's insistent study of her own image highlights her strongly regressive, dreamlike (and therefore maternal) quality, itself mirrored in the
photographic portrait as a genre. "The photograph is the advent of myself as
other," wrote Barthes.[45] That is, it forever repeats the moment of what
Lacan called the "mirror stage of development," the moment at which the
other is inscribed in the self as a constituent part of the ego.[46]

Gina's play with her photographs thus depicts an uncanny nexus, both at
the level of character and at the level of metacinema, of the themes of both
identity and Oedipal desire.[47] As the locus of incest (with Fabrizio), Gina
represents the impossible union with the mother that is desired in the male
child's Oedipal phase. As photograph, she repeats the present tense of cinematic images "which resonates in us without any possibility of consummation." As a potentially incestuous mother figure, she invites and repulses the
tendency to fantasy that is normally activated by cinema itself. If Clelia
represents the static acceptance of romantic illusionism in cinema, Gina
constantly pushes toward a self-conscious analysis of the viewer's status
in cinema.

As though conscious of her status as image, Gina at one point rather
insistently places herself in front of a television screen, so that she appears to
be (but is not quite) a televised image. A similar play with Cesare's radio
directs our attention to the relative "reality" of voice and image. Gina repeatedly voices in this film messages that can be understood to be addressed
both to Fabrizio (at the level of voyeur and incestuous son) and to the film's
viewer as *voyeur* (at the level of both dream and metacinema).

In their first sequence together, Fabrizio continues his bookish ways,

Figure 2. Gina (Adriana Asti) gazes intently at a series of photographs on her bed. Courtesy The Museum of Modern Art/Film Stills Archive.

begun in his judgmental sermons to Agostino, as he sits, immobile, statically framed at the dinner table opposite Gina. After describing Agostino and his "myth," Fabrizio complains, "Sometimes I stupidly use the same words as Cesare hoping they will be more limpid than mine . . . but I never understood Agostino at all" (*Primo*, 17). The camera several times cuts to Gina, who alternately holds her hands over her ears in a gesture that refuses this stolid language, then holds one hand over one eye, a gesture that clearly "flattens" Fabrizio, making him, like Clelia, merely two-dimensional, without depth. Her gestures "speak" cinematically in a visual refutation of Fabrizio's literary verbosity.

In their next scene together, Gina speaks the first in a series of double messages to her nephew and the audience. After attempting to amuse Fabrizio without success, Gina commands, "Don't look at me with those eyes." This self-consciousness is repeated moments later when she says:

> Please forgive me. . . . Don't try to probe. I am so delicate,
> I would immediately feel like I was in prison. I don't know whether

there is only curiosity in you or something else, something more.
. . . But I've noticed that you've noticed. Your face goes dark all of
a sudden. Your face goes bright all of a sudden. There's only one
remedy for my troubles. Others. People. You. You follow me. . . .
Don't try to understand. [*Prima*, 20]

Gina's self-conscious position as *character in a film* excites her realization
that we, as audience, are peering at her. Her voice speaks (off) while images
of villas, trees, countryside, and sky seen from the moving automobile
alternately *lighten* and *darken* our faces opposite the screen. Her fragility as
a character makes her feel as though she is in prison, another allusion to the
tower prison central to Stendhal and one which will recur later in the film in
a specifically metacinematic way.

In the next sequence, she continues this double address. Like Fabrizio, we
watch as she dresses in the empty room that once contained a printing press
and is now the locus of the image of incest. Gina suddenly accuses the
curious: "You wanted to watch me while I dressed, while I pulled up my
stockings, my panties. Fantastic, isn't it? Did I disappoint you? . . . Your
mother is different, but she's built like me" (*Prima*, 22). Voyeurs, the
cinema functions as *our* dream, our primal scene. We sit in a darkened space
and watch a scene of incestuous love, where child has replaced parent, where
mother betrays. Suddenly the subject of the scene addresses us: "Your
mother is different, but she's built like me."

Bertolucci's clearest allusion to the metapoetics of Stendhal's prison/prism
occurs in the only scene in *Prima* to take place in a tower. Interestingly
enough, Clelia's role has been usurped by the more incestuous Gina in the
cinematic transcription, and the metapoetic *content* of Stendhal's novel has
been replaced by an act of cinema. In the same tower from which Stendhal's
Fabrice watched Clelia, Fabrizio seats Gina at a sort of wooden table and
declares, "This is called an optical chamber—it's a game of mirrors. It's both
magic and true. But it's magic all the same" (*Prima*, 24). In this Renaissance
game of mirrors, the Technicolor image that suddenly appears in contrast to
the black and white photography of the rest of the film has "something
fabulous in its authenticity" (ibid.). Within her view of the square below
appears the image of Fabrizio, who jumps and dances. Yet he remains only an
image, for Gina reflects, "How nice it is, this machine that makes me talk
with you when you're not there" (ibid.). "This machine" is of course cinema
itself, and Gina can again be understood to be addressing the film's audience.

This burlesque allusion to Stendhal's tower prison scenes indicates how thoroughly Bertolucci has understood those passages as a commentary on the absent presence of the image. Again, as if conscious of her own status as image in a finite film, Gina declares: "You're happy now . . . but it won't last. I know it won't last. You'll end up remembering me as if I were dead. Then more time will go by, and you'll have forgotten me. Finally you'll hate me. It's not my fault; I never promised you anything. . . . Where are you?" (ibid.).

At one level, *Prima della rivoluzione* can be understood in its entirety as an anti-Bazinian meditation on the absent presence of cinema. The genius of Bertolucci's appropriation of this focal element of Stendhal's novel lies, however, in his transformation of this scene of love, a "problem of content," into a "matter of style" and in the way that very style becomes a "moral fact" when reinscribed into the thematics of imitation, authority, and revolt.

As locus of an incestuous fantasy about the mother, Gina resembles dream and dreamwork. Just as Fabrizio seems to descend toward the "gates of dream" at the beginning of the film (*Prima*, 8), Gina seems constantly to enter and reenter the film through mirrors. Her first mise-en-scène occurs through the mirroring of her double, Fabrizio's mother. Next she gazes intently at the series of photographs on her bed, and in subsequent scenes Bertolucci places Gina before mirrors in an almost obsessive fashion. She is seen through a mirror in the bar where she talks with Fabrizio about how difficult it is to return, because "things are never the same . . . and people and places too" (*Prima*, 18). She is mirrored in store windows in both the shopping scenes and the emotional breakdown sequences. In the long night scene in her bedroom, she seems transfixed by the mirror and even attempts to arrange the hair of her mirrored image. When she and Fabrizio meet after her affair with Luigi, she appears to speak to him through the mirror and exits from the mirror and from the spectator's view simultaneously. Mirrors frame and surround their last meeting in the opera house foyer.

From the precedents of Lewis Carroll and Jean Cocteau, it is clear that mirrors are intimately tied to dreaming and death.[48] Gina's own connections between dreams of her father's death and her own death reinforce this connection: "I'm thinking of my fa—— of your grandfather's burial. I dreamed of his death so often, and in the dream, I always died too. . . . We are so alive next to the dead. . . . we can't share it with them, enter their coffin. We're more alive than ever" (*Prima*, 18).

As the major persona of dream, Gina doubles Fabrizio's mother, but she also doubles little Evalina, the girl in the tower. Like Evalina's, one of Gina's photos is taken against a tree. Gina refers to her little tormentor as "a little devil with disheveled hair" and to herself in the mirror of her bedroom as "a monster with disheveled hair." Both engage in totally obsessive acts. Evalina maniacally chants a song whose every verse contains the phrase, "Turn the page and see," and Gina obsessively collects photo magazines in a subsequent scene.

Psychoanalytic analyses of dreamwork show a similar tendency for doubling among the dream's personae and also reveal that, in dreams, the element of condensation allows not only for logical opposites to exist simultaneously but also for our normal chronological sense of time to break down.[49] As locus of dream and the irrational, Gina constantly makes self-contradictory statements and twice proposes that chronological time does not obtain for her. "I want everything to be fixed," she says in the optic chamber. "Look, no more May, June, July, August, September" (*Prima*, 24). At Cesare's she declares, "Time doesn't exist," and proceeds to illustrate this assertion with a fable (*Prima*, 28).

The sequences between Gina and Fabrizio center on a dreamlike reenactment of the entire Oedipal struggle.[50] In the sequence in which Fabrizio's family visits Agostino's family to offer condolences, Gina remains in the car with Fabrizio, who has just refused his father's order to accompany him inside. Gina reminisces on her life in Milan, unconsciously articulating the latent structure of dream: "I engage in transmission of thoughts. I have an infallible gift. I play the triangle. . . . I cry ceaselessly. . . . I laugh ceaselessly. . . . I don't like big people. Adults . . . No, they're never seductive. . . . At least look in my direction" (*Prima*, 17).

The camera is unusually active in this sequence. Traveling shots of the car's windows are interspersed with close-ups and three-quarter shots and zooms. Suddenly Gina, last seen in the back seat of the car cheek to cheek with Fabrizio, is shot outside the car tapping at the window and refuting each of her previous assertions. The dislocated and self-contradictory nature of this sequence is quite oneiric and becomes increasingly so as Gina repeats Agostino's earlier scene verbally: "It's not true that I know how to ride a bike. I always fall." And immediately she passes out of range of the camera. Again, Bertolucci's highly active camera is "unable to follow" and accentuates the cinematic moment. Following this quotation of the earlier scene,

Bertolucci introduces a metaphoric and metacinematic version of the same theme: Gina is shown in six different pairs of strange spectacles without transition. As film spectators, we see through only that prism that Bertolucci has chosen. Like Gina, we take on a series of different optics as the film presents them.

The most memorable and dreamlike of all of these oneiric scenes is the "imaginary" love sequence between Gina and Fabrizio. By a subtle use of montage, the two appear to occupy the same bed and move as if transported by a shared expression of physical desire. The jump cuts from one bed to another, a technique borrowed from Jean Vigo's *L'Atalante*, reintroduce insistently the theme of absent presence situated at the center of Bertolucci's meditation on Stendhal and at the nexus of the problematics of dreams. If there is an insistence on the oneiric here, it is pursued in order to dissuade us from participating in the traditional, romantic illusionism of the cinema and direct us toward a deeper level of reality. Although this fantasy ends in the apparent reality of lovemaking, Gina brings this fantasy to a painful conclusion several sequences later when she picks up the stranger and takes him to the Hotel du Coq d'Or. When Fabrizio discovers this "infidelity," the camera reenacts insistently Gina's earlier statement about her unfailing gift for *playing the triangle*: Gina stands on a street corner and looks repeatedly at Luigi and then at Fabrizio, each located, but blurred, at points of a visual triangle, with her body as the fulcrum. Once again, Bertolucci plays out the primary Oedipal conflict in purely cinematic terms, passing through desire and betrayal, moving to the nexus of dream.

These oneiric sequences do not depart grammatically from other sequences of the film; that is, they are not set off through dissolves, washes, or other traditional dream effects. They function in the isotopy of the film's realism and as such possess an equal weight and significance with those scenes not obviously oneiric.[51] Each of these scenes treats an incipient Oedipal revolt against family tradition which, at the level of content, leads only to the desire for an impossible union with the mother, fantasized quite patently as accomplished without disturbing her. Such is the deepest level of Oedipal dreams, according to Freud.[52] Pontalis suggests further that the very locus of dream is the mother.[53] But if Fabrizio remains trapped at the manifest level of the dreamer in this film, the film itself seeks, through an insistent self-consciousness, to move toward the latent level of dream, toward analysis, toward the possibility of change, and ultimately toward the discovery of a new language that might transcend the strictures of tradition and family structure.

It is in this light that we can understand where filmmaker and character diverge. Fabrizio's evolution in this film is circular and ends in an impasse. A disciple of Cesare (who is clearly an allusion to Cesare Pavese),[54] Fabrizio compares himself to one of the pigeons that flock to the foot of the statue of Garibaldi: "My Garibaldi is Cesare who also has his pedestal" (*Prima*, 18). Rather than equality and comradeship, Fabrizio prefers a slavish, static, and almost mindless adoration of a paternal figure.[55] His movement into political engagement leads almost immediately from this imitative position through angry, self-righteous sermonizing of others to a stolid acceptance of his status as bourgeois.

He castigates Puck for never working and for indulging in false sincerity: "It's too easy," Fabrizio jeers, "to begin to examine one's conscience once one has no more money in his pockets. . . . Cases like yours are too numerous in Italy" (*Prima*, 39). Later he extends his criticism to the party and the proletariat: "The people accept everything blindly. In the last twenty years, the people haven't developed even a shadow of consciousness" (*Prima*, 44). He criticizes the party for not helping Agostino and proclaims, "I wanted a new man, a humanity of sons who could be parents for their parents" (ibid.).[56]

Cinematic self-consciousness invades even the scene in which Cesare and Fabrizio discuss the failure of Fabrizio's revolutionary ideals. No sooner has Fabrizio said, "Everything's going to Hell; people blindly take what they are given," than he is interrupted by two female party workers who interject a discussion of the suicide of Marilyn Monroe. Cinema is again interjected into a discussion of politics. And, almost like a deus ex machina of the classical theater, a huge ungainly cart is rolled on camera in which William and Enore reenact their gestures from the earlier scene of Agostino's suicide. This purely visual association (like a dreamwork), coupled with the Agostino leitmotif, provides the cue for Fabrizio's next comment: "What did the party do for Agostino?" Once again, a purely verbal, that is, literary, discussion of political disillusionment is contrasted with a cinematic tour de force.

Caught in the essentially literary nature of his traditional framework, Fabrizio's "vision of a new humanity" reduces to a version of the Oedipal struggle recounted in *Totem and Taboo*, where the sons usurp their father's role without effecting any real change in the role structure. Freud reminds us that the desire to become one's own father is but a disguise for the desire to have one's mother to oneself.[57] Cesare is not blind to the implications of Fabrizio's vision: "You're on the outside, and you think you're more on the inside than anyone else. Your problem lies elsewhere. If you had more courage, you would talk about Gina" (*Prima*, 44).

Gina herself tells her nephew he is "stupid and presumptuous" and adds, "You talk, you talk, you think you understand everything, but you don't understand anything or anybody" (*Prima*, 39). Indeed, speaking and order both belong to the primarily literary orientation that limits Fabrizio's understanding of the world. Ultimately, his political position vis-à-vis the party and the people never transcends the level of his primarily Oedipal relationship to Gina. It is a passing youthful flirtation with revolt that is never pursued as a real action. In both, he dreams of overthrowing paternal order, but he can only think of replacing the paternal system with another of similar structure: "sons who could be parents for their parents."

In this respect, it is significant that the film reaches its own dénouement with that of Verdi's *Macbeth*. Fabrizio's vision of revolt is more mythical, regicidal, and sterile than revolutionary and potential. This type of rebellion and usurpation is but an illusion of Marxist progress through revolution. Everything is mediated through a literary tradition: "I speak like a book because I have to speak like a book to be convincing" (*Prima*, 29). Thus can Fabrizio merely recapitulate the past. Finally he recognizes that

> I have a fever . . . which makes me feel a sort of nostalgia for the present. Although living, I feel the moments I live as though very far away . . . So I don't want to transform the present. . . . I take it as it comes . . . But my bourgeois future is in my bourgeois past. Thus, for me, ideology was a kind of vacation or sabbatical . . . I thought I was living the years of the Revolution . . . whereas I was living the years before the Revolution. Because one is always before the Revolution when one is like me. [*Prima*, 45]

Fabrizio ends, like Stendhal's images in the tower, by being but another absent presence, a faceless image or reproduction of his milieu. Thus his "nostalgia for the present" is exactly that of the absent presence of the photograph, without moral style to give it direction. His vision is patterned after the books he has read and the order he must impose on those around him.

Bertolucci, however, has used the notion of absent presence in a much more revolutionary way. Rather than following the *content* of his authorizing model, he seeks to reinterpret that tradition through a stylistic revolt. Rather than overthrow the authority of the book in order to *take its place* (the revolution come full circle, back to stasis or mere repetition), Bertolucci operates within the context of that authority to subvert it by a revolution in vision, by an attempt to devise a new language and a new style appropriate to a new medium. We must understand Bertolucci's relationship to Stendhal as profoundly ambivalent and ambiguous: He remains "faithfully subversive" by carefully reinscribing the deepest literary structures in Stendhal into truly cinematic elements.

I will return to Stendhal's novel one last time to better appreciate the nature of Bertolucci's subversive fidelity. Fabrice's own genealogy is, much like *Prima*'s, thoroughly ambiguous. Born several months after the withdrawal of the Napoleonic occupational force, Fabrice is forced to occupy the house and use the name of the marquis del Dongo, his presumed father, a pusillanimous fop. His natural father, we are led to believe, is Lieutenant Robert, a dashing French soldier, responsible for "the prevailing high spirits and the expansion of every heart" (*CP*, 10). Stendhal notes that "The departure of the last Austrian regiment marked *the collapse of the old ideas:* to risk one's life became the fashion. People saw that, in order to be really happy after centuries of cloying sensations, it was necessary to love . . . with a real love and to seek heroic actions" (*CP*, 4). "Lieutenant Robert's story was more or less that of all the French troops. . . . they were loved" (*CP*, 9). Like the ambiguity of Fabrice's Franco-Italian paternity, the film's models are double: Pavese and Stendhal. Bertolucci manages a stance of subversive fidelity to each, for the film eschews an open revolt against the reigning bourgeois power structure (thus imitating Cesare's [Pavese's] deeds and failing his doctrine) in favor of an individual and purely stylistic refusal to accept the prevailing aesthetic vision of the world (imitating Stendhal's content only at the level of style).

We may better understand Fabrizio's advice to Agostino, "Poetry, politics, everything can serve! But you have to fight *from within*" (*Prima*, 10, 12). Following the example of Godard and Pasolini (again a transalpine fatherhood), Bertolucci, through the "ambiguity and uncertainty" of his relationship to Stendhal, had begun to raise the revolutionary question: "What does it mean to make a film?"[58]

Certainly it did not mean a decision to copy the plot and imagery of a literature offered as model; rather, it meant a reexamination of the deeper structures of literature in appropriate cinematic terms and through a specifically cinematic style, in order to promulgate a new understanding of those deeper levels of psychology and politics.

Although Fabrizio cites the concluding section of Marx's *Communist Manifesto* when he says, "The communists don't try to hide their opinions and their plans. They openly proclaim that their goals can only be attained by the violent overthrow . . . ," and Cesare concludes for the weeping young bourgeois, "of the entire traditional social order"; the younger man can nevertheless not commit himself to political action. In his portrait of Fabrizio's failure to enact this *textual* program, Bertolucci was pursuing a line already proposed by Pasolini, "that it is just as necessary and legitimate for the left-wing intellectual to express his own ideological and sentimental crisis as to contribute overtly to the class struggle."[59] Fabrizio's failure at the level of character as one of those "who have remained bourgeois with the violence and the inertia of a psychology determined by history" is sufficiently dramatic to point to the need for a "new poetry."[60] Beyond Fabrizio's impasse, one senses Pasolini's call for this new poetry and Bertolucci's initial response in terms of a new "moral style."

Moral film, then, was emerging for Bertolucci as a revolutionary notion that based morality not on staid traditions of bourgeois ethics but on an attempt to realize and maximize the full potential of the medium. "The fundamental thing in films," he said, "is continually to reinvent and rediscover them."[61] In so doing, he was obeying a deeper revolutionary tendency that lies at the heart of the artistic endeavor: "Of all our cultural artifacts," notes Guy Rosolato, "art, above all, demands an exemplary mobility vis à vis the law: we might say rather that its rules must constantly be invented, or appear to us as inexhaustibly new; in this respect artistic creation always carries its revolution within it."[62] By redirecting Stendhal's problematics to a meditation on what and how we see and the relation of (cinematic) perception to deeper oneiric and psychological configurations, Bertolucci had begun a revolution that he was to carry on in a very different way in *Partner*.

The theater will never find itself again except by furnishing the spectator with the truthful precipitates of dreams, in which his taste for crime, his erotic obsessions, his savagery, his chimeras, his utopian sense of life and matter, even his cannibalism pour out, on a level not counterfeit and illusory, but interior.

ANTONIN ARTAUD

3 *DOUBLING* THE DOUBLE

Partner as Imitation and Opposition

"When I was making *Prima della rivoluzione*," Bertolucci mused, "I found myself confronting the fear of clarifying my ideological position and the desire to exorcise it. My adhesion to Marxism which was passionate and romantic was the sign of the fear of being reabsorbed, sooner or later, into the bourgeois atmosphere from which I'd emerged. The character of Fabrizio represents the exorcism of this fear."[1] In *Partner*, Bertolucci seems to have been concerned with accomplishing the opposite: exorcism of the fear of falling too far into a radicalism that left no stability whatsoever.

The years of waiting that separated *Prima* from *Partner* were "four years of thought and inactivity, of theoretical reflection never accompanied by practice."[2] During that period, Bertolucci found it impossible to find financial backing for a film, but he was not completely inactive. He made a short documentary for Italian Television entitled *La via del petrolio*,[3] wrote the screenplay for Sergio Leone's *Once upon a Time in the West*,[4] and conceived a film, never to be realized, called *Natura contra natura*.

This last was to have been the story of three young men who meet by chance: a poet, a homosexual, and a political extremist. The three make a pact that they will split up, accomplish a difficult ordeal, just as in certain fairy tales, and then meet to discuss the success of their ventures. The poet's task is to read his poetry to the person he considers (without ever having met

Figure 3. Fabrizio (Francesco Barilli) exorcising political fears: "My
bourgeois future is my bourgeois past." Courtesy New Yorker Films.

him) his "master": Pasolini. The militant must organize a political action
group in the countryside around Rome, and the homosexual must exchange
pants with one of the kids he makes love with. "But his task," Bertolucci
adds, "is the one that today [in 1982] I remember least well—in terms of
either detail or significance."[5]

Ultimately, all three fail in their tasks: The poet, just as he is preparing to
throw some of his poetry into Pasolini's garden (hoping to pretend the wind
blew it there),

> finds himself suddenly by chance face to face with Pasolini and is so
> taken aback that he doesn't dare show him his work. The militant
> takes control of a train leading from the center of town out to the
> suburbs, baptizes it "Potemkin," and preaches a sermon of political
> indoctrination to a group of tough kids. His sermon is so
> misunderstood that he is forced to run away, taking refuge in a little

country church, and succeeds in escaping from the angry kids, thanks to an extremely humiliating strategy, that of disguising himself as a priest. The homosexual ends up in an amusement park where he is forced to participate in a motorcycle acrobatics show called "The Madman of Death."[6]

Of this project, Bertolucci says that each figure "fit the fantasies and desires of the movement of '68: the revitalization of poetry, need for political engagement, and the beautification of homosexuality. . . . *Natura contra natura* had in fact a lot in common with *Partner*."[7]

Indeed, not only do the three characters end up exchanging roles to a very great extent (the homosexual becomes involved in a group, whereas the militant ends up in an exchange of clothes and the poet ends up "face to face" with the man who "beautified" homosexuality), but all come together without exactly merging in the character(s) of Giacobbe in *Partner*. It is undoubtedly because Giacobbe is unable to integrate these conflicting tendencies—militant/poet/homosexual—that he(they) says "I have failed" and walks out of a window at the conclusion of the film. Giacobbe's poetic-romantic side enters into such conflict with his militant position and with his evident homosexuality that he first strangles the soap salesgirl and then *puts his pants* on her and ends up dispatching Clara in a similar fashion on a bus in the Vatican City.

"Nature isn't natural," says Giacobbe as he steps from a urinal along the banks of the Tiber, clearly an allusion to the double of *Partner, Natura contra natura*.[8] This statement and the very title of the project alluded to suggest how thoroughly schizophrenic is this entire film. Indeed, Bertolucci lamented that, because of the long period of inactivity that preceded it, "*Partner* was my least natural film . . . was a schizophrenic film about schizophrenia."[9] To be sure, this schizophrenic quality was due not only to the multiplicity of levels at work in the earlier project but also, and perhaps more significantly, to the literary source of the film, Dostoevsky's novella, *The Double*.[10]

Like *La Chartreuse de Parme* in *Prima della rivoluzione*, the anecdotal presence of *The Double* in *Partner* seems almost too slight to merit the coincidence of characters' names. The careful progression of character disintegration charted by Dosteovsky seems almost entirely overlooked as a progression and is pushed to the film's margins by a plethora of elements completely foreign to the Russian original.

Whereas Dostoevsky's Yakov Petrovich Golyadkin is a clerk in an accounting firm and experiences difficulties with his look-alike at work, ultimately losing his position to his more aggressive and playfully vicious offspring, Bertolucci's Giacobbe is (apparently) a professor of political drama at the University of Rome and does not experience any difficulties with his rival at work. Not only is Dostoevsky's Yakov displaced in his professional life, but the "self-styled Mr. Golyadkin" insinuates his way into "our hero's" fiancée's house and becomes a rival for Klara Olsufyevna's heart. Yakov senior's progressive character disintegration centers around his humiliation at Klara's house, and it is there that he is found by the mysterious and terrifying Dr. Rutenspitz and whisked away in a carriage along a dark and unknown road. Although Bertolucci's Giacobbe is unceremoniously ejected from Clara's house for, among other things, lying upside down on the stairs, crowing like a rooster, and dancing a solo tango, he nevertheless manages to "elope" with Clara in a stationary car, "driven" by the former prompter Petrushka, who imitates the sounds of a moving vehicle while Giacobbe brutally "seduces" Clara in the back seat. Following that scene, there is scant use of Doestoevsky's text elsewhere in the film. It is as though the entire matter were simply forgotten. In short, Bertolucci turns Dostoevsky's story from comic tragedy to black comedy and allows the place of the Russian novel to be usurped by other considerations.

As in his use of *La Chartreuse de Parme* in *Prima*, Bertolucci's reduction and distortion of the originating text raise many questions about the reasons for his choice of Dostoevsky's novella as a model. That choice can be clarified by an understanding of what is distinctive about Dostoevsky's text, as well as the particular use Bertolucci made of its distinctive features.

In *The Double*, Dostoevsky presents a narrative structure that remains unique in the literature of the double. Composed in 1846, the work appears to employ a thoroughly traditional framework: An omniscient narrator recounts the misadventures and psychological collapse of Yakov Golyadkin. Throughout the text, the narrator provides many familiar narrative signposts. "It was a little before eight when Yakov Petrovich Golyadkin, a minor civil servant . . . opened his eyes after a long night's rest" (p. 3). The events are situated chronologically, the character is named and placed "on the fourth floor of a large tenement house in Shestilavochnaya Street in the capital city of St. Petersburg" (p. 3). The narrator appears to maintain this objective distance throughout, following Golyadkin at the third-person level, using quotation marks to distinguish Golyadkin's voice from his own, introducing logical, causal, and chronological notations (e.g., "The reason for this was . . ." [p. 7] or "Every tower in St. Petersburg . . . sounded midnight as Mr. Golyadkin rushed out, demented, onto the Fontana embankment" [p. 38]). The narrator frequently emphasizes his cognizance of the demented state of his character. Often he labels Golyadkin, ironically, "our hero" (pp. 69, 74, 95, 109, 115, et al.) or, more objectively, "our minor civil servant" (p. 75) and carefully distinguishes the initial character from his double by referring to them as "Golyadkin senior" and "Golyadkin junior" (e.g., p. 115). Occasionally the narrator intervenes to reaffirm the realistic limits of his narratological position: "Would I were a poet . . . But I must confess, and confess freely that it would be beyond my powers to depict the full pageantry" (p. 27). At pains to insist that his narrator is not a poet, the author has nevertheless labeled his novella "A Poem of St. Petersburg," and it is precisely in the space between these two contradictory stances that Dostoevsky has created a thoroughly *uncanny* structure.

What begins narratologically as an objective account of a highly *subjective* experience is slowly and insidiously eroded by the delusions of the character. Rather than saying, "Our hero thought he saw his double," Dostoevsky's narrator recounts all elements of the narrative, both quotidian and fantastic, in the same psychological isotopy. Whereas at one point the narrator recognizes that "the adventures of Mr. Golyadkin . . . are . . . very curious in their own way" (p. 29), this objectivity is totally lost one page later when for an entire paragraph the narrator's and Golyadkin's positions merge:

> There was nothing wrong with his standing there [concealed under the back stairs at Olsufy Ivanovich's]. . . . He was quite all right. . . . Here he was concealing himself until the appointed hour and meanwhile merely following the general course of things as an outside observer. He was just watching. . . . He could go in if he wanted. . . . after all why shouldn't he? [P. 30]

By an extremely subtle game of narrative duplicity, the narrator has both established his objective position adhering to a rigorous set of narrative grammatical rules *and* violated these rules at every turn. Significantly, not only has the narrator's voice and point of view become enmired in Golyadkin's inner debate, but he unwittingly describes Golyadkin as having usurped his *own* role—that of the "outside observer . . . just watching."[11]

Just as Golyadkin has discovered a double within the narrative (Golyadkin junior), the narrator has just as completely, though more subtly, revealed himself as yet another double of Golyadkin.

Dostoevsky's labeling of his doubles as Golyadkin *senior* and *junior* further reinforces the second double relationship with the narrator. Golyadkin junior acts out an Oedipal fantasy of imitation/obedience followed by betrayal and usurpation. This "other Golyadkin" (the very name "Jacob" implies usurpation and rivalry) insidiously usurps his senior's place professionally, financially, sexually. The double is the epitome of duplicity. This pattern of obedience to seniorial primacy giving way to intense rivalry is subtly but surely imitated at the level of narration until the narrator's point of view is itself inextricably entangled with and undermined by that of his creation.

Ultimately this narrative device tends to involve the reader in a disorientation analogous to that of Yakov Golyadkin. By seeming to create while subtly undermining any critical distance the narrator implicates the reader as another double of Golyadkin, thereby producing a complex meditation on the relationship between psychological and narratological levels.

Bertolucci's adaptation of Dostoevsky initially evolves from this meta-narratological position as it implies and is implied by the double.

Partner opens with a close-up of Giacobbe (P. Clementi) reading the screenplay of Murnau's *Nosferatu*. Bertolucci immediately recapitulates the ambiguity inherent in Dostoevsky's text between narrator and character. Giacobbe's reading is disturbed by faint noises, and only when he removes a set of earplugs can the spectator identify the noise as the voice of a waiter. A traditional grammatical rule of cinema dictates that, unless otherwise specifically indicated, point of view (that which corresponds to the narrator in the novel) belongs to the "eyes" and "ears" of the camera and soundtrack. (Just as the narrator of a novel directs our attention to specific aspects of story and character, camera and sound/synch focus our visual and auditory attention on various images to be "read" in sequence.) By reducing the sound level to imitate the effect of Giacobbe's earplugs, Bertolucci has displaced the unique authority of the narrator from the camera to a position shared by camera and character. What renders this effect all the more powerful is the concurrent reduction of sound level of the musical accompaniment. Giacobbe's earplugs have reduced not only those sounds he as a character would be expected to hear but also those (the music) traditionally added for the viewer only. In blurring the character–narrator dichotomy Bertolucci cleverly reduplicates the narrative ambiguity of Dostoevsky's text where narrator and character are subtly merged.[12]

Although signaled initially by a violation of objective and subjective conventions of the soundtrack, this blurring of "narrator's" and "character's" wills invades other areas of the film as well: composition, camerawork, and ultimately "content." As Giacobbe becomes increasingly split, so do Bertolucci's compositions. For example, when Giacobbe leaves the cafe of the opening scene, he crosses a street and our view of his destination is momentarily split by a tree trunk, which both *divides* our perception and *addresses us* politically. Tacked onto this dividing point of the screen is a poster about Vietnam, dramatically split into red and blue halves. Following this, split-screen phenomena reappear as frequently as does Giacobbe's double: Giacobbe himself is split horizontally by a pile of books in his room, and the room is split vertically by the same means. During his invasion of Clara's party, the screen is again split, by a step in an open staircase, which appears to divide Giacobbe from Clara. Once ejected from the party, Giacobbe and his shadow are partitioned by a tree, on either side of which they carry on their boxing. Immediately thereafter the screen is split horizontally by a garden wall. When a monstrously large shadow appears and seems to chase Giacobbe in the nightscape, the composition is segmented by another brick facade and by a white stripe. Such compositional dispersal continues throughout the film.

Another narrator–character confusion occurs during Giacobbe's "deliciously personal parenthesis" at Clara's party. As he dances by himself, the camera quits the longer shot in favor of a series of close-ups of Giacobbe's and Clara's faces. As a set these close-ups (like the "bedroom" scene composed of separate takes of Fabrizio and Gina in *Prima*) serve to give the impression that Giacobbe and Clara are actually dancing together. Here again, Bertolucci has artfully merged Giacobbe's desire with a visual, apparently objective rendition of that fantasy.

This merger of points of view leads to a cinematic mise-en-scène of the double, which the text does not achieve. Dostoevsky insists of course on the physical identity of the two doubles to the point of their indistinguishability *for others* (e.g., "Not a soul would have undertaken to say who was the real Mr. Golyadkin and who the counterfeit, who the old and who the new, who the *original* and who the *copy*"—p. 48; italics mine). Thus, although

Dostoevsky's narrator and protagonist "conspire" to convince us that Yakov has indeed seen his double, nevertheless these two always remain textually separable, the intruder inevitably distinguished by such appellations as Golyadkin junior or "Mr. Golyadkin's perfidious friend." Bertolucci's merger of character and narrator coupled with the characteristics of cinema allow a doubling process that ultimately erases all certainty as to the distinction of (and therefore *primacy* of) original and imitation. Although some viewers of the film have attempted to define Giacobbe's characteristics (e.g., "one of nature's ineffectuals who yearns for the ability to persuade, even to command") from his double's (e.g., "a strong identity side by side with the weaker Jacob"),[13] there is ultimately no sure ground on which to make this distinction. Both doubles enter and reenter their artificially decorated room without the benefit of any textual labels. If, in Dostoevsky's text, the other characters become confused about the identities of Golyadkin senior and Golyadkin junior, the author always allows his reader his certainty on the issue. Bertolucci robs his viewer of precisely this certainty and thereby in the very matter of identity creates a difference from the original. In that difference, in fact, lies a crucial difference between textual and cinematic semantics.

When the two images of Pierre Clementi occupy mirrored positions on the screen, there is no longer any *reasonable* solution to their identities. Indeed, the spectator is cleverly integrated into the characters' ontological uncertainty, engendering a sense of the fantastic.[14]

That this ambiguity should be linked to perception and the *visual*, is even more significant.[15] The mirroring here not only breaks down all *reasonable* structures of visual organization but assimilates this fantastic scene to the thematics of scopophilia and the "transgression of the look."[16]

Although apparently far from the concerns of *Prima* and its multileveled approach to the problem of seeing and being seen, the appearance of the double in this film reintroduces a series of meditations on the complexity of perception itself, be it specular (the doubles in the mirror), psychological (the doubles as they express conflicting views of the world), political (master or "original" and slave or "copy"), or aesthetic (the oppositions of word/text vs. image/cinema).

Bertolucci's meditation on the relationship of the double and perception begins in the opening scene of the film where Giacobbe is seated at a cafe table. Placed in front of a window where a reflection copies and distorts his image, Giacobbe is first seen looking at a copy of the scenario of Murnau's *Nosferatu*—itself a fantastic film about love–hate conflicts and cruelty. In response to an unheard question from the waiter, Giacobbe replies, "I was looking at the pictures." This (otherwise gratuitous) mise-en-scène functions as a metaphor for Bertolucci's relationship to Dostoevsky (and to models in general). The response reopens the meditation on the relationship between novels and film already begun in *Prima della rivoluzione*. What can be adapted from texts into film (and vice versa) lies precisely at the level of mental images; the metaphorical nature of the word must be compromised (as must the materiality of the cinematic image). This form of translation implies an apparently equal degree of imitation (at the level of the signified) and rejection (at the level of the signifier).[17] Like Golyadkin's doubling of his original, the imaging of a text through film and, inversely, the "writing" of a film must almost inevitably constitute a double-edged figure: Imitation at first thought to be faithful must always already constitute a form of rivalry and an attempt to "re-place" the original.

But if Bertolucci appears to have reopened here "old" questions, already encountered in *Prima*, he now relates them to a much more vigorous examination of political cinema in general and to the recent French aesthetic revolution of 1968 in particular.

Giacobbe's book in this first scene contains and conceals a gun: It appears as both part of and separable from the text, as that to which the political text aspires (ability to affect life in explosive/radical ways) and to which it may lead. As the difference between the power and immediacy of text and political action, the gun symbolizes the gap between literature and its double, life. Because the gun is used *to shoot the piano player* it also signals ironically the film's inability to speak of anything but itself—of its other doubles—in this case the post–New Wave French cinema.

Although the most obvious reference here is to Truffaut's film of 1960, *Partner* as a whole contains a plethora of allusions to the "master," Godard. Already in *Prima*, Fabrizio's "friend" had extolled Godard for his "moral" and "politically engaged" cinema, and Bertolucci had experimented with some of his French counterpart's visual techniques and theories. *Partner* can be read as a long tribute to—if not an exorcism of—Godard's importance as a political filmmaker. Since 1963 and *Le Petit Soldat*, Godard had brought out such highly political pieces as *Les Carabiniers* (1963), *Pierrot le fou* (1965), *Deux ou trois choses que je sais d'elle* (1966), *Masculin-féminin* and

Figure 4. Giacobbe (Pierre Clementi) with the book containing a gun.
Courtesy The Museum of Modern Art/Film Stills Archive.

La Chinoise (1967). In the last three in particular, Godard had abandoned
and was pushing cinema away from bourgeois "cooptation" toward a position of pure "irrecuperability." *Weekend* (1968) concluded ambiguously
with the words "Fin du cinéma," but there was nothing ambiguous in
Godard's subsequent efforts (with Gorin) to render his cinema unmarket-
able. If *Partner* indulged generally in Godard's anti-Aristotelianism it also
displayed many more specific allusions to Godard's work.[18]

Already in *Le Petit Soldat*, Godard had made much of the relative power of
Malraux's *La Condition humaine* versus a gun, a scene to which *Partner*'s
opening sequence clearly alludes. In that same film, the actors throw off their
enslavement as actors by symbolically jumping from a window, a scene that
prefigures the two Giacobbes' exit out the window at the end of *Partner*.

Godard's presence can also be felt in the scene of the soap salesgirl, whose
equation between capitalism and prostitution refers both to *Masculin-*

féminin, where Catherine, as a child of "Marx and Coca-Cola," understands sex as a market product and responds to the heavy publicity in her laundromat, and to *Deux ou trois choses*, where an assemblance of soapboxes becomes a metaphor for the entire cityscape. In another scene of *Deux ou trois choses* piles of books in a cafe preview Giacobbe's need to use literature as a barrier to feeling.

In *La Chinoise*, Godard had turned most clearly toward a marriage of static imagery with large doses of quotation. The film is constructed almost as a treatise on political and historical issues, and the actors—in particular Jean-Pierre Leaud, whom Bertolucci was to use ironically in *Last Tango*—walk about holding books from which they read in a most declamatory and bombastic style. While Godard was resurrecting Brecht, Bertolucci was using many of Godard's discursive methods to rediscover Antonin Artaud.[19]

Just as Leaud opens *La Chinoise* in a self-consciously declamatory fashion, Pierre Clementi as Giacobbe appears early on in *Partner*, partially hidden behind a pile of books, reading histrionically from Artaud's *Theater and Its Double*: "And if there is still one hellish, truly accursed thing in our time, it is our artistic dallying with forms, instead of being like victims burnt at the stake, signalling through the flames."[20]

As he sits in this space, which he later calls his *chambre obscure* (i.e., camera), Giacobbe switches the light on and off in an alternation that recapitulates *au ralenti* the shutter movements of a camera or movie projector. In addition, then, to the political content we would expect in such a borrowing from Godard, Bertolucci immediately adds his own signature, a metacinematic meditation that cannot be divorced from the political one. Bertolucci noted that

> the movie theater is also a kind of *camera obscura*. Often in my films there are characters looking, and many times the optic of the film—the objective regard of the camera—can be exchanged or identified with the subjective view of the character. Sometimes the camera looks at things subjectively, like a character who, however, at a certain point enters the scene and becomes prisoner of his own looks.[21]

Giacobbe's "imprisonment" within his own looks (i.e., his double) makes him, like Artaud's martyr at the stake, a victim signaling to his other double, the film spectator. Bertolucci constantly plays Artaud's political and aesthetic concerns through the optic of cinema.

The patently false painted decor serves as a loaded backdrop for the next passage from Artaud, in which Giacobbe proclaims:

> We abolish the stage and the auditorium and replace them by a single site, without partition or barrier of any kind, which will become the theater of the action. A direct communication will be reestablished between the spectator and the spectacle, between the actor and the spectator, from the fact that the spectator, placed in the middle of the action, is engulfed and physically affected by it. [Artaud, p. 96]

The irony of quoting such a passage *in a film*, and from the mouth of a character who is situated in a patently artificial decor, engulfed not by action but by books, again serves to point at the cinematic process itself. Only in the cinema would we be so conscious of the *artificiality* of this decor, for it contrasts with photography in "natural" settings. Not so in the theater, where decors are always, by necessity, artificial and are therefore proposed and accepted *as natural*. This irony is heightened in the next quotation from Artaud.

Giacobbe again holds up Artaud's text and *reads*, "We shall not act a written play, but we shall make attempts at direct staging, around themes, facts, or known works" (Artaud, p. 98). Clearly Giacobbe violates this dictum by reading it verbatim—yet Bertolucci's use of known works (i.e., Dostoevsky and Artaud himself) as themes represents an equal degree of fidelity. Bertolucci's relationship to Artaud becomes explicitly double in Giacobbe's next quotation:

> To the crude visualization of what is, the theater through poetry opposes images of what is not. However, from the point of view of action, one cannot compare a cinematic image which, however poetic it may be, is limited by the film, to a theatrical image which obeys all the exigencies of life. [Artaud, pp. 98–99]

The relative power of theater and cinema will, of course, long be debated. What Jacob creates here, however, is a tension of ambivalence with Artaud's text (could Artaud ever have imagined this passage cited in a film?), which once again recapitulates every structure of the film thus far examined. "Theater!" "Theater!" "Theater!" Jacob and his double repeat no less than fifteen times to each other. But as the image of Jacob's double fades from view, it whispers, "Cinema!"

Figure 5. Giacobbe in a patently artificial decor engulfed in books.
Courtesy The Museum of Modern Art/Film Stills Archive.

This little dialogue recapitulates *in nuce* the tension of Bertolucci's ambivalence about cinematic realism. As filmmaker, Bertolucci was constrained by the limitations evoked by Artaud, yet he attempted to work against these limitations through a consciously antitextual and improvisational approach:

> Improvisation has an important weight in the making of my films. When I'm writing the scenario, I'm extremely meticulous and exacting. I am continually rewriting and am never completely satisfied . . . All this in order to have a final copy as close as possible to my idea of the film. Then, when the moment comes to shoot the film, I don't even open the scenario or look at it at all. . . . For me improvisation is the opposite of anarchy and is born of the conviction that you can't lie to the camera. Improvisation is the conscious marriage of fiction and documentary.[22]

Improvisation in *Partner* may not be evident per se for the viewer of the finished product, but there is clearly an attempt to "marry" a documentary or cinéma vérité style (the many shots of the streets of Rome) with fiction (Bertolucci's "fidelity" to the Dostoevsky story). This attempt at improvisation pushes *Partner* forcefully in the direction of a "living theater" and toward an uncomfortable political stance.[23]

Much of Jacob's role as drama teacher at the university is given over to a Brechtian demystification of the realism of cinema, by such means as exposing the machinery of illusion (e.g., the machine that makes "spider webs") and the techniques of acting.

He also uses his drama classes to depart from traditional notions of theater and move toward another, more potentially violent form. His careful explanation of how to make a "Molotov cocktail" is followed by lessons in guerrilla theater conducted at rush hour in the streets of Rome.

In the film, masks blind and conceal; posters dichotomized in red and blue split the screen, reminding the spectator of the divided Vietnam emblematic of the deeper divisions in society. The soap salesgirl's painted-on eyes separate expression from feeling as she tells Jacob how she has been transformed into a whore by the insidious workings of capitalism.

At the end of the film, Giacobbe delivers a speech on American imperialism (much of which was cut from the final version) and then berates the film's audience with the insult/exhortation: "Admit it. You've understood nothing. Look around you. Giacobbe is in you. Unleash this wild animal. This is only a beginning."

If Bertolucci has violated Artaud's anticinematic position by the very act of creating a film, clearly he is faithful to Artaud's basic ideals in many aspects within his film. Thus, although betraying Artaud's text even as it speaks it, the film engages in a quest for Artaldian cruelty through means that constantly recall Godard. Jacob unleashes a hysteria on both his students and his lover, provoking the first to social action with the call, "Il faut arracher les masques!" and then unexpectedly murdering the second. Not only is this cruelty a bacchanal, it teaches Artaud's deeper meaning of cruelty: "We are not free. And the sky can still fall on our heads. And the theater has been created to teach us that first of all" (Artaud, p. 79).

Socially, politically, psychologically, and aesthetically, Bertolucci's *Partner* proposes a reinscription of cultural artifacts operating like (and unlike) Artaud's plague, seeking to test and arrest our notions of reality and replace them with that double of reality Artaud dreamed of:

> It is a question, then, of making the theater in the proper sense of
> the word function: something as localized and as precise as the
> apparently chaotic dream images in the brain. The theater will never
> find itself again except by furnishing the spectator with the truthful
> precipitates of dreams in which his taste for crime, his erotic
> obsessions, his savagery, his chimeras, his utopian sense of life and
> matter, even his cannibalism pour out on a level not counterfeit and
> illusory but interior. [Artaud, p. 92]

This double of the theater, dream, lies at the nexus of all of the various
levels of the film. If Dostoevsky's *Double* is an important source for *Partner*,
it is not only because of the narrative ambiguities discussed at the outset of
this chapter but also because *The Double* is very much a dream text.

The novella opens as "Yakov Petrovich Golyadkin . . . lay motionless in
bed, like a man as yet uncertain whether he is awake or still asleep, whether
all at present going on about him is reality or a continuation of his disordered
dreams" (p. 3). This uncertainty between the real and the dream worlds is
precisely the uncertainty of dream itself. When Golyadkin meets his double
for the second time, the narrator notes,

> Sitting opposite, was the terror of Mr. Golyadkin, the shame
> of Mr. Golyadkin, his *nightmare* of the day before, in short,
> Mr. Golyadkin himself. . . . No. This was a different
> Mr. Golyadkin, quite different but at the same time identical with
> the first. . . . "Is it a dream or isn't it" wondered Mr. Golyadkin.
> [P. 48]

This oneiric uncertainty is never to be resolved; despite the narrator's
"heroic" attempt to establish spatial and temporal chronology, Golyadkin
repeatedly finds himself in unexpected places without knowing how he got
there.

> Golyadkin . . . took a look around and noted to his astonishment
> that he was in the vestibule. . . . Nor was this the only thing that
> had escaped his notice, for he had no memory or recollection of how
> he came suddenly to be wearing his overcoat and galoshes, and hold-
> ing his hat. [P. 109; cf. p. 125]

At other times Golyadkin is propelled through space in unusual ways:

"Our hero did not run, he flew, bouncing off and bowling over men, women and children as he went" (p. 117). Elsewhere, like Alice, Golyadkin experiences alterations in size due to a most peculiar logic: "He seemed in some strange fashion to have shrunk—probably in the effort to hear better" (p. 110). Events overtake him—"it was all just happening in some inexplicable way, and it would be vain and so much wasted effort to protest" (p. 117)—exactly as they do in dreams. The language of dreams, so apparently logical during the dream yet so vague and bizarre in the light of day, becomes habitual for Golyadkin: In making his case to His Excellency (an otherwise unnamed paternal figure), "our hero" says, " 'Such and such a thing,' I said, Your Excellency" (p. 130). Elsewhere he wonders, "What am I to do now? . . . Be bold, speak out, of course—but with a certain nobleness of manner. 'This and that,' I'll say, 'and so on' " (p. 139).

Ultimately Golyadkin's experiences are indistinguishable from those events he himself identifies as dream. Golyadkin's long dream (pp. 94–95) occupying the center of the tale begins, like the text itself, with imaginary triumphs but ends with "shame and despair":

> The ruined but rightful Mr. Golyadkin fled blindly wherever fate might lead. But as often as his footfalls rang upon the granite pavement, an exact image of Golyadkin the depraved and abominable, would spring up out of the ground. And each of these exact images would come waddling along behind the next, in a long procession like a gaggle of geese, after Golyadkin senior. Escape was impossible. The pitiable Golyadkin grew breathless with terror. In the end there sprang up so fearful a multitude of exact images that the whole capital was blocked with them. . . .
> Our hero awoke, stark frozen with horror. And stark frozen with horror, he realized that his waking hours were hardly any better.
> [P. 95]

Later the narrator further blurs dream/reality distinctions when he remarks that "everything was happening just as in Golyadkin senior's dream" (p. 104). When things are even worse, Golyadkin realizes that "There was something familiar about what was happening to him. For a moment he tried hard to remember whether he had not had some presentiment or other the day before—in a dream for instance" (p. 117).

It is worth noting here that Golyadkin's misadventures are dreamlike in the very terms that Dostoevsky himself posits for dreams:

> Dreams, as we all know, are very curious things: certain incidents
> in them are presented with quite uncanny vividness, such detail
> executed with the finishing touch of a jeweller, while others you leap
> across as though entirely unaware of, for instance, space and time.
> Dreams seem to be induced not by reason but by desire, not by the
> head but by the heart, and yet what clever tricks my reason has
> sometimes played on me in dreams! And furthermore what
> incomprehensible things happen to it in a dream. . . . Why does my
> reason accept all this without the slightest hesitation? . . . In
> dreams you leap over space and time and the laws of nature and
> reason and only pause at the points which are especially dear to your
> heart.[24]

To insist on the oneiric structure of the work is not, as is often done, to
remove it from reality but to inscribe it in a deeper level of psychological
reality where primary processes predominate. Using the mechanisms of
condensation, doubling, and displacement, Dostoevsky removes his tale
from the merely anecdotal and initiates an inquiry into the recesses of the
psyche as well as into the narrative structure that is likely to ensue from any
serious attempt to recount the oneiric.

As Jung has noted, the personages of dreams are almost always projections
of the dreamer: "The whole of dream work is essentially . . . a theater in
which the dreamer is himself, the scene, the player, the prompter, the
producer, the author, the public and the critic. . . . All the figures in the
dream are personified features of the dreamer's own personality."[25] In
recounting his dream, then, the dreamer inevitably narrates a tale of
doubles.[26]

Moreover, if we are to believe Jung, the dream always contains the symbolized unconscious compensatory *complements* of conscious elements: that
is, it is a symbolized double of the conscious life.[27] According to Charles
Rycroft, the very act of dreaming (even assuming its *contents* were not
double) involves the dreamer in an unusual kind of psychic division:
"Dreaming is a special case of reflexive mental activity in which the self
becomes two-fold, one part observing, arguing with, reflecting upon, resist-
ing the implications of . . . ideas presented to it by the other . . . in non-
discursive symbolism."[28] According to Rycroft, then, voyeurism would
seem to be integral to the very structure of dreaming, yet another connection
between dreams and cinema at a very deep level.

Dostoevsky's doubling of narrator and main character clearly reduplicates this oneiric division between observer and actor. Furthermore, in collapsing his narrator into the psychological abyss of the character of Golyadkin, Dostoevsky implies a relationship between the act of recounting (*narrer* in French) and the state of madness (*Narre* in German). To remove oneself from the world sufficiently to recount the world involves a process of alienation and doubling. Golyadkin's dream ultimately functions as a hyperbole of the ellipsis opened by the alienation and reduplication implied in the act of narration.

Like Dostoevsky's *Double, Partner* is ultimately best understood as the precipitate of a dream. The film progresses by no recognizable narrative principles, jumping from one all but incomprehensible scene to another: from Giacobbe's assassination of a never-to-be identified piano player, Bertolucci cuts to Giacobbe sitting in his darkened room, where trompe l'oeil paintings of furniture are partially concealed behind immense walls of books. Another cut shifts to Petrushka reminiscing about his role as prompter in the good old days of theater. Yet another takes us to Clara's house. From there the film moves back to Giacobbe's rooms where he addresses his image in the mirror. Again a cut returns us to Clara's where Giacobbe lies head downward on the stairs and makes crowing noises to Clara, then dances with himself in an elaborate, narcissistic tango. In the night air, Giacobbe boxes with his shadow and then flees in terror from this shadow suddenly become autonomous and enormous. The rest of the film lurches abruptly and associatively through various implausible and oneiric decors and moments. No progression is evident. Once Jacob's double is introduced, the two become virtually indistinguishable, further diminishing any sense of coherence. The murders, guillotine fantasies, illogicalities, fade-outs, 360-degree pans, and ultimately the close of the film cannot be restored to any narratively logical order. Just as Dostoevsky's narrator becomes involved in the process of delusion, so Bertolucci's narrative undergoes the condensation, fragmentation, and associative structuring of a dream. And, like a dream, it has no dénouement; it simply fades from consciousness.

As noted earlier, cinema is an ideal mode for rendering the structure of a dream. *Partner* comes particularly close to Havelock Ellis's belief that "the commonest kind of dream is always a living and moving picture . . . a constantly revolving kaleidoscope."[29] Rycroft furthers our understanding of *Partner*'s unusually oneiric structure when he confirms, "dreams are more like moving-pictures than passages of print . . . are less organized, less unified, less condensed. . . . They more often resemble someone who is groping for the appropriate metaphor than someone who has found it."[30]

Figure 6. Giacobbe boxes with his shadow suddenly become autonomous.
Courtesy The Museum of Modern Art/Film Stills Archive.

A relatively unstructured, kaleidoscopic, and fragmented film like *Partner* thus tends to approach very closely the basic structure of dreams. In his writings on dreams, Dostoevsky warned against the temptation to over-structure the dream's manifest message in the process of secondary elabora-tion.[31] As if faithful to Dostoevsky's thinking, Bertolucci has produced a relatively unstructured "manifest content" so highly symbolic as to verge on what Michel Tournier calls the "diabolic," where "symbol, no longer bal-lasted by anything, proliferates, insinuates itself everywhere, and shatters into a thousand meanings that don't mean anything anymore." Like Giacobbe at the end of *Partner*, Tournier warns of the diabolic: "Don't try to understand it—don't try to find the thing to which each sign refers. For these symbols are diabols and no longer symbolize anything."[32] The "latent con-tent" of this "dream" can thus best be deciphered by resource to the repeti-tive structure rehearsed by character and author alike. Bertolucci's Giacobbe, like Dostoevsky's Yakov, functions as the exact replication/rejection of an original. Unlike that original, but like Artaud's notion of the double, he does not rival and destroy that original so much as betray him more subtly by becoming indistinguishable from him.

The very structure of ambivalence implied in the cinematic rendering of a text recapitulates the structure of the double at the heart of Dostoevsky's original. In adapting the film as an alternative to or usurpation of the printed text, Bertolucci has discerned and faithfully imitated the deeper ambivalent structure of the original. His ambivalence is perfectly bivalent: In this combination of anecdotal rejection and structural fidelity, Bertolucci ex-presses yet another level of understanding of Dostoevsky's text, the sym-bolic formulation of the relation between the double phenomenon and the Oedipal configuration. Otto Rank synthesized the psychoanalytic implica-tions of the double phenomenon as follows: "The double, who personifies narcissistic self-love, becomes an unequivocal rival in sexual love; or else, originally created as a wish-defense against a dreaded eternal destruction, he reappears in superstition as the messenger of death."[33]

As a smaller version of his father (and created out of an age-old parental desire to defeat death through extension into one's children), the male child in the Oedipal stage imitates his father, becomes in fantasy the father's rival for the mother, and fantasizes replacing the father in everything. The phe-nomenon of the double in *Partner* involves a more pathological *acting out* in mirror form of the Oedipal conflict, involving, first, the raising of the child to the equal of the father, subsequent rivalry, and ultimately the fantasized annihilation of the original figure.

"A film is a dream," said Bertolucci categorically, "and the director is the dreamer. All the characters of a dream are always the dreamer. The dreamer is the father and the sons."[34] In this "dreamaturgis,"[35] the father and sons are pushed toward a kind of equality. Successful resolution of the Oedipal stage tends toward the recognition of a necessary equilibrium between both of the conflicting emotions—imitation and rebellion. Bertolucci (if not Giacobbe) succeeds in just such an understanding of his relationship to the authority of Dostoevsky and Artaud.

Like Artaud's theory of the double, Bertolucci's film strives through cruelty to question accepted notions of reality. But unlike Artaud's ideal (yet like Dostoevsky) Bertolucci voluntarily accepts the limits of a prescribed form. In his relationship to the dual models of Russian and French authors, Bertolucci thus constantly recapitulates an inevitably ambivalent structure of imitation and rejection. In the heightened consciousness he brings to our understanding of the entire phenomenon of the double, he raises his own work to a level at least equal in authority to theirs. In so doing, he realizes an identical structure at both the artistic and the characterological levels of his work. Like his two Giacobbes, his own work and that of his models stand in a new relationship: the ambivalence of an imitation so structured as to equal rather than repeat its model, so that, understood at its deepest structural levels, "not a soul would have undertaken to say who was . . . the old and who the new, who the original and who the copy" (Dostoevsky, p. 48).

Thus the film adumbrates a successful resolution of the Oedipal conflict implicitly symbolized by the double configuration. In just such a discovery of the possibility of a balanced ambivalence about authority as we find in *Partner* lies the child's first instinctive solution to his "frenetic search for an identity."[36]

Admittedly, this resolution lies hidden beneath a series of manifestly disturbing images—the character splitting, the violent rejections of women, the guillotine, and the final exit of both partners onto a window ledge.

Like the wealth of material dredged up in a dream, the film has a plethora of "perverse" elements. Indeed, Bertolucci said of *Partner* that it was "the film that made me suffer the most."[37] Part of that suffering surely had to do with "the relationship that we tried to theorize between film and spectator [which] was a perverse relationship, built with the foreseeable mechanism of sadomasochism."[38]

The rationale for this position lay in the continued pursuit of the concerns begun in *Prima*, that is, what and how the spectator sees in the cinema:

> Behind our film was the sadism of a cinema that imposed on the spectator the obligation of distancing himself from his emotions, which was supposed to force him at all costs into *reflection*, which placed him in violent conflict with his insufficient cinematic preparation.[39]

Yet his imitation of Godard's political "irrecuperability" and Artaud's notions of cruelty had pushed Bertolucci into a very different relationship with his spectator than the one he had enjoyed in *Prima*. More than self-conscious reflection, *Partner* evoked a self-abnegating rejection:

> It was a form of masochism to do things that nobody wanted to see, to make films which the public refused. The fear of an adult relationship with the public forced us to take refuge in a *perverse* and *infantile* cinema. From this point of view, *Partner* was a sort of manifesto of the cinema of 1968. The idea of alienation that the film assumes and tries to impose is equivocal on the cultural level because of a bad reading of Brecht.[40]

Partner best represents a necessary step in the dialectic of Bertolucci's development of a new cinematic language. If *Prima* represented an attempt to exorcise Bertolucci's fear of falling into the bourgeois traditions in which he had grown up, it also constituted the arena for the struggle of two cinematic styles. Likewise, *Partner* can be read simultaneously as the exorcism of a radical tendency into which Bertolucci could not ultimately fit and a similar leftward shift of his earlier stylistic struggle. Here Bertolucci's individualistic creativity was to do battle with Godard's fragmentary and politically uncompromising influence. Of this struggle Bertolucci concluded:

> Even in *Partner*, which I consider my most unresolved film, there is an abandonment to the magic of cinema, the desire of a repressed and suffocated visionary. *Partner* is the cry of one who has been skinned alive, a schizophrenic film about schizophrenia, just as, a few

years earlier, but with more felicitous results, *Prima* was an
ambiguous film about ambiguity.[41]

Ultimately, Bertolucci's encounter with Godard parallels those with
Dostoevsky and Artaud—and Stendhal before them. To imitate a model is
not and cannot be simply a double of that model. Again, Bertolucci's struggle
with the authority of his sources leads him to an understanding of the nature
of representation itself.

As Jacques Derrida would phrase it, "Representation does not double anything." Film, like all representation, is "a double which does not redouble
anything simple, which nothing precedes, nothing that is, in any case, not
already a double."[42] However disturbing, this complex interplay of origins,
doubles, narrative structure, and psychological necessity produced, at the
very least, a catharsis of Bertolucci's hyper-Godardism, freeing him to continue his meditation on personal and cinematic identity in other films,
equally rich—often equally disturbing.

The retina is a spider web woven of the slenderest, most delicate, most sensitive of the body's nerves lining the back of the eye.
DENIS DIDEROT

4 *THE VILLA BORGES*
Labyrinths in *The Spider's Stratagem*

"Even in *Partner*, which I consider my most unresolved film," Bertolucci had said, "there is an abandonment to the magic of cinema."[1] If *The Spider's Stratagem* vies with *Partner* in its lack of resolution—Bertolucci called it "a film on the ambiguity of history"[2]—it is nevertheless a film whose "magic" is much more evident and accessible than its predecessor.

In many ways the two films are conceived in the same paradigm. Both are intensely dreamlike, both deal explicitly with doubles, and both are fashioned loosely after literary models. Yet *The Spider's Stratagem* is as much a reaction to *Partner* (as the tarantella is to the tarantula) as it is a repetition. Depending, of course, on the spectator's degree of identification with Bertolucci's splitting character, *Partner* is likely to be perceived as a hell of incomprehensible anguish, ending in a general breakdown of the narrative process. Without some more effective structuring process than is evident in *Partner*, the portrayal of personality fragmentation—a theme evidently necessary to Bertolucci's creative development—is likely to end in a mere incomprehension. Clearly, it became imperative for Bertolucci to find a structure on which he could build an artistic representation both intelligible to his viewer and yet faithful to what is finally an irrational process. In *Spider* Bertolucci had discovered an idiom in which he seemed completely at ease with his material and with his audience.

Some of this change may be attributable to the fact that in 1969 Bertolucci had begun his analysis and that for him "*Spider* represented the beginning of an opening . . . the attempt to move from a cinema of monologue to a cinema which allowed a dialogue."[3] If so, the progress of analysis might perhaps be measured in terms of a movement from subject doubles (as divided parts of the ego) to object doubles (as self and other). As subject doubles, the two Giacobbes in *Partner* would represent aspects of the ego at war with itself. As object doubles, the two Athos Magnanis of *Spider* move to another level of psychic conflict, one that engages literature itself, its relation to film, and that of film to the viewer in an entirely original way. Here, instead of a generalized guerrilla conflict waged indiscriminately on all cultural artifacts, Bertolucci chooses as his vehicle a voyage of return.

The film's protagonist, Athos Magnani (Giulio Brogi), returns after a thirty-six-year absence to Tara, his birthplace, at the behest of his dead father's "official mistress," Draifa (Alida Valli). She has summoned him, we learn during their first encounter, to find the murderer of his father. Athos senior (also played by Giulio Brogi) had been a celebrated member of Tara's antifascist movement—in fact, the town abounds in street names, cultural centers, and monuments to the memory of Athos senior, "Hero Vilely Assassinated by the Fascists, June 15, 1936." As the film progresses, Athos junior learns that his father and three comrades, Gaibazzi, Rasori, and Costa, had plotted the assassination of Mussolini during Il Duce's projected visit to Tara on June 15, 1936, to dedicate the new municipal theater. The assassination was to have taken place during a performance of *Rigoletto*, at the very moment when Rigoletto sings, "Ah, la maledizione!" But Athos also learns that the plot was betrayed, and the conspirators narrowly escaped imprisonment. Athos is disturbed to discover a remarkable coincidence: His father was "vilely assassinated" during the very performance of *Rigoletto* and at the very moment that Mussolini was to have been killed. Believing the three co-conspirators and Draifa to have been his father's assassins, Athos junior flees, hoping to catch a night train out of Tara. At the train station, however, the music of Verdi's *Rigoletto* filters mysteriously through the night air, drawing him back into town, into the municipal theater, into the very seat his father had occupied when killed on this very night (June 15) some thirty-six years previously. Athos spies the three "assassins" in a box opposite his own, then notices that each in turn has disappeared from his seat. Panic-stricken, he glimpses in the mirror facing him their images in the doorway behind him. "I understand now," says Athos bravely, "why my father made no attempt to escape: his murderers were men known to him." But the three reveal to him that his father was not the hero the town believes.

Athos senior had betrayed their plot to the police and then, to expiate his crime, had decided that his own death should appear to have been a heinous act committed by the Fascists. The son decides not to reveal his father's treachery but instead makes a speech to the citizens of Tara, in which he attempts rather lamely to reaffirm his father's heroism. When he returns to the train station to take his leave, the train is announced to be ten minutes late, then twenty minutes, then half an hour behind schedule. Idly walking along the tracks, Athos notices that tall grass has covered them, that no train could have passed for weeks, perhaps longer. To properly understand this voyage of return, a number of formal aspects of the film must first be analyzed.

As the film opens, Athos emerges from a train in a manner nearly identical to that of a sailor. The two walk in uncannily parallel fashion along the platform, then through the station. Athos watches as this militarily dressed "double" executes a pseudomilitary maneuver that seems to designate an imaginary boundary beyond which he will not pass, then collapses on a park bench calling out, "Tara!"—seat of the mythical Irish kings,[4] name of the lost plantation in *Gone with the Wind*, the first two syllables of the most dreaded of spiders, thus an evocation of what Freud has termed the family romance, nostalgia and danger.

Athos continues on his way, entering a town that is remarkably labyrinthine, "a dream city" reconstructed constantly by Bertolucci's remarkable camerawork and editing.[5] Walking through two fifteenth-century galleries, Athos spies two old men gainsaying each other repeatedly in almost slapstick fashion; next, a very old man sitting directly under a sign announcing "Circle of Youth for Athos Magnani"; then, two other octagenarians sitting in adjoining chairs facing in opposite directions. It is of course the nature of dreams to juxtapose contradictory elements as if there were no conflict. This series of visual contradictions thus functions as a kind of early announcement of the dream structure Athos has entered.

In one of the most striking sequences of the entire film, the camera closes in on *the back of Athos's head* as if seeking to enter it, then focuses on the street sign he is reading, and moves from right to left, so that the film's viewer is forced to read the words "Via Athos Magnani" backward! In Tara, "City of Kings," this "via reggia" would be Freud's royal road to the unconscious: dream. Here, the camera's reversal of the via, making it a voyage backward, the placement of this voyage within the faceless head it is straining to penetrate, and the image of a man reading his own name on a street sign all further reinforce the oneiric, indeed, surreal nature of the moment as regressive, interior, and egocentric.

This shot constitutes the first of many allusions in this film to the work of the surrealist artist René Magritte. Magritte painted a series of uncanny portaits of backs of heads, and his *La Reproduction interdite*, whose title resonates curiously with the content of the entire film, is structurally very similar to this moment. In it (see fig. 7) a man seen from the rear is peering into a mirror and sees only the back of his head where his face should be. Bertolucci's allusion to Magritte here is both proleptic and uncanny: proleptic in that Athos will discover the "truth" about his father/himself by looking in the mirror in the theater; uncanny because, as traditional portraiture and the film's close-ups are linked to the mirroring phenomenon, the film viewer becomes inevitably enmeshed in this oneiric process in which the self is viewed as other in a distorting mirror.[6]

La Reproduction interdite could almost be a metaphor for the cinematic experience. Nick Browne noted of the spectator's work of identification in the film act that

> the place of the spectator in his relation to the narrator is
> established by, though not limited to, identification with characters
> and the views that they have of each other. More specifically, his
> "place" is defined through the variable face of identification with the
> one viewing and the one viewed . . . [as in a traditional mirror
> image, I might add]. The spectator's figurative position is not stated
> by a description of where the camera is in the geography of the scene.
> On the contrary, though the spectator's position is closely tied to the
> fortunes and views of characters, our analysis suggests that
> identification, in the original sense of an emotional bond, need not be
> with the character whose view he shares, even less with the
> disembodied camera. Evidently the spectator is in several places at
> once—with the fictional viewer, with the viewed, and at the same
> time in a position to evaluate and respond to the claims of each. This
> fact suggests that, like the dreamer, the film's spectator is a plural
> subject: in his reading he is and is not himself.[7]

This single sequence, then, contains a nucleus of meaning linking the contents of *Spider* with the dynamics of dream and with those of the cine-

Figure 7. René Magritte, *La Reproduction interdite*, 1937. Collection
Museum Beymans-van Beuningen, Rotterdam.

matic act itself. Clearly then, although Bertolucci had abandoned the frenetic, almost schizoid, search enacted in *Partner*, he had not slowed his meditation on the nature and style of the medium.

Magritte's presence in the film cannot be overestimated. Bertolucci recounts that

> I proposed doing *The Spider's Stratagem* to Storaro in 1969. From the first discussion I understood that it was useless to talk about warm or cold tones or about contrasting lighting. I had to show him examples. I bought a book on Magritte and studied it at length with Vittorio. Other than Ligabue and some naive Yugoslav painters, Magritte was the inspiration for the lighting in *Spider's Stratagem*, and in particular one painting by Magritte: *The Empire of Lights*. I was interested by a nocturnal light full of azure reflections, the light of those nights in which you can see everything. All the blue moments of *Spider's Stratagem* were shot between light and dark at dusk.[8]

Not only is dusk an archetypal moment of dreaming, but Magritte's use of that moment (and consequently Bertolucci's) represents a hyperbole of the dream state, surrealism which, for André Breton, was based on "the omnipotence of dream . . . a certain point of the mind at which life and death, the real and the imagined, past and future, the communicable and the incommunicable, high and low, cease to be perceived as contradictions."[9]

Several other allusions to Magritte's work further the dreamlike quality of this film. Toward the end of the film particularly, when Athos returns to the station intending to leave Tara, the camera focuses on him through two pairs of windows with a strangely eerie result, recalling Magritte's *Eloge de la dialectique*. As Athos leaves the station, drawn back into town by the strains of *Rigoletto*, he passes a series of frozen, immobile figures, including two elevated on a chair as if weightless, much like the Magritte painting *Golconda*. When he is sitting in the opera house during the performance, the camera zooms in and out four times on the "conspirators" in the box opposite Athos, with, each time, a disappearing act, the four moments recapitulating sequentially Magritte's *Now You See It, Now You Don't* or *L'Homme au journal*.

These various allusions to Magritte's work are themselves part of a larger pattern of oneiric effects that produce a resemblance between the structures of film and dream. Adult dreams are often characterized by an irrationality of point of view, by condensation of different places into one, by odd juxtapositions of rationally unconnected scenes, by displacement, and by doubling. *Spider* is characterized generally by the bizarre activity of the camera. If dreams are structured by an unconscious process that appears to be autonomous, independent of rational thought, Bertolucci's camera could be thought of as an instrument of this process. He has said of his camera, as one might say of the unconscious itself, "What is important is what happens *inside* the camera. . . . Sometimes the camera forgets the characters and goes to look at something completely unrelated."[10] Normal film grammar prescribes that a film be shot by stationary cameras that allow the spectator to take a fixed point of view vis-à-vis the world observed. If the camera tracks, pans, or zooms, it moves from a point well-identified to another fixed or stable location. To break these rules excessively is to deprive the viewer of the coherence and organization offered by a set point of view. Bertolucci's camera verges on such excessive movements throughout the film. For example, in the scene following his first visit to Draifa, Athos walks his bicycle down a long lamp-lit corridor toward two men engaged in lively conversation. As Athos passes the two men, they recede, sandwiching him, and he appears to pass into the camera. Next, the camera switches position 180 degrees, making Athos appear to retrace his steps. The shift would be totally disorienting were it not that the position of the two old men has been reversed and the viewer can resituate himself through this rather subtle change.

Such oneiric dislocations are frequent in *Spider*. During Athos's first conversation with Draifa, a photographic portrait of Athos senior is displayed on the wall behind or beside the two speakers. Virtually every time the camera captures this portrait, it has changed slightly: Either Athos senior's hair style has changed, or he has donned a tie. No rational explanation is or can be given for such disjunctive effects. In the same scene, while they are in conversation, the light outside changes from daylight to night without explanation. When Draifa leaves the table and passes through the doorway to the next room, the tracking camera follows her, paralleling her advance. Just as it had done with Agostino in *Before the Revolution*, the camera "misses" the fact that she faints in the doorway. This sense of inability to follow, the vain attempt to see the essential, and the frequent dislocation (achieved in *Spider* by frequent jump cuts that catapult Athos from one location to another without explanation) are all common to dreamwork.

The editing of the flashbacks further serves to disorient the already shaky narrative purpose of the film. Each of the flashbacks coincides with a version of the stories told by Costa, Gaibazzi, Razzori, and Draifa. Whereas the traditional film grammar restricts flashbacks to "true" memories of an event, each of *Spider*'s flashbacks has a disturbing tendency toward anachronism, "not making the slightest effort at flashback illusionism."[11] In each of these flashbacks, the characters appear to be the same age as they are thirty-six years later. The most dreamlike of all of these follows directly Athos junior's complaint to Draifa that Costa, Gaibazzi, and Razzori have all prearranged their stories. Draifa sits in the maize and tells Athos of an incident in which his father was scared by a lion. There are a series of rapid cuts back and forth between Draifa and Athos senior and Draifa and the son. At one point, Draifa, sitting in her room with the father, speaks directly to the son, saying, "That was the last time I saw him alive," clearly an inadmissible "mistake" in logical film grammar.

Bertolucci's style is the first indication that these stories are entirely contrived. Indeed, the composite of these tales presents both at the level of style and at the level of content a remarkable similarity to the manifest content of a typical dream, about which Freud noted:

> Almost everywhere noticeable gaps, disturbing repetitions and obvious contradictions have come about—indications which reveal things to us which [the dream] was not intended to communicate. In its implications the distortions of a [manifest dream] text resemble a murder: the difficulty is not in perpetrating the deed but in getting rid of its traces. We might well lend the word distortion the double meaning to which it has a claim, but of which today it makes no use. It should mean not only "to change the appearance of something" but also "to put something in another place, to displace." Accordingly, in many instances of textual distortion, we may nevertheless count upon finding what has been suppressed and disavowed hidden away somewhere else, though changed and torn from its context. Only it will not always be easy to recognize it.[12]

Displacement is certainly the central mechanism of *Spider*, for, if the dream is a veiled language that can be interpreted only by searching for what is hidden in the interstices of the manifest content, so too are the stories provided to Athos about his father. As Athos will discover, all of the stories are intended to hide the traces of his father's betrayal and, at the same time, lead him to the discovery of that crime. If dreams are opaque webs made of strands so translucent as to allow us a glimpse of the "light" behind them but so constructed as to hide the danger at the center, so too are the myths woven by Athos's "friends" in Tara. The manifest content provided by Draifa, Costa, Gaibazzi, and Razzori is itself an artificial tissue of fictions carefully composed so as to simultaneously conceal and reveal: a spider's stratagem.

Norman O. Borwn reminds us that

> in Vao [mythology] the newly dead man is believed to arrive before the entrance to a cave . . . where he encounters a terrible female monster, seen as spider woman, man-devouring ogress . . . with immense claws, or a giant bivalvular genital organ, and which shuts to devour. In front of the cave mouth is a maze-like design called "the Path," traced on the sand by the monster. As the dead man approaches, she obliterates half of the design, and he has to restore it, or else be devoured.[13]

Draifa clearly functions in a remarkably similar way to the Vao spider woman. She is both Arachne, the architect of, and Ariadne, (false) guide to, this labyrinth of stories through which Athos must feel his way toward the monstrous truth about his father. As Ariachne,[14] she assumes a double role of guiding heroine and self-serving traitor of Athos's project. The mythical strand she proffers as a lexicon of the maze slowly metamorphoses into a mimesis of the maze, a mystifying and intricate web.

The film initially displays this function of Draifa in a most graphic way. Draifa lives in a villa so overgrown with flowers that it appears to be a nest or a tomb. When Athos arrives for the first time, the camera does a 180-degree pan that follows the *circle* of her courtyard and ultimately locates her at its center. Draifa is first seen to be standing, as though waiting for the attention of Athos, the camera, and the film's viewer to focus on her. Only then does she very self-consciously begin her processional, never looking at Athos, leading him toward the inner recesses of her space. Once he has penetrated to an inner garden, she suddenly turns and holds him in her gaze, saying, "Don't be afraid!" She then leads him through another series of enclosures and places him next to a photograph of his father, saying, "Look how much you resemble him! You are Athos resuscitated!"

She immediately captures Athos in a web of identification with his father from which he seems unable to escape. And it is hardly a comfortable position. Like the child in the Oedipal stage—or the dreamer's regressive fan-

Figure 8. Draifa (Alida Valli) leads Athos (Giulio Brogi) to her villa become spider's web. Courtesy New Yorker Films.

tasy—Athos repeatedly hears the message, "Be like your father, but don't try to be too much like him !" Athos wrestles constantly in this film with the conflicting messages of seduction by this mother figure and the overweaning and deflating myth of the father. Surrounded by mementos of her dead lover, Draifa proposes to the son that he become the new hero of Tara by uncovering the murderers of the father. Terrified by the prospect of re-duplicating his father's position to such an extent, Athos threatens to pull away, whereupon Draifa faints, feigning death, like a spider. Athos turns to help and is caught inexorably in her traces. Draifa's self-conscious theatrics and Bertolucci's self-conscious cinematics in this scene—the stylized circular pan, the abrupt shift from day to night, the changing decor, and the camera's failure to "see" Draifa's fall, which is a direct allusion to the stylistic tour de force of *Prima*—all contribute to an invitation to meditate on the relation-ship of this psychological dynamic to that of cinema itself.

The web once begun is spun out through a series of "yarns" about Athos's

father. Draifa's contributions to these "memories" invariably include messages for Athos himself. In her version of the episode with the runaway lion,
Draifa visually recounts her last hours with his father in a way that signifies
her own intense ambivalence about the elder Magnani. When he insults her
sexual prowess, she winds Athos senior into a medical sarape, spinning him
around and around, in a gesture that recalls both the action of a reel of film
being *embobiné* and a spider mummifying and embalming its prey. Bertolucci's own version of male–female relations was once expressed in very
similar terms:

> In nature it is usually the female that devours. Genetically, over
> the centuries, some males have understood her mechanisms, have
> understood the danger. Some spiders just approach the female, but
> stay within safe distance. Exciting themselves with her smell, they
> masturbate, collect their sperm in their mouth and wait to regain
> strength after orgasm. Because that is how they get devoured, when
> they are weak after ejaculation. Later, they inseminate the female
> with a minimal approach and thus she cannot attack them in the
> moment of their weakness. . . . What can develop (between a man
> and a woman) is only possessiveness . . . the destruction of the
> loved object. [15]

There is clearly a warning in this scene in both its cinematic (reel) and its
offscreen (real) implications: Distance is a requirement of pleasure. Bertolucci reinscribes this warning into the fabric of the film at other moments as
well. At Razzori's house, Athos sits down to an enormous plate of tripe while
two women stand at the window of a locked door, carefully kept at a safe
distance. Other than these two carefully sequestered women and Draifa,
there are *no other women in all of Tara!* The only other time that women are
glimpsed, they have been carted into town as if they were livestock on a
trailer and sit *outside the theater* during the performance of *Rigoletto*. Athos
meets only old men who proclaim their fraternity: "Qui tutti son amici"
("Here all are friends"). Even the name Athos itself evokes the most famous
monastery in Greece, from whose territory all females, animal and human,
are excluded. Everything in this town appears to point to the lesson that
distance is a prerequisite for continued enjoyment of this drama and for film
itself.

Uncannily, Bertolucci has once again introduced an implied understanding of his viewer's relationship to his film. If, as has been amply theorized,[16] the cinema spectator is a kind of voyeur, his relationship to the screen is congruent to that of the voyeur and his perceived object.

Symbolically, once again, Bertolucci has subtly but convincingly succeeded in doubling the film's major character and spectator in a structure of identification. Like Athos, the film's spectator is symbolically *embobiné* in a relationship that guarantees that our pleasure will be carefully "bound" by the rules governing the cinematic experience. As cinematic voyeurs, we choose a place carefully established at a minimum distance from the filmic event. Our "present absence" combined with the "absent presence" of the projected images constitute the conditions requisite for pleasure: an identification carefully uncommitted and a consummation inevitably deferred.

Having thus proffered a vision of the father's entrapment and symbolic castration, Draifa states emphatically, "That was the last time I ever saw him." She then proceeds to attempt alternately to reduce Athos to a child and to elevate him to his dead father's position. Her gestures always seem equivocal—like her name, Draifa, a feminine Dreyfus, the symbol of ambiguity between traitor and hero in France. When he follows her home, she brushes him away as if he were a three-year-old nuisance, saying, "I'm busy." At other times there is a concomitant effort to mold him into the form of his father, including both a virilization (clothing him in his father's old jacket and scarf) and an emasculating entrapment: "You cannot go away any more."

Gaibazzi, Costa, and Razzori each reinforce these conflicting messages in their versions of the myth of Athos. The dead father "was more intelligent. . . . He overshadowed us all. . . . Your father led an exceptional life." Yet Athos is encouraged to pursue the *rescue* of his father, which projects him in psychoanalytic terms into the role of his own father, his mother's lover. He simultaneously receives the message that he could never achieve his father's mythic status. The myth of the overpowering and vengeful father is mercilessly repeated, with variations, by the spinners of this tale: Draifa cites *Macbeth, Julius Caesar, Othello; Gaibazzi evokes *Hernani*, as well as Sam and Tom of *A Masked Ball*, in which the hero is killed by his best friend. Costa tells his tale standing near a movie poster of "L'Occhio caldo de cielo," that is, Apollo. The name Athos itself may refer to Dumas's character in *The Three Musketeers* who was betrayed and poisoned by a friend.[17] Throughout the film, the music of Verdi's *Rigoletto* provides a steady obbligato of mythic dimension. "Verdi corresponds for me—and thus for the son of Athos Magnani—with a mythic dimension," said Bertolucci, "and that works very well with the mythical structure of the father. Mythic music for a mythic personage."[18]

All of the mythic references—and there are legions of them!—correspond perfectly with the Borges story from which the film was adapted, "The Theme of the Traitor and the Hero." In Borges's text, Ryan discovers "facets of the enigma . . . of a cyclic nature: they seem to repeat or combine events of remote regions of remote ages."[19] Among these reenactments emerge elements from *Caesar, Macbeth, Hernani,* and so on. In Borges's story, the father was "killed in a theater, but the entire city was a theater as well, and the actors were legion and the drama crowned by his death extended over many days and many nights." (Bertolucci's Athos senior very self-consciously repeats this phrase of Borges's story as he stands in the tower surveying the town shortly after his betrayal has been discovered by the three friends.) As in the Borges text, Bertolucci's Athos becomes aware of a "pattern of repeated lines" and "circular labyrinths" too contrived to be accidental. There are simply too many clues given for him to fail to discover the truth: that the assumed hero had in fact betrayed his companions. As in the story, "he suspects that the author interpolated them so that he too forms part of the plot."[20]

These discoveries are at one with the nature of the Oedipal configuration because resolution of the Oedipal conflict in the male child involves the discovery that the father is *both* hero (as father to be imitated and emulated) and traitor (as seducer of the mother). They also reproduce the very nature of dreams and their interpretation, inasmuch as the circularity of the film metaphorizes the circularity of the tangled, multiple, and often conflicting identities of the "family romance" in the nexus of the (Oedipal) dream.[21] The impasse for the child is complete. Confronted with the father's duplicity and fallibility, the child has no choice but to remain silent or to acquiesce to the myth, for to broadcast his discovery is, the child believes, to risk castration or to threaten the father's very being and risk usurping his place. Such a "murder" (Freud's term) would cast the son as the father (for he has already projected himself as an imitation of the father), that is, as traitor and hero himself!

The Spider's Stratagem rather brilliantly demonstrates the double bind that seems inexorably to condemn the son to repeat the father's image no matter which choice he makes. Compelled to find the murderer of his father, Athos's quest leads him to the theater and the very box in which his father was killed. Sitting in his father's seat, he suddenly realizes with horror, "My father *recognized the murderer in the mirror* which explains why he made no attempt to escape !" Athos at first misunderstands the (otherwise obvious) implications of this discovery, believing that his father had seen the images of his three friends in the doorway behind him. But in fact the "other" in the mirror is, like the spectator in the darkened cinema and like the child in Lacan's mirror stage, *himself*.[22] In arriving at this discovery, Athos *repeats* his father's experience, and ours, and thus symbolically doubles his father in the mirror. As double of his father he in turn both recapitulates and usurps paternity; that is, he is a hero (in fantasy) and a traitor (in his refusal of engagement). No matter which way he turns he seems destined to encounter yet another structure of repetition.

His fear of the three friends causes him to double his father's attempt to escape them, and this flight through the woods is captured in a remarkable demonstration of parallel cutting in which Bertolucci repeatedly moves from father to son and back again.

Aware that the father has been reduced to a mere fraternal rival by Draifa, frustrated that his own desire to recover a sustaining authority seems to lead only to the disillusionment of repetition, realizing that the attempt to return to origins leads only to the discovery of the same, Athos attacks the symbol of family history, his father's tomb. He first erases his father's birthdate (1900) and then, coincidentally, his own (1936), for his father's death is coeval with his own birth, and finally desecrates his father's (and, inevitably, his own) portrait. Father and son have collapsed in on each other as one identity, destroying, or rather "destorying," family history. Without hierarchy and authority there can be no progression, no history, no story. It is also a scene that was predicted in the most uncanny mise-en-scène of the entire film. When, earlier, Athos approaches the painted bust of his father, he tries to walk around it, to "get behind" this mystery of identity. But the statue rotates as Athos walks, forever blindly throwing back Athos's own features in a maddening surface image of sameness.

The pessimism of this set of structures at first seems to parallel *Partner*, which is so thoroughly situated in a "modernist" aesthetic, with its insistence on discontinuous (rather than hierarchical) structures, on metonymic (rather than metaphorical) tropes, and on fraternal (rather than

Figure 9. Athos Magnani approaches the bust of his father/double.
Courtesy The Museum of Modern Art/Film Stills Archive.

paternal) relationships.[23] Yet, curiously, Magritte's presence in this work suggests another, less pessimistic interpretation, for if his work signifies the oneiric, it also forcefully raises the issues of representation and illusion. There is a scene in the film that directly evokes this other aspect of Magritte's work. Costa agrees to meet Athos in his open-air cinema. As he tells of Athos's father, he walks to the large empty screen at one end of the courtyard and raises the screen to reveal the lush green landscape hidden behind it—and which it is presumably the function of many of the films shown there to represent. Many of Magritte's paintings raise just this issue. Canvases that render indistinguishable the painted scene from its model are in fact meditations on the act of representation itself.

In *This Is Not a Pipe*, Michel Foucault discusses the difference between *resemblance* and *similitude* in Magritte's work in a way that shows it to be uncannily pertinent to the fundamental structure of Bertolucci's entire film. In such paintings as *Representation,*

> Magritte dissociated similitude from resemblance, and brought the former into play against the latter. Resemblance has a "model," an original (in its most transitive sense, that is, not only "first" but also generative") element that orders and hierarchizes the increasingly less faithful copies that can be struck from it. Resemblance presupposes a primary reference that prescribes and classes. The similar develops in series that have neither beginning nor end, that can be followed in one direction as easily as in another, that obey no hierarchy, but propagate themselves from small differences among small differences. Resemblance serves representation, which rules over it; similitude serves repetition, which ranges across it. Resemblance predicates itself upon a model it must return to and reveal; similitude circulates the simulacrum as an indefinite and reversible relation of the similar to the similar. [24]

Although Athos's relation to the image of his father seems to entrap him, much like his father in Draifa's "reel" of linen, in an inescapable labyrinth of similitude, endless repetitions that seem to allow no progression, Bertolucci's film, like *Prima* and *Partner* before it, bears another kind of relation to the text it is intended to "represent." Borges's text is fashioned on the figure of repetition, on "patterns of repeated lines" and "circular labyrinths," reenactments of previous myths, tragedies, opera, and legends. Certainly Bertolucci's text plays Athos in some ways similar to Borges's, for the film certainly does *repeat these repetitions.* Yet it is Bertolucci's genius to have incorporated these internal repetitions without repeating the structure of the whole.

Spider differs from the Borges text in several capital ways. Whereas the Borges text necessarily remains always at the level of potentiality ("I have imagined this story plot which I shall perhaps write someday"), Bertolucci has his enacted and realized in a film. Of course it is true that Borges "tells" the story he promises someday to tell, but it is told in an abstract and conditional way. Rather than repeat this feature in a sterile simulacrum of the original, Bertolucci has once again transcended the limitations of textual imitation by translating the very potentiality of Borges's text, itself emblematic of the unrealized nature of all written texts vis-à-vis the images of reality they seek to elicit, into a cinematic style that is both "realized" and pro-foundly original. Magritte's presence in the film serves notice that cinema is hardly a copy or repetition of some preexistent reality but an adaptation of it *on its own terms.* Once again, Bertolucci's dialogue with Bazin is evident. The very potentiality at the heart of Borges's narrative strategy has here been replaced by its cinematic equivalent: a dreamlike structure that elevates every element of the "original" narrative from the status of the "potential" to the level of images that enjoy the force of the "reality" of dreams. In this move, Bertolucci has reasserted what is fundamental to cinema: its dream-like structuration, which allows the viewer to engage in creative (and not simply passive) seeing. He even manages to figuralize this difference visu-ally! When Athos meets Beccarria in the municipal theater, Bertolucci's antirealistic editing has them jump from seat to seat without transition or explanation. This scene metonymically signals the film's potential to be a creative construction and metaphorically reproduces what Nick Browne calls the film viewer's "ability to be in many places at once."[25]

The entire film, then, functions at one level as a metaphor of the very *difference* of cinema from literature. Nor is it merely an attempt to film a dream. Although clearly oneiric in its presentation, it is hardly a mere repetition of the structure of dreamwork, for the stylistic effects that so forcefully lead toward this oneiric interpretation are also recollections of Bertolucci's earlier edicts on film style. This self-consciousness about the medium and its relation to dreams should alert us to the fact that *The Spider's Stratagem* is not merely an illustration of a dream; it is *about* the relation-ship between dreaming and cinema and about the problematics of repre-sentation that are at the heart of any interpretation.

At the conclusion of the film, Athos is left to contemplate the tall grass, which weaves yet another confining web over the train tracks, signaling that there will be no train to enable him to escape his struggles with the identity of the parents and the inexorable contemplation of *similitude.* This too was foreseen by Borges, but in another text:

> Music, states of happiness, mythology, faces balabored by time, certain twilights and certain places try to tell us something, or have said something we should not have missed, or are about to say something; this imminence of a revelation which does not occur is, perhaps, the aesthetic phenomenon.[26]

If *The Spider's Stratagem* seems to be a remarkably faithful visual representation of this other text, this "imminence of a revelation which does not occur" belongs to Athos rather than to Bertolucci. If the nexus of this dream is, in Freud's terms, a "tangle which cannot be unravelled"[27] (I am tempted to say "last tangle," but that would be premature), that nexus, the unconscious itself, is also a matrix, a womb whose role, as John Perry has noted, "is one of destroying *and* recreating, of dissolving *and* resynthesizing, of devouring *and* giving birth."[28] The film's genius, it seems to me, is to have worked at the level of anecdote with a version of the Oedipal struggle as impasse while simultaneously managing at the level of cinematic style to go beyond the authoritative model to affirm the creative process itself.

However the thing might have been, whether it had really happened, it was nevertheless a dream because it was not to be explained in a rational manner.

ALBERTO MORAVIA

5 THE UNCONFORMING CONFORMIST

"*The Spider's Stratagem* and *The Conformist* have in common the theme of betrayal, the presence of the past that returns, and the weight of the paternal figure," said Bertolucci of his two films released in 1970. "The difference is that in *The Conformist* the son, Trintignant, betrays Professor Quadri (the father figure) whereas in *The Spider's Stratagem* it is Athos the father who has betrayed. In any case the films treat two parricides which suppose a past and a memory."[1] Seeing these two films as, in some sense, doubles of each other allows an appreciation of the many ways in which "betrayal" can be understood as fundamental to Bertolucci's larger project of this period. This movement from focusing on the betrayal of the father to concentrating on the son's treachery is rich in implications for the film itself, for the development of Bertolucci's larger work, and for the understanding of the dynamics of cinema itself.

At the anecdotal level of the film, the dynamics of betrayal are only too obvious in *The Conformist*. Once Professor Quadri's best student, Marcello Clerici (Jean-Louis Trintignant), journeys from Rome to Paris on his honeymoon in order to betray and murder his former mentor (Enzo Tarascio). Quadri himself is certainly a paternal figure for Clerici, who has "lost" his own father to an insane asylum. The young Fascist's recollections of his professor are highly ambivalent: Quadri was, on the one hand, the butt of his students' jokes. As an intellectual presence, however, he had a lasting impact on Clerici despite their grave political differences. As an antifascist, living in exile in Paris, Quadri is, like Athos's father, a figure of questionable loyalty: Is he traitor or hero? Clerici cannot decide. He ultimately betrays Quadri, his own fascist ideals, and himself, for when it comes time to act he will simply watch from a car as others assassinate Quadri and his wife in the woods of Savoie. At the moment of crisis, he is not only incapable of acting on his fascist convictions, he is unable to lift a finger to save the woman who has inspired his life's greatest passion. His motives for this plan will remain a mystery to the Fascist bosses who have sent him on this expedition. Clerici can indeed be compared to Athos Magnani senior, because both are the architects of plots to assassinate father figures who have become political enemies, yet neither is able to act on the plan he has devised. In both films an intimate connection between treason and self-betrayal and between the separate identities of father and son considerably clouds the definition of Bertolucci's main character.

In *The Conformist* several other levels of betrayal are also at work. There is one scene in particular that considerably illumines several other aspects of this film. When, during their evening together in Paris, Professor Quadri asks Clerici to deliver a letter for the antifascist cause, Clerici, as a loyal Fascist, refuses. Quadri unexpectedly thanks him for that refusal and reveals that the request was a test to see whether Clerici would accept the letter and then betray its contents. This incident is remarkable at many levels. It is a prime example of betrayal at *both* paternal and filial levels, for Quadri has acted to trap Clerici by means of a clever ruse, yet Clerici's refusal to take the letter ironically appears to vindicate him at the very moment he is most committed to Quadri's destruction. The incident figuralizes the theme of appearance versus reality that has been the very center of an earlier discussion between the two.

Taken directly from Moravia's *Il conformista*,[2] this scene contains a significant deviation emblematic of Bertolucci's entire relationship to the original. Whereas in the novel Quadri simply thanks Clerici for refusing to take the letter (p. 260), in the film Quadri shows the letter to Clerici, revealing it to be a blank page. Quadri's letter, then, functions as a gratuitous sign—gratuitous precisely in terms of its relation to the Moravia original and of its necessity to the action of the film—of the unreliability of texts. Proffered by the professor whom Marcello feels he must betray in order to establish his own identity, this letter may also be interpreted as the Moravia novel itself in relation to Bertolucci's film.

Virtually every instance of writing in this film is highly charged: Literature functions constantly as a trap or contains empty, false, or indecipherable writing; in short, texts never seem to be reliable.

Of the four explicit mise-en-scènes of texts in this film, two involve Marcello's real father. In both cases, writing emphasizes the conflict and the ambiguity surrounding the paternal relationship. In the first instance, Giulia's mother produces an anonymous letter claiming that Marcello has inherited a syphilitic disease from his father, that is, that father has betrayed son through sexual activity. But Giulia guesses that the author of this infamous letter is "Uncle" Perpuzio, the father figure of her youth who had taken advantage of her when she was fourteen and then held her in sexual bondage for years. As signifier, the letter spells paternal betrayal at a variety of levels. Though it is true that this incident is included in Moravia's text, its reinsertion in the context of the cinematic narrative gives it an entirely different and, as it turns out, ironic connotation. As text, it produces a conscious denunciation of the authority of Marcel's father, and at an unconscious level it constitutes an autodenunciation of both text and author/ parent Perpuzio. Moreover, the simplistic equation between psychology and (biological) destiny, despite its inclusion in Moravia's novel, can, in this context, be interpreted as a critique of the novel itself, which indulges in exactly this sort of theorizing at the level of narrative. If the son is the betrayer in this film, the father or authority figure is hardly without blame.

The second example of paternal writing even more clearly establishes Bertolucci's ambivalent relationship to author-ity. When Marcello visits his father in the asylum, the old man is sitting in a huge forum—architecture ironically reminiscent of the Fascist authority's office—writing madly. In Moravia's novel, the son listens rather disinterestedly to the father's mad ramblings. In the film, Clerici seizes his father's manuscript and holds it up to ridicule, then takes his father's pen hand in his own and guides it in the writing of his father's signature on his wedding banns, giving father as origin and son as progeny equal authority. Next, Marcello taunts his father with recollections of the father's former crimes of torture and murder while an Italian resistance fighter, goading him until he breaks down and demands to be straitjacketed. Here Marcello creates another, albeit unconscious, equation between his father and himself, for he will soon repeat those crimes in the service of another political regime. He will, moreover, repeat this autoaccusation for the church father in the scene of the confessional. The entire scene convincingly portrays Marcello's obsession with repudiating and imitating authority simultaneously.

Clearly, writing, for Bertolucci, continues to be the locus of conflict and intense ambivalence. Even his own script of the film, as text, became a battleground:

> Often cinema is merely an illustration of a story. That is the
> biggest danger you face when you make a film from a novel. That was
> my problem when I made *The Conformist*. Many filmmakers use
> their scripts as if they had started from a novel; they simply make an
> illustrated film of the script. On the other hand, I, too, start from
> a very precise script, but only in order to destroy it. . . . To write
> a script for me is a literary experience. . . . when I'm writing, I can't
> think of shooting because to write is to write. Words are words, not
> images. . . . I must be completely free when I'm shooting. I can't
> follow the script.[3]

Clearly, the vocabulary chosen here is not one of indifference: The text is not something to be ignored; it is something to be *destroyed* in order to gain one's freedom. The battle lines drawn so many years earlier continue to feel as fresh as when, Bertolucci muses, "I first began to want to make films in the desire, the need, to do something different from what my father did. He was a poet and I wanted to compete with him, but not by doing the same thing. I used to write poetry myself, but I realised that I would lose that battle, so I had to find a different terrain on which to compete."[4]

The filial-paternal conflict, so firmly drawn up around the themes of the paternal logos versus the filial image, continue to haunt and animate *The Conformist*. But Bertolucci, however clever and expedient these visual critiques of texts may be, is not content to leave the issue there. The central scene of this film, the confrontation with Quadri over the interpretation of Plato's dialogue on the cave, moves the level of Bertolucci's critique to another plane altogether. In Quadri's apartment, Marcello reminds his former professor of his lectures on Plato and quotes:

> Picture a sort of subterranean cavern with a long entrance open to
> the light on its entire width. Inside are men who have been there
> since childhood. Chained together they are forced to face the interior
> of the cave. Light glows from a fire some distance behind them.
> Between the fire and the prisoners imagine a long low wall has been
> built, as the exhibitors of puppet shows have partitions before the
> men themselves, above which they show the puppets.[5]

Marcello's "faithful" recollection of Quadri's lectures on Plato appears as a homage to their earlier master–disciple relationship, but is in fact merely an attempt to blind the professor to Marcello's real perversity.

As he quotes this passage from Plato's *Republic,* Quadri is silhouetted as if on a screen against the harsh light of the open window behind him and consequently gives the impression of being merely a shadow on a "wall" of light, inadvertently illustrating the most celebrated text in Western culture on illusion and reality as tragic elements of our human condition. This cinematic tour de force brings many levels of this film together: As Quadri warns Clerici about the dangers of his own illusions, the professor is rendered merely an illusion by the lighting of the scene, subtly undermining the strength of his message.[6] By this visual insistence on the link between a darkened cavern and a lighted puppet show, Bertolucci uncannily displaces the subject of the Platonic text from the human condition to a series of other meanings.

If, as Jean-Louis Baudry has theorized,[7] in both Plato's and Freud's depictions of the "other scene" the illusions discussed are actually deformations or "symptoms" in Freudian terms, then Plato's prisoner is, no less than Freud's psychotic, a victim of hallucinations in the waking state. The defense against such illusions turns out, ironically, to be conformity itself. Indeed, Joyce McDougall argues that "Normality is an overadaptation to the real world" and that "no one doubts that conformity erected as an ideal is a well compensated psychosis."[8] The scene in question becomes, then, a metaphor for Clerici's entire conforming approach to the world.

As a metaphorical prisoner of Plato's cave, Clerici takes on the additional representation of passive viewer, analogous in many instances to the film viewers themselves. Indeed, it is precisely this similarity between the cave and the cinema that Baudry develops in his essay on the origins of the cinema. Plato's insistence on the immobility of his prisoners is congruent, Baudry argues, to the first such immobility we experience, that is, "that of the child at its birth, deprived of resources of movement, and also that of the sleeper who repeats, as is well known, the postnatal state and even intrauterine life, and it is also the immobility that the visitor to the darkened movie theater experiences settled deep in his seat."[9] Bertolucci later confessed that the scene was indeed about cinema, "because when you read the cave of Plato's, the cave is exactly like the theater and the background is the screen and Plato says there is a fire and people walking in front of the fire and the fire projects the shadows in the background of the cave. It's the invention of cinema."[10]

Now this multileveled interpretation of the "cave scene" of *The Conformist* suggests that, once again, Bertolucci has not only brilliantly conducted a meditation on the difference between the written text and the cinema but centered that meditation in the relation between the ontology of the cinema and that of man. Bertolucci "betrays" two texts here (Plato's and Moravia's) and in so doing hardens his position on writing—but in the very methods of his subversion he illustrates in a remarkably condensed form just how the cinema, in a language all its own, involves the viewer in the most fundamental of experiences.

There is yet another level of "betrayal" at work here. The allusion to cinema and the reduction of Quadri to a black and white, two-dimensional image suggest that the professor may symbolize one of Bertolucci's cinematic mentors. Indeed, Quadri's address and phone number—given as 17, rue St. Jacques; telephone: MED–15–37—belonged in 1971 to Jean-Luc Godard. Bertolucci confessed, in fact, that

> *The Conformist* is a story about me and Godard. When I gave the professor Godard's phone number and address, I did it for a joke, but afterwards I said to myself, "Well maybe all that has some significance. . . . I'm Marcello and I make fascist movies and I want to kill Godard who is a revolutionary, who makes revolutionary movies and who was my teacher."[11]

This "killing" of Godard *and* his father the poet left Bertolucci on very new ground indeed: The challenge clearly lay in charting a path between the radical rejection of narrative proposed by Godard, which so isolated the French filmmaker, and conformity to written texts, a path that lay in a conscious or unconscious imitation of another French filmmaker, who had managed to synthesize a more traditional narrative with a new, much more self-consciously cinematic aesthetic. François Truffaut had provided a model in *Tirez sur le pianiste*, already alluded to in *Partner* and directly imitated in this film (especially in the sequence of Quadri's assassination). The thrust of Bertolucci's creativity was clearly directed once again toward working out a cinematic style that would render, without slavishly imitating it, Moravia's novel.

Because Moravia most obviously constitutes the textual authority being explicitly imitated and implicitly contested in this film, it is crucial to understand in what other ways Bertolucci has adapted the novel to a specifically cinematic style. Remarkably, Bertolucci is more "faithful" to the anecdotal level of this novel than he is in any of his other films based on literary texts. Perhaps, by the time he made *The Conformist*, he felt less anxious about the relationship between film and literature. In this film, he managed to retain many of the elements of Moravia's narrative, choosing to situate his meditation on the specificity of cinema in other, more subtle elements of his film. Clearly, Bertolucci's first and most dramatic departure from Moravia's novel was his refusal to imitate the novel's insistently systematic chronology and causality, composed as though the novelist had to demonstrate a particular theory of psychoanalytic determinism.

From Marcello's first sadistically violent games in his parents' garden to his ultimate betrayal of Quadri, Moravia follows the progress of his protagonist with an almost deadening chronological rigor and proleptic foreboding. His parents' neglect of Marcello leads to the child's symbolic castration of "a fine clump of marguerites covered with white and yellow flowers, or a tulip with its red cup erect on a green stalk, or a cluster of arums with tall, white fleshy flowers . . . leaving the decapitated stalks standing erect" (p. 7).

Moravia's narrator stresses that it is "inevitable" that Marcello should pass from these symbolic acts to a massacre of dozens of lizards, and from this frenzied agitation to the "murder" of the family cat. In this last act, Marcello perceives "an unmistakable sign that he was predestined, in some mysterious and fatal way, to accomplish acts of cruelty and death" (p. 19). These fatal signs of Marcello's abnormality serve as the context for the central psychological moment of the novel. All too willingly seduced by Lino, a pederastic chauffeur, Marcello takes up the pistol constituting and symbolizing the exchange that was to have taken place and "kills" the perverse Lino.

The rest of Moravia's novel painstakingly charts Marcello's misguided attempt to atone for this childhood "crime" through a life of "well-defined, barren, reserved, benumbed, grey normality" (p. 72). He dedicates himself to total conformity by marrying the most apparently ordinary, uninspired, materialistic, middle-class woman he can find; by going to confession in order to be married ("a further link in the chain of normality," adds Moravia [p. 96] in case we should have missed the point), and by joining the Fascist party, "as an abstract whole, as a great, existing army held together by common feelings, common ideas, common aims, an army of which it was comforting to form a part," despite the fact that, as individuals, he finds it "impossible to recognize himself in them and feels at the same time both repugnance and detachment" (p. 77).

It is of course heavily ironic that the Fascist party sanctions Marcello's plan to betray (and symbolically to murder) one of his former professors during Marcello's honeymoon in Paris. Rather than anonymity and atonement, Marcello finds within the Fascist ranks an ever more murderous destiny, so that "the figure of Judas, the thirteenth Apostle, became confused with his own, coalesced with its outlines, in fact *was* his own" (p. 193). Moravia not only exposes fascism as a barely repressed perversion but also raises a more general question about the nature of conformity. Each time Marcello believes he has espoused normality, he discovers a new form of perversion. His "normal" bride turns out not only to have been the illicit child concubine of a well-known Roman lawyer but also to have carried on a lesbian affair immediately preceding their marriage. The priest who hears Marcello's confession rather perfunctorily exacts a few prayers of penance for the "murder" of Lino but expresses avid interest in the particulars of Marcello's sexual encounter with the chauffeur. Moravia's Quadri "sacrificed [his antifascist initiates] quite coolly in desperate actions . . . that . . . involved a cruel indifference to the value of human life" (pp. 182–83). Quadri's wife Lina not only doubles the perverted chauffeur of Marcello's "original sin" in name but repeats Lino's homosexual seduction on Marcello's much too willing wife (p. 231). Fleeing this discovery, Marcello seeks seclusion on a park bench and ends up being approached by an older man with a large black limousine. Moravia's novel hammers doggedly away at the overwhelmingly evident message of *Il conformista*: Normality, as Marcello imagines it, is an illusion. Society is a composite of polymorphously perverse individuals in a

> topsy-turvy sterile world in which merely sensual relationships occurred from the most natural and ordinary to the most abnormal and unusual, [between] ambiguous figures of men-women and women-men whose ambiguity when they met was mingled and redoubled. [Pp. 233–34]

Moravia insists repeatedly on this theme: Virtually every character becomes a distorted double of every other. Lino as homosexual chauffeur with a coveted pistol is redoubled by Orlando (and the Fascist authorities), the mother's lover (and therefore by extension Marcello's father), the old man in the park, and Lina. Lina is also portrayed as a double of a whore in Ventimiglia (and therefore Marcello's promiscuous mother), as well as a double of Giulia. Quadri doubles not only Marcello's father but also Orlando and the Fascists. Moravia single-mindedly builds an enormous but simple equation in which all the characters collapse into a composite image of the bad parent.

This repetitive explicitness, frequently bemoaned by Moravia's otherwise sympathetic critics, is mirrored by the author's overly insistent use of destiny. Moravia repeatedly alludes to Greek tragedy in general and to the Oedipus myth in particular. From his first taste of violence, Marcello discovers in it "an unmistakable sign that he was predestined, in some mysterious and fatal way, to accomplish acts of cruelty and death" (p. 19), a passage that bears but superficial resemblance to Borges's "Theme of the Traitor and the Hero."[12] Whereas Borges devises in "a pattern of repeated lines" an uncanny relationship between literature and its double, Moravia constructs a weighty monument to an unimaginative version of Freudian determinism. Marcello is caught, Moravia insists on reminding us, in

> a trap of which you have been forewarned, which, even, you can see clearly, but into which nevertheless, you cannot help putting your foot. Or just a curse of . . . blindness that creeps into your movements, your senses, your blood . . . an intimate, obscure, inborn, inscrutable fatality . . . which stood like a signboard at the opening of a sinister road. He knew that this fatality implied he would kill somebody; but what frightened him most was not so much murder as the knowledge that he was predestined to it, whatever he might do.

"Like a signboard at the opening of a sinister road," Moravia's insistence on certain themes leaves little to the imagination. The novel in fact offers an excellent foil for Bertolucci's adaptation for the screen, for it engages in a kind of hyperbolic *literalness*. Clearly, the doubling, the Oedipal configurations, and the mythic level of Moravia's novel all attracted Bertolucci to a text that was for him like a "memory of my own memory."[13] But for the film director that memory was now inexorably filtered through film itself. If *Spider's Stratagem* was influenced by "life and by memories of childhood:

Baccanelli, Sabbionetta, the countryside when I was a kid," *The Conformist* was influenced "by cinema . . . by the memories of American and French films of the 30s."[14]

If, on the anecdotal level, what attracted Bertolucci to Moravia's novel was "the ambiguity of the main character,"[15] at the stylistic level Bertolucci clearly wanted to experiment with editing as a cinematic adaptation of Moravia's literariness. Previously Bertolucci had considered editing a kind of autopsy or castration of the living material of the camerawork. With *The Conformist* he was to discover that, "even in editing, one can leave the door open to chance, that one can improvise, that rather than being only a moment of analysis, editing can reveal secrets hidden in the belly of the film that we never would have seen otherwise."[16] Thus, to the deadening chronology of Moravia's novel, Bertolucci opposed improvisation and revelation; to Moravia's literariness, he proposed the "memory of my memory": a remembrance of films past, a cinema recaptured. To the figure of doubles in Moravia's text, he responded with a meditation on the primary doubling, always already accomplished, which is, according to Christian Metz, the nature of the cinematic signifier itself.

The film opens with Marcello (Trintignant) sitting somnolent on a bed in a darkened room, periodically illuminated by a red neon sign outside his window which spells ESTAN, a kind of present participle of the verb "to be." In this initial position, he has coincidentally assumed a position nearly identical to that of both Charles Aznavour in the opening scenes of Truffaut's *Tirez sur le pianiste* and of the film viewer watching him, on whose face the same colored lights are intermittently reflected. When the phone beside him rings, he awakens from his reverie and reaches for the phone with a surprising suddenness. Hanging up the receiver, he grabs his hat from its perch on the nude posterior of the unidentified woman sleeping beside him and heads for the door. In the street below, he hails a 1930s-model car, leaps in, and begins the pursuit of another car through the mist of a snowy Paris morning. It is an exposition worthy of the American detective films of the forties, a salute to Dashiell Hammett, whose *Red Harvest* Bertolucci has, for years, wanted to film.

Nothing is explained, and nothing will be explained through traditional narrative exposition and chronological sequence. The viewers must garner whatever understanding they can from a system of flashbacks out of a point of time given as the film's "present" (the car ride out of Paris) to a series of moments that themselves do not proceed chronologically. Bertolucci's use of flashbacks is unusual not only for its disregard of chronology but also for the tendency to use flashbacks out of flashbacks. Progression occurs clearly by association rather than logic. Each scene presents images and/or information that must be stored and read associatively rather than analytically. The viewer is forced to watch in the way an analyst listens, for clues that can later be pieced together to form an interpretation. What is most cinematic about this arrangement is that the narrative "authority" of the film has been vested both in the associative process of the main character *and* in an omniscient camera. Rather than imitating Moravia's omniscient narrator, Bertolucci has, to use Nick Browne's phrase, situated the spectator simultaneously in many places in the film's text, imitating instead the multiple identities of dreams.

The first of the film's flashbacks jumps the spectator into a recording studio where Marcello is, characteristically, listening and watching. Indeed, his own status as passive viewer is emphatically marked by the wall of glass that separates him, like Razzori's glazed doors, from the women singing in the studio. Bertolucci frequently captures Marcello's reflection in the glass of the studio, perhaps alluding to the mirroring function of cinema itself. During this episode, Marcello listens to a group of women singing, a speech glorifying fascism, and a man doing bird calls—a potpourri of programming that puts a serious strain on the spectator's belief in the realism of the scene. Interspersed in this jumble of elements are shots of Marcello dwarfed by enormous Fascist architecture on which yet another text, this time a Latin lapidary inscription of Hadrian (the Roman emperor who managed, unlike Caesar—and Quadri—to escape an assassination attempt), resists adequate deciphering. Whatever "warning" there may be in this text is lost on the viewer partly because of the force of the image itself and partly because of the rapidity of the editing of these sequences. It is impossible at a first viewing to situate these scenes logically or chronologically: Only at subsequent viewings do the pieces of this assemblage create a proper cinematic sequence. A sudden cut returns to the radio station, now darkened, where Marcello awakes (perhaps from the dream the film viewer has just witnessed) to find himself opposite a mysterious personage whose entry into the studio we have not witnessed. From their conversation, it ultimately becomes clear that this character is a Fascist agent sent to inform Marcello that his plan for a "working" honeymoon in Paris has been approved. Another cut projects

Figure 10. Marcello (Jean-Louis Trintignant) dwarfed by Roman
architecture. Courtesy The Museum of Modern Art/Film Stills Archive.

Marcello just as inexplicably into a different Fascist architectural immensity.
Flashes back and forth to and from the car ride out of Paris further confuse
whatever narrative thread can be followed.

In direct contrast to the careful chronology and rational presentation of
Moravia's text, Bertolucci presents the viewer with a content and a structure that can only be described as oneiric and implicitly cinematic. These
scenes not only lack causal and chronological coherence but proceed by
association, condensation, displacement, and doubling, all techniques of
latent dreamwork.

The clearest example of these dream structures involves the uncanny reappearance of Dominique Sanda in three different roles. Unlike Moravia's
text, which is reduced to making Lina's double an explicit and therefore
consciously authorian device, here the impact, possible interpretation, and

indeed the very fact of Sanda's reappearance in several different roles without commentary are left entirely to the film's spectator to measure. The cinematic rendition of this doubling thus succeeds to a much greater degree than does the novel in placing upon the viewer the task of associating and organizing the visual material. Sanda is most prominently cast as Anna Quadri, wife of the professor whom Marcello inexplicably wants to kill. Notably, the first reference to Anna in the "present tense" of the film (the automobile trip to Savoie) comes *via Marcello's dream*: "I just had a strange dream. I was blind. You were taking me to a clinic in Switzerland. Quadri was operating on me. The operation was a success; I got my sight back. Then I ran off with Anna."

In this dream, Marcello condenses his own character with that of the older Italo, who is blind and whom he will feverishly denounce at the end of the film; with his father, a madman in a clinic; with Hitler, whom he has previously referred to in terms that perfectly describe his own father; and with Quadri, for Marcello takes Quadri's place in the dream. It is an Oedipal scenario complete with an allusion to the infant's castration anxiety (blindness) and a manifest threat of that anxiety (Quadri's operation), followed by successful union with the mother figure, Quadri's wife. Notably, Manganiello (Gastone Moschin) figures in the dream as chauffeur and therefore a double of Lino, the pederastic chauffeur who seduced the child Marcello. Marcello's blindness may also signify a denial of both male seduction fantasies and dreams of murderous revenge. Switzerland, that is, the mountains of Savoie, condenses the destination of their present trip (where Marcello will indeed kill Quadri) with a state of neutrality, the perfect conformity that has blinded everyone to Marcello's perversity—what Joyce McDougall has called "a well compensated psychosis."[17]

Remarkably congruent in content and structure to the entire film, each of the elements of this dream appears in manifest or latent form in the film, and each undergoes a similar degree of primary process distortion, or dreamwork. Condensation, displacement, and doubling are the structural counterparts of the series of fantastic and/or oneiric elements permeating the narrative.

When Marcello first visits Giulia's apartment, a confluence of decor, costume, and lighting gives the entire scene an obsessive and inexplicable striped effect, suggesting the emotional ambivalence predominant in Marcello—and, undoubtedly, the prison of marriage he is about to enter. On their train ride to Paris, the decor outside the compartment window is patently unreal. Bertolucci says that he

> wanted to have two levels. One was the realistic level inside the train and the other one was a sort of film in the film. A window like a magic lantern. So, outside the time is very surrealistic, very magic, because in two minutes you have sunset and night, and [there are] also some dissolves in the window but not in the train.[18]

Fantastic voyage indeed! Bertolucci underscores the undecidability of Marcello's position by having him recite, during this train ride, a poem of D'Annunzio, who supported fascism yet is famous for his decadent poems in which he passionately celebrates sensual pleasures without any real concern for morality or conscience.

The bordello in Ventimiglia is inexplicably grandiose; the desk and bookshelves of Raoul's office, for some never-to-be-explained reason, are lined with walnuts, and on leaving that offiice Marcello makes three utterly uncharacteristically grandiloquent gestures with the pistol, ending in a mock gesture of suicide. Dominique Sanda's brief appearance in this "brothel" is uncanny, for the viewer has but fleetingly glimpsed her in the arms of a Fascist minister and has not yet encountered her in her role as Anna Quadri. Thus the "recognition factor," to the degree that the viewer succeeds at all in this, can be exercised only hazily and in retrospect and cannot be verified except by a second viewing of the film. Indeed, many viewers of *The Conformist* are surprised to learn that Sanda is cast in three roles. Ultimately, the effect of this chronology produces a kind of subliminal, rather than explicit, identification of Anna as "whore" and "Fascist mistress"—an effect specific to the properties of cinematic montage and all too explicit in the novel.

Once in Paris, Anna accepts Marcello's sexual advances despite her obvious dislike of him, a scenario that one would expect only of a dream script. When he attempts to discover the address of her dance class, he finds a perfectly new label announcing that address attached unrealistically to an otherwise well-worn pair of ballet shoes. Dreams are notorious for mixing past and present and generally ignoring such logical contradictions. During the soirée with Quadri and Anna, Marcello again takes up our posture of inactive spectator as Anna and Giulia perform one of the most sensual and visually rich dances ever filmed. When Marcello does join the dance, it is in a

Figure 11. Dominique Sanda appears in the first of three roles, here as the minister's mistress. Courtesy The Museum of Modern Art/Film Stills Archive.

"paranoid" fashion: The entire population of the dance floor makes a human reel (reminiscent of the "embobinage" of *Spider's Stratagem*), rolling him up like a mummy—or the body of a dreamer—in the middle. This scene, moreover, evokes associations of two earlier scenes, one in which Marcello is set upon sexually by a group of schoolboys and a later one in which the body-guards in Quadri's apartment suddenly surround him on all sides and escort him to the professor's study. A photo of Laurel and Hardy appears mysteri-ously on the window of the dance hall in Montmartre almost as a road sign: "Ricorda: cinema!"

In light of the extensive dreamwork permeating the entire film, we may appreciate the fantastic rendering of Quadri's assassination as a kind of oneiric extension of the dream Marcello has just moments before reported to Manganiello. The entire scene is self-consciously patterned after two separate but significant moments: on the one hand, the various cinematic versions of the murder of Julius Caesar in the forum, another powerful if implicit allusion to the Roman architecture that houses the Fascist leader-ship; and, on the other hand, the final scenes of Truffaut's *Tirez sur le pianiste* in which a car nearly identical to Quadri's ascends a winding, snow-covered Alpine road toward a tragic destiny in which a woman is shot by several assassins as she flees through the snow. This subtle homage to Truffaut's cinematic retranscription of an American gangster novel rein-forces Bertolucci's alignment with experimental yet popular cinema and his rejection of Godard's expressly unpopular political film stance.

The mist shrouding this scene is the closest Bertolucci comes in any of his films to a cliché of dreaming. Quadri's examination of the still figure in the car blocking their way couples silence with immobility in an uncanny way. The several assassins who appear from nowhere out of the mist are filmed in such a way that their knives seem to cut endlessly into Quadri's body—almost an "active" freeze-frame device that causes time to seem to stand still without stopping the action. Curiously, despite these many stab wounds, inflicted in balletlike cadence, Quadri's sweater reveals but a superficial amount of blood. In contrast, Anna, shot in the back by her pursuers in the woods, reveals a face unrealistically smeared with what is unmistakably red paint. Bertolucci said of this scene: "I thought that this exaggeration of blood on Anna was sort of a compromise with my old meaning, so audiences could think, 'It's not true, it's not true, it's not true. . . . The murder of the father is a fantasy. . . . It's imaginary.' "[19]

Figure 12. Marcello is encircled in a human reel on the dance floor.
Courtesy National Film Archive, London.

What makes this scene particularly metacinematic is Marcello's immobility. He sits throughout the entire assassination watching through the windshield, again a spectator to this classic drama. Even when Anna rushes to the car and presses her face to the glass, he sits unable to move—like Plato's enchained slaves, or like the dreamer he has personified throughout this film. This posture of an "actively passive" complicity in repressive and mortal violence most forcefully metaphorizes Clerici's fascism and painfully implies the potential fascism of the so-called apolitical position of the spectator in the film act. Once again, as film viewers we are forced to identify with and reluctantly imitate Marcello's behavior when confronted with such violent images, and, once again, Bertolucci pushes us to contemplate our relation to these images. When Anna leaves the car and flees through the woods, Bertolucci's hand-held camera takes up *exactly* the position of the assassins, running after her, losing sight of her, awkwardly leaping over

Figure 13. The assassins' knives appear to cut endlessly into Quadri's
body. Courtesy The Museum of Modern Art/Film Stills Archive.

obstacles and, finally, after contemplating her dying figure, slowly turning
away. From passive complicity we have subtly but surely been mobilized to
active repression, a further uncomfortable reminder of the possible implications of our own tendency as film viewers to identify (like the dreamer) with
all the positions offered by the film. This is undoubtedly the reason behind
Bertolucci's lighthearted autoaccusation: "I'm Marcello and I make fascist
movies and I want to kill Godard who is a revolutionary." Each filmmaker,
however, has his own way of drawing our attention to the dynamics of
spectator response to the manipulations of cinema.

Anna's fantastic "death" culminates a presentation of character that never
strays far from the oneiric. As the object of desire of Marcello's dream in the
car, she already holds a powerful and inexplicable attraction for him as of
their "first" meeting. Within minutes of his arrival at their Paris apartment, he draws Anna into an empty room, pulls her to him, and kisses her.

Figure 14. Marcello watches the assassination as though a spectator at a film. Courtesy National Film Archive, London.

Visually, however, as I have noted above, this is not their first encounter. Marcello has already glimpsed this woman in the arms of the Fascist minister who authorizes his murder of Quadri. This earlier scene is itself remarkable, for it is choreographed as a classic primal scene. During his visit to the palatial offices of the minister, Marcello suddenly finds himself quite inexplicably peering through a set of curtains, like a curious child, down the length of an enormous hall where a woman, legs dangling over the edge of the minister's desk, glances pointedly at Marcello and then lies provocatively full length on the desk while the minister explores her body. For the third time in the film, Marcello occupies the film viewer's position both structurally and psychologically. Later in the film, Marcello's mother's legs will be filmed in exactly the same manner, dangling out of her bed, while her son fishes for her shoes and the syringe that symbolizes her sexual oppression.

Immediately following the scene at his mother's house in which his mother's lover is eliminated, Bertolucci cuts to a shot of Marcello in the car on the road to Savoie, who says, "We have to save her." The object of this rescue fantasy could equally well be Anna or his mother.

As I have indicated in another context, Sanda reappears in yet another role during Marcello's inexplicable layover in Ventimiglia. The brothel he visits is a grandiose architectural space visually analogous to both the minister's office and Marcello's father's asylum. As whore in this setting, she cries "I'm crazy!" from Manganiello's Fascist arms, evoking both the primal scene previously witnessed and the condition of Marcello's father. Thus when Marcello reencounters her in Quadri's apartment in Paris, she has already, if *subliminally* for the viewer, become the object of his desire: mother/whore/victim. As the condensation of sexual partner of various figures of authority, she becomes, by definition, desirable. The Anna figure elicits fantasies of love, betrayal, and rescue consistent with those normally experienced by the male child in the Oedipal phase. Marcello's feelings of revenge and rescue are thus quite simply displaced onto Quadri from this condensation of his earlier "experiences" with Anna.

Another major condensation in *The Conformist* involves the characters of Lino, Manganiello, and Alberi. The Lino incident, central to Moravia's novel, occurs there as a logical and fated moment in the progression of Marcello's violent tendencies and as the unique and consciously felt explanation for his obsessive conformity. In Bertolucci's dream structure, Marcello's seduction by Lino appears as a flashback rather late in the film, and only then as an involuntary association produced by an analogous moment during the trip in Manganiello's car.

Only in retrospect can the viewer understand that Marcello has already projected the Lino role on Manganiello as well as on his mother's sexually exploiting chauffeur, for when Manganiello in his big black limousine first follows Marcello along the street toward Signora Clerici's house, the viewer has not yet seen the Lino seduction scene to which this scene alludes. Bertolucci's editing here clearly keeps the "secret in the belly of the film" but alludes to it by a kind of "symptomatology": The entire scene is filmed with the camera tilted at a forty-five-degree angle, suggesting that something in this sequence creates a disequilibrium. Marcello flees from Manganiello's car and succeeds in closing a large wrought-iron gate similar to those he passes through as a child in Lino's limousine. Marcello then suggests that Man-

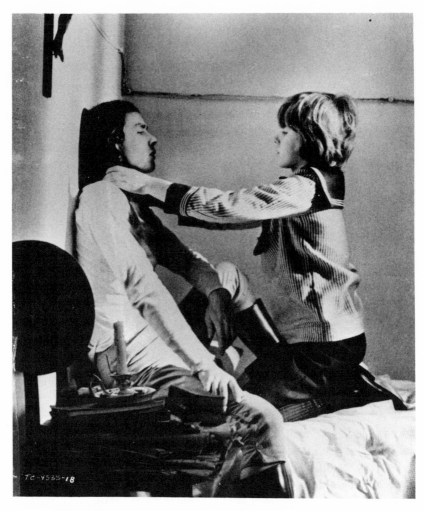

Figure 15. Lino (Pierre Clementi) seduces the child Marcello. Courtesy Paramount Pictures.

ganiello get rid of Alberi, his mother's chauffeur, an act that symbolically condenses revenge on Lino (dressed identically to Alberi), the source of his original sense of guilt, and on Manganiello himself, as a double of Lino. Here again, Marcello does not act; he whispers his wished for solution to the imposing Manganiello and then scuttles away, behaving exactly like the child who, covering his eyes, believes he is invisible. What keeps this doubling from becoming heavy-handed is Bertolucci's editing: The Lino affair occurs in the film after the Manganiello scenes, illuminating them only in retrospect, in the same way that a dream will jumble chronology and "make sense" only after interpretation.

The Lino relationship functions as Marcello's particular obsession, even repetition compulsion. The most striking occurrence of this repetitive structure involves Anna (whom Moravia heavy-handedly named Lina). In her seduction of Giulia, she reproduces with extraordinary fidelity—but with the positions reversed—the gestures Lino had used in seducing the child Marcello: She kneels "innocently" between the seated Giulia's legs, head on knee. Bertolucci places Marcello in a darkened hallway and joins the film viewer in a voyeuristic appreciation of this primal scene, just as he had done when Marcello had spied on a double of Anna in the minister's office. The difference here is that Marcello watches the uncanny repetition of his own seduction as a child, here acted out in a feminized version. It is worth recalling that, in the "original" version of this event, Lino lets down his long hair, calls himself Mme. Butterfly, and instills enough sexual ambiguity into the event to make Anna's seduction even more uncannily repetitive. Moreover, her reduplication of the seduction with the positions reversed itself alludes to Marcello's imitation of Uncle Perpuzio's seduction of Giulia as confessed to Marcello during the train ride to Paris. Whereas Giulia was the victim in her confession, she takes the dominant position in the re-creation of the scene during the train ride.

The scene of Anna's seduction of Giulia thus effects, without ever explicitly stating it, an extraordinarily rich condensation of levels and characters in the film, for Anna compositely doubles Lino (as homosexual seducer), mother, whore, and Marcello himself, given his unconscious tendency to project the elements of his early relationships onto all those around him. The scene also manifests the dream's tendency toward multiple determinations by engaging in a wish-fulfillment fantasy of seduction, for if Anna doubles Lino then, structurally, Marcello's deeper fantasy would involve being seduced by her! Finally, Marcello's position of voyeur in this scene repeats the stance he has taken repeatedly throughout this film: Time and time again, he prefers to watch rather than act and thus doubles the position of the film's spectator, allowing the spectator to project him/herself into any or all of these condensed roles. While developing a tale of political intrigue and psychological complexity, Bertolucci has interwoven subtly but surely a critique of his viewer's (and his own) conformity to roles prescribed by the very nature of the cinematic experience, where a primary doubling at the level of the image always already precedes the doubling at the level of character. Although the content and imagery of his film differs dramatically from his earlier works, a continuing concern with the specificity of cinema pervades, with remarkable consistency, all of his works through *The Conformist*.

This scene of voyeurism is to be repeated one more time: at the end of the film when Marcello discovers Lino alive, engaged in the seduction of another young boy, using the same language he had used with Marcello so many years before. Marcello's reaction is immediate: If Lino is not dead, then he is not a murderer and cannot be guilty of murdering Quadri. But Quadri is dead, and someone must be responsible: The most obvious solution is for Marcello to project his guilt onto the blind Italo, and he begins violently to denounce his helpless friend, symbol of the blindness and fascism he has for so long adopted. In the final shot, we see Marcello looking ambiguously at the bed on which lies the naked boy just propositioned by Lino: another double. The glance and the relationship are as ambiguous as every other gesture made by Marcello, who has never stopped using authority figures as scapegoats for a crime uncommitted and a desire unassuaged.

The fragmented, uncanny, and oneiric quality of the entire film, then, can be understood as "a memory of my memory," a thoroughly and unmistakably cinematic transcription of Moravia's literary effort. By rearranging Moravia's chronology to conform to a purely associative process, Bertolucci not only escapes many of the narrative limitations of the novel but effects a remarkable demonstration of pure cinema. By locating the primary point of view both in Marcello *and* in an omniscient camera, Bertolucci practices a diffusion of identities that is particularly oneiric (and cinematic). In this way, elements in the novel's objective structure that tend to overly strain the reader's credibility can be comprehended as the mental associations or dreamwork of a single consciousness and so predispose the film's viewer to identify not only with that consciousness but with the film's very fabric. In so doing, Bertolucci directly, if implicitly, educates the viewer to the (potentially fascist) implications of the act of viewing.

The genius of Bertolucci's film is that it succeeds in transforming Moravia's rather traditional narrative elements into a new and more meaningful structure while at the same time subtly but surely addressing the issue of the relationship between original text and film at every level of the work. Unlike *The Spider's Stratagem*, the son in this film is no longer enmeshed in the father's history. If it is his "destiny" to kill the father, Bertolucci succeeds where Marcello has not: He manages his "murders" (of Moravia and Godard) on a purely symbolic and creative level.[20]

As copy and as parricide, Bertolucci's *Conformist* not only invites us to reconsider the necessarily ambivalent relationship theorized between authority and creativity but extends that theory to a new and important realm: the relationship between text and image. As such it is a logoclastic and iconocentric enterprise.

It might be well, then, to give another level of meaning to Marcello's dream, which we recall as: "I was blind. You were taking me to a clinic in Switzerland. Quadri was operating on me. The operation was a success; I got my sight back. Then I ran off with Anna." As film viewers, we only really comprehend the nature of films through the fantastic voyage within a psychologically protected space (which is the operation of this film) and specifically through the optics of Quadri's discourse on Plato's cave. Once we comprehend our position as viewers, we can appreciate the dynamics of desire and fantasy at work in the cinema.

It remained for *Last Tango in Paris* to extend and deepen this meditation on the nature of the cinematic experience.

I hear the echo of those tangos
I watched danced on the pavement
On an instant that today stands out alone
Without before or after, against oblivion,
And had the taste of everything lost,
Everything lost and recovered.
JORGE LUIS BORGES

6 "A TURBID, UNREAL PAST, IN CERTAIN MEASURE TRUE"

Last Tango in Paris

"Tonight we improvise!" shouts a gleeful Jeanne (Maria Schneider) as she enters the apartment in the rue Jules Verne for the third time. Despite the allusions to Pirandello and Verne, the film represented a watershed for Bertolucci, for he was no longer tied to a literary model. His direct engagement with literature seemed to end with the series of films that had occupied his energies from 1961 through 1970. With the completion of *The Conformist* Bertolucci had proved that the cinema had a style and a language of its own, fully capable of expressing its own version of the literary model in its own way. The ghost of Atilio/Laertes was at least temporarily pacified.

"You must always leave a door open on the set through which an unexpected visitor may enter. That is cinema!" Jean Renoir was to tell Bertolucci a few years after the completion of *Tango*. But his younger Italian friend had already discovered this lesson for himself. Marlon Brando (as Paul) and Maria Schneider (as Jeanne) were given enormous freedom to invent their roles as the film unfolded. If we are to believe actors and director, the door remained open throughout.

The visitor to whom Jean Renoir alluded, however, was an unusual one. Bertolucci was to say, "The modern word for the Greek concept of fate is the unconscious. My unconscious is the fate of my movies." From his unconscious emerged a character from Greek myth who was to structure this film in a way that was deeply coherent despite the degree of improvisation carried out by the actors. An intricate series of allusions to the Orpheus myth and to various modern versions of the myth thoroughly permeates the film.

According to the myth, Orpheus's wife Eurydice was fatally bitten by a serpent while fleeing the advances of her lover, Aristaeus. Inconsolable at her death, Orpheus managed to charm the infernal deities with his poetry and music and obtained permission to descend to Hades to get her back. But the gods of the underworld diabolically imposed one condition on this permission: that Orpheus should not turn back to look at Eurydice as he led her out of the underworld. Orpheus of course broke this command and lost Eurydice, this time forever.

Parallels between the characters in the film and those of the myth are not immediately obvious because, like the adaptations of the myth by other modern artists such as Jean Cocteau, Jules Verne, Marcel Camus, and Tennessee Williams, Bertolucci's work is as much a perversion as a restatement of the myth. Recourse to an analysis of the film will elucidate the many connections with the mythic structure.

Last Tango in Paris in simplest terms presents a man (Paul) and a woman (Jeanne) who encounter each other in an apartment near the Quai de Passy in Paris. We learn during the course of the film that the man's wife, Rosa, has just committed suicide, and, grief-stricken, he seeks hopelessly for a way to get her back. With Jeanne, Paul acts out a series of violently erotic fantasies. When the couple leave the apartment for the last time, Paul pursues Jeanne to her own apartment where she shoots him in the genitals and kills him.

One of the keys to understanding the structure of this film occurs late in the work when Paul sits beside Rosa's bier and conducts a long apostrophe of anger, resentment, and guilt. This scene is particularly difficult because initially it is not clear whether Paul has left the Jules Verne apartment or whether he is in the brothel owned and operated by the late Rosa. Nor is she visible as the scene begins. This ambiguity allows the viewer at least momentarily the impression that Paul is addressing Jeanne with whom he has just finished a scene of enormous emotional impact, telling her that she must "fuck a dying pig" for him. The apostrophe to Rosa's body is crucial, for it

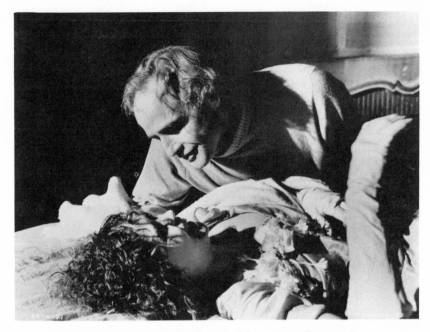

Figure 16. Jeanne (Maria Schneider) in bridal costume recalls Rosa on her bier. Courtesy Jerry Ohlinger.

retroactively elucidates Paul's relationship with Rosa and provides a comprehensible underlying motive for his otherwise inexplicable search for an apartment and his complex affair with Jeanne. Beside Rosa's beflowered bier, he intones a lament that gradually becomes a terrible but impotent accusation: Rosa was a "goddam fucking whore" and a "pig-fucking liar," her suicide (accomplished with her lover Marcel's razor) a betrayal. Paul raves at her impassive remains, " 'Even if the husband lives two hundred fucking years, he's never going to be able to discover his wife's true nature. I mean, I might be able to comprehend the universe, but I'll never discover the truth about you, never. I mean, who the hell were you?' "

The repetition of this question of the parents' identity, already posed so insistently in *The Spider's Stratagem* reinforces both the obsessive need for, and the inaccessibility of a response. Paul must thus search elsewhere for communion, understanding—and revenge. He chooses for his purposes one of Bertolucci's most persistent themes: the double. The immediate repetition of the violent epithet "pig-fucker" as well as many other visual and verbal repetitions demonstrate that Jeanne functions for Paul as a double of his dead wife. The erotic-aggressive ambivalence expressed toward Jeanne can thus be understood as a displacement of Paul's frustrations and anger with Rosa. Bertolucci uses the Orpheus myth to explore many of the deeper implications of Paul's attempt at recuperation or psychic recovery of this wife/mother figure.

The film opens with a series of highly symbolic and deliberately allusive camera shots. Our first view is of Paul, then of Jeanne, who overtakes and passes him. The camera then pans to a shot of the bridge and the river, deliberately emphasizing their transition across the river.[1] (According to Greek mythology, we should recall, one was obliged to cross the river Styx to reach the gates of hell.) Jeanne thus precedes Paul onto the Quai de Passy, whose very name constitutes an allusion to death: Passy—passage—trépasser ("to die"). The camera records this from an angle that emphasizes the cavernous tunnellike structure of the bridge. It then quickly cuts, several times, to groups of riot police, who appear to be guarding the far bank, in what I believe to be an early allusion to another well-known interpretation of the Orpheus myth. In Jean Cocteau's *Orphée* (1950), the same aggressively militaristic uniformed French police deliberately represent the personal guardians of Death's kingdom.

Once past these guardians of the other bank (who include an old hag who literally bares her teeth at the young woman), Jeanne finds herself in the rue Jules Verne, an apparently innocuous detail until one realizes that the geography of Paris has been deliberately scrambled. The actual rue Jules Verne is situated far from the Quai de Passy, in the heart of the Eleventh Arrondissement. Once again, Bertolucci alludes to Cocteau's celebrated film of 1950 in which he effected the creation of an imaginary city out of Paris. In that earlier film, Orpheus got out of his car at Grenelle (alluded to in *Tango* in the name of the metro station where Jeanne and Tom meet and fight), walked up the Buttes-Chaumont, and arrived at the Place des Vosges. The choice of rue Jules Verne constitutes in itself an allusion to the myth, for Verne's novel *Le Château de Carapathe* is also a retranscription of the Orpheus legend.

Just before entering the heavy iron gates of the apartment building, Jeanne pauses very insistently to consult her watch, another allusion both to Cocteau's film in which the Princess repeatedly stops to consult her watch as

Orpheus follows her through the streets of Paris and to Lewis Carroll's *Alice in Wonderland* whose Mad Hatter is also preoccupied by time immediately prior to his descent down the hole leading beyond the looking glass.

Once inside the gates, Jeanne suddenly encounters the sinister West Indian concierge who raspingly intones, "Some funny things going on around here." Denying at first any knowledge of the vacant apartment, she grudgingly produces a "double" of the key and then seizes Jeanne's hand and holds her prisoner for several anguished moments, laughing hysterically. According to Greek legend, the vestibule of hell is traditionally guarded by the Eumenides, who sit in cages and harass every new arrival. Similar witch-like figures can be found in both Marcel Camus's *Orpheu negro* and Tennessee Williams's *Orpheus Descending*, filmed as *The Fugitive Kind*.[2]

Robert Alley's "novel" based on the film describes the concierge's voice as "immensely old. It was as if Jeanne was attempting to gain entrance to some shadowy and threatening netherworld, and the gatekeeper was bent on preventing her. This old woman, like Charon at the gates of Hades, demanded payment before admitting suppliants; Jeanne wondered if she would disappear in the depths of the building." The place becomes a "place out of time where there were no real people doing the things real people did, just the deformed and the almost-dead."[3] Indeed, Jeanne turns just in time to see a disembodied hand place an empty wine bottle next to a row of others and then retreat noiselessly into the apartment across the hall.

Jeanne's entry into the apartment, whose living room has a Dantesque circular shape, becomes yet another allusion to previous recent versions of the myth. As she passes through the doorway, the camera shifts from a direct to a mirror-reflected shot of Jeanne, so that she appears to pass through the looking glass to enter. Cocteau's Orpheus had also to pass through the mirror of his bedroom in order to visit Hades, and in that film, "Mirrors are doors through which death comes to get souls." Thereafter, each time the two return to the apartment, they are projected into it by means of jump cuts, which break the normal time–space continuum in a most disconcerting way. Just as disconcerting is the insistence of camera shots that record their faces and actions via a mirror.

When Paul tells the unknown telephone caller, "There is no one here," he is announcing their symbolic death and finalizing the separation from their normal social roles and identities, preparing the intricate relationship they are to share within this "privileged space."[4] The rest of their first meeting

Figure 17. Paul (Marlon Brando) tells the caller, "There is no one here."
Courtesy United Artists.

continues the mirror's allusion to an almost infernal world, removed from
and somehow parallel to accepted reality.

This parallelism is further reinforced by the fact that, as we later learn,
Paul has left behind in his hotel a double of himself in Marcel.[5] The series of
homing rituals that follow (the discussion of where the armchair should be
placed, use of the toilet and telephone) begin to establish Jeanne's role as
Rosa's surrogate. Significantly, too, in the later scene in which mysterious
movers carry in unannounced and unaccountable furniture, one of them
addresses Jeanne as if she were Paul's wife.

The unexpectedly abrupt sexual encounter that terminates this scene
further and most obviously contributes to the Jeanne/Rosa doubling, both in
identifying the former as Paul's mate and in typing her as a whore, the accusation Paul will later level at the dead Rosa. In that her relations with Paul
constitute a betrayal of Tom, she also imitates Rosa's betrayal of Paul.

Later, in the bloodstained room where Rosa has committed suicide, a maid languidly describes and reenacts for Paul Rosa's suicide. Following her description of the wrist slashing, she explicitly reintroduces the theme of the double, saying, "I did everything just like her." Paul angrily seizes her wrists and neck but quickly pushes her aside and leaves. This momentary anger at an explicit double of Rosa's reestablishes the element of displacement that is so fundamental to the entire film.

When we return to the apartment, the intimacy now established leads Jeanne to ask Paul his name, thereby eliciting the sacred law governing their continued existence together. Paul furiously proclaims, "You don't have a name, and I don't have a name either. No names here. . . . We don't need names here. . . . We're going to forget everything we knew . . . All the people, all that we do wherever we lived . . . Everything!" This absolute interdiction to consider each other's identity and past life metaphorically parallels the divine command to Orpheus not to look back. Paul's subsequent violation of his own rules as they recross the bridge at the end of the film will fatally doom their relationship as inevitably as Orpheus's disobedience. When Paul reveals his identity there, Jeanne screams, "It's finished!" and flees. In an uncanny parallel to the Orpheus legend, the revelation of her identity coincides precisely with Paul's ultimate failure at the recovery of this maternal figure. In response to his demand to know her name, she whispers, "Jeanne" at exactly the same moment that she fires a pistol into his abdomen. Like the myth again, Jeanne has metamorphosed from Eurydice to castrating Maenad.[6]

Yet the mere presence of these allusions does not in itself provide an explanation of the film. To translate these mythic figures into interpretation, it is necessary to search behind the myth, as Freud did with the Oedipus legend, recognizing that myths are actually paradigms of mental processes, namely, "distorted vestiges of the wishful phantasies . . . the secular dreams of youthful humanity."[7] Because the Orpheus myth is most obviously the reenactment of a rescue fantasy, I shall turn first for a deeper understanding of the work to that aspect of mental functioning.

The first and most obvious question to arise is: Who is being rescued? By his insistent allusions to Cocteau's use of the Orpheus myth, and particularly through insistence on the passage through the mirror, Bertolucci suggests an answer to this question, for obviously in Cocteau's *Orphée* and *Sang d'un poète* the mirror serves primarily to reflect oneself, and to pass

Figure 18. Paul angrily seizes the maid's wrist and neck. Courtesy
United Artists.

through the mirror represents a fantasy of self-exploration. Michel Serres
has demonstrated how, in another version of the Orpheus myth alluded to in
this film, Jules Verne's *Château de Carapathe*, the Orpheus figure pursues
his own image into a "sacred space," perceives the image of his loved one (in
this case *himself*) on a screen, and plunges through the screen, causing an
explosion of the entire inner space and ultimate madness.[8]

Tango is remarkably similar. The key to Paul's self-recuperation lies not
only in the use of mirror-imaging (to which I shall return) but also in the cor-
rect identification of the Rosa/Jeanne figure. Rosa, we must remember,
functioned primarily as a mother/wife figure for Paul. She had "adopted"
him and supported him for years but had never given him her complete
attention. Paul knows all too well that Rosa has a lover who is to some degree
a double of himself, and as "readers" of Bertolucci's work we cannot fail to
see a reference to the doubling of Athos Magnani in this configuration. Rosa,

like Draifa, becomes an object of intense ambivalence—a desired love object and a hated betrayer. This mother role is reiterated visually when the chambermaid, a remarkable look-alike of Rosa's *mother*, reenacts Rosa's suicide, saying, "I did everything just like her." Later, before Rosa's bier, Paul will observe sarcastically, "You're your mother's masterpiece!" And to Rosa's mother, he intones, "Rosa was a lot like you. . . . People must have told you often. . . . Isn't that right, Mother?" Rosa's mother answers, "Two sisters." Paul will vent his feelings onto both the maid and the mother at several different points in the film.

D. W. Winnicott has noted the mother's function as mirror in child development: "What does the baby see when he or she looks at the mother's face? . . . himself or herself. In other words the mother is looking at the baby and what she looks like is related to what she sees there."[9] Such a function is normally greatly transformed in adult behavior and would be over-interpretive in this instance were it not for several factors: the insistent presence of mirrors in the film—especially in scenes weighted with problems of either self-definition or regression; the emphatically regressive sexual behavior of Paul in the apartment; and the allusion to Francis Bacon that opens the film.

The several Bacon paintings successively occupying the screen at the outset of the film immediately set the problematics of identity that will pervade the entire work. Winnicott insists on Bacon's allusion to the mirror and identity in his essay on the mother's mirror role:

> Francis Bacon . . . the exasperating and skillful and challenging
> artist of our time who goes on and on painting the human face
> distorted significantly . . . is seeing himself in his mother's face, but
> with some twist that maddens both him and us. . . . Bacon's faces
> seem to be far removed from perception of the actual; in looking at
> faces he seems . . . to be painfully striving towards being seen,
> which is at the basis of creative looking.[10]

Winnicott quotes one of his patients as having said, "Wouldn't it be awful if the child looked into the mirror and saw nothing?"[11] Transposed into Winnicott's own terms, the question may be posed, "Wouldn't it be awful if I looked at Mother's face and was unable to see my own being?" Bertolucci has uncannily captured this very moment in the scene at Rosa's bier. She is an expressionless mask to whom Paul turns for some sign of identity, both hers and his own.[12] Her mother (whose resemblance to Rosa is an obsession for Paul) wears a similar mask in life. And there is a further allusion to Rosa's blindness while alive. As Paul leaves the room of his double, Marcel, he muses, "I wonder what she ever saw in you." By condensing this expression of anxiety here displaced onto an explicit double, we may understand, "I wonder what she ever saw in me."

In discussing Bacon's presence in the film, Bertolucci said, "I took Marlon [Brando] to the exhibition of Bacon's paintings and said, 'That's what you should be.' "[13] That may be generally true of Brando's face, which manages to look so plastic and tortured throughout, but it is nowhere more true than when he first confronts the scene of Rosa's absent presence. In the bathroom covered with Rosa's blood, Brando passes behind a screen of frosted glass so that his face appears to take on the same distortions as the Bacon paintings. It is clearly the moment at which Paul most desperately seeks a lost maternal image. Later, after his most intense punishment of Jeanne and the notion of family—that is, his sodomizing of Jeanne—Bertolucci's camera again captures Brando lying twisted on the floor in exactly the position of the first Bacon painting to be glimpsed. This reference to Bacon with Jeanne most convincingly reemphasizes the doubling of Rosa by Jeanne and Paul's double failure to get her back. Notably, Jeanne's face remains hidden to Paul in this scene.

The Orpheus rescue fantasy, then, would respond to a thoroughly ambivalent retrieval of Rosa using Jeanne as surrogate: to get her back in both recuperative and vengeful terms. This double motive would explain why Brando plays such an impenetrably mercurial role throughout, moving from tenderness to sudden fits of sadistic and punitive behavior. Paul's need for recuperation is, as I have suggested above, most tellingly revealed by the mirroring of the mother role: a project of self-rescue, an effort of recovery of identity. Also, to the degree that Jeanne performs simultaneous roles as sex object and mother surrogate for Paul, we may sense that there is another level of self-rescue at work here:

> The mother gave the child life, and it is not easy to find a substitute of equal value for this unique gift. With a slight change of meaning, such as is easily effected in the unconscious and is comparable to the way in which in consciousness concepts shade into one another, rescuing his mother takes on the significance of giving her a child or making a child for her—needless to say, one like himself. This is not

too remote from the original sense of rescuing, and the change in meaning is not an arbitrary one. His mother gave him life—his own life—and in exchange he gives her another life, that of a child which has the greatest resemblance to himself. The son shows his gratitude by wishing to have by his mother a son who is like himself: in other words, in the rescue phantasy he is completely identifying himself with his father. All his instincts, those of tenderness, gratitude, lustfulness, defiance and independence, find satisfaction in the single wish *to be his own father*. [14]

Again, it is possible to understand how fully the presence of *A Spider's Stratagem* permeates *Last Tango in Paris*. As a double of Paul and as Mother's/Rosa's lover, Marcel occupies a structurally identical position to that assumed by Athos Magnani in the earlier film. If, as Bertolucci has claimed, the entire relationship between Paul and Jeanne is "an obvious search for authenticity," it becomes evident that this search cannot be conducted without the (impossible) clarity about the identity of mother *and* father. [15] The apostrophe to Athos père, "Who was Athos Magnani?" is now addressed to the mother as well.

In this privileged space, womblike in shape and color, a remarkable representation of the unconflicted part of the ego, Paul announces the Orphic command of refusal to look back and thereby attempts to eliminate memory, culture, civilization, and all that they mean in terms of taboos, inhibitions, repressions, and defenses. Just as in primitive language or in the language of dreams, where "contradictory concepts have been quite intentionally combined, not in order to produce a third concept . . . but only in order to use the compound to express the meaning of one of its contradictory parts," this command simultaneously prohibits (on the explicit level) and encourages (on the unconscious level) a particular form of behavior. Paul is thus free to experiment in regression to earlier stages of sexual development; pure Oedipal desire, onanism, [16] anal eroticism, and even bestiality (with the dead rat). The ultimate expression of this regressive and thoroughly narcissistic desire occurs during their last moments together in the apartment, when Paul exclaims (ironically, as it turns out, describing himself):

> You want this gold and shining powerful warrior to build you
> a fortress where you can hide in. . . . Well, then it won't be long
> until he'll want you to build a fortress for him out of your hair and

your smile—and it's someplace where he can feel—feel comfortable
enough and secure enough so that he can worship in front of the altar
of his own prick.

Nor is this the only example of Paul's primarily narcissistic urge. At one
point Jeanne screams at Paul, "Why don't you listen to me? You know, it
seems to me I'm talking to the wall. Your solitude weighs on me, you know.
It isn't indulgent or generous. You're an egoist." We know that narcissism is
to some degree a constant in all creative work, in dreams and fantasies,[17] and
that under stress a narcissistic person may regress from socially transformed
to primary forms of object relations.[18] What should impress us is the intricacy with which Bertolucci has woven the reflective aspects of narcissism (the
themes of self-rescue and the mirror) together with the deeper significance of
the Orpheus myth.

In a most perceptive essay on the nature of Orpheus, Jean Normand has
described the mythic bard in Tennessee Williams's play as:

> poet, pariah, pervert become martyr. . . . He represents . . . a
> free, nomadic, and irresponsible life, sexuality without complexes,
> which he can only have by renouncing all security and taboos. He is
> the man from somewhere else who brings with him his freedom. His
> three traits are his guitar [read *bongos* here], his wings, and his
> animal nature. He is an ambiguous animal whose blood is hot or cold
> according to his mood (or metamorphosis). "O dieses ist das Tier, das
> es nicht giebt," the nonexistent beast of Rainer Maria Rilke's
> *Sonnets to Orpheus*, who fascinates women and disturbs men. . . .
> Orpheus is that which has no name, no face, no expression, that
> which is hidden, unknown, that which in man is foreign to man, at
> least so he believes, his unconscious, his intuitions, the dreams he
> dares not recall or realize, poetry, the poem he carries within with
> which he does nothing or which he destroys. . . . The truth of
> Orpheus is the truth of the poem, a life work which one must snatch
> from the powers of death—it is the eternal struggle of Eros against
> Thanatos. Orpheus is, like other men, split between the creative and
> the destructive drives.[19]

Significantly, Bertolucci's Paul refuses names, prefers animal grunts and
crows to language, and pursues his erotic dream ever closer to death, pro-

claiming finally to his willing/unwilling Eurydice, Jeanne, "You're all alone. And you won't be able to be free of the feeling of being alone until you look death right in the face. I mean, that sounds like bullshit and some romantic crap. Until you go right up into the ass of death—right up his ass—till you find a womb of fear. And then, maybe then you can—you'll be able to find him." For Paul, the association of love and self-love seems to lead directly to a confluent description of anality, the maternal womb, and death, a verbal prefiguration of his own fetallike position as he dies.[20]

Bertolucci comments on this relationship among sex, narcissism, and death as follows: "I quickly realized when shooting, that when you show the depths . . . you drown yourself, as it were, in that feeling of solitude and death that attaches to a relationship in our Western, bourgeois society. . . . Sex is very close to death in feeling."[21] The film becomes a vertiginous dance conducted on the frontier that so narrowly separates Eros from Thanatos, a voyage so persistently Orphic as to be uncanny.

In his various versions of the Orpheus myth, Jean Cocteau repeatedly insists on the relation of primary narcissism to death. "Mirrors," Cocteau once wrote, "are doors through which Death enters our soul, and through which Orpheus enters the kingdom of Death."[22]

Earlier, Francis Bacon's allusion to the mirror was noted. Bertolucci extends that allusion to include a notion of decomposition and death: "Marlon Brando resembles Francis Bacon's characters. . . . his face has that same plasticity of life in decomposition." And he quotes Cocteau, "Faire du cinéma, c'est saisir la mort au travail [To make films is to catch Death at work]."[23]

But Bacon's work constitutes another kind of reference point for Bertolucci as well. Not only do the Bacon paintings seem to signal issues of identity and the relationship between narcissism and death, but they bring these several themes together with another ongoing and fundamental issue for Bertolucci: the identity of the cinematic process itself. First of all, Bacon's work has much to do with mirroring, for "to look at a painting by Bacon is to look into a mirror and to see there our own afflictions and our fears." John Rothenstein also notes that Bacon's preference for glazing his paintings derives from "his belief that the fortuitous play of reflections will enhance his pictures . . . by enabling the spectator to see his own face in the glass."[24] Winnicott relates Bacon and a more fundamental historical process in the child: "In looking at faces he seems . . . to be painfully striving towards

being seen, which is at the basis of creative looking. I am linking appercep-
tion with perception by postulating an historical process (in the individual)
which depends on being seen. When I look I am seen, so I exist. I can now
afford to look and see. I now look creatively and what I apperceive I also
perceive."[25]

Viewers of *Last Tango in Paris* also look at/through a kind of glass. In his
previous films, Bertolucci has compellingly *alluded to* the spectator's role as
voyeur and *suggested* the intricacies of the dynamics of the film experience.
In *Last Tango* Bertolucci presents an analysis that is no longer merely
allusive.

It is Bertolucci's genius to have raised issues in the content of the film that
are fundamental to the film experience itself. It is even more extraordinary
that he uses a single nodal point in the film—indeed, at the very margins of
the film—to allude to so many different but intensely related issues: seeing,
mirroring, identity, ontology. The mirroring suggested in the Bacon paintings brings us back to the issue of doubles in the film, this time to a double
whose function is almost entirely metacinematic.

Thus far I have explored the double relationships linking Paul with Marcel
and Jeanne with Rosa, for these inform most directly the anecdotal level of
exchange in the film. Tom, however, serves as the most intricate double of
all, for in his character are linked the psychological and metacinematic levels
of the work.

In the scene of Tom's arrival in Paris, the arched metalwork of the Gare
St. Lazare repeats the visual effect of Jeanne's first meeting with Paul under
the Passy trestle. Jeanne's fiancé, Tom (Jean-Pierre Leaud), emerges from a
train at the Gare St. Lazare and attempts to capture Jeanne with an en-
thusiasm and unquestioned license equal to Paul's but here displaced onto
the medium of cinema itself. In this first encounter, a film technician thrusts
a phallic-shaped microphone into Jeanne's face while Tom declaims on love.
Each time Tom and Jeanne meet, this sadly artificial phallus (always proffered by one of Tom's crew) replaces Paul's "hap-penis." Throughout the
film we are to witness the same explicit parallelism of behavior between Paul
and Tom with, in each case, Tom's version of Paul's behavior expressed in
terms of displacement from a purely sexual (pornographic) to a purely visual
(photographic) form of interaction. Jeanne at one point exasperatedly reminds him, "I'm supposed to marry *you*, not the camera." Ironically, too, it
will be to Tom and not to Paul that Jeanne complains, "You should have

asked my permission. . . . You take advantage of me and make me do things I've never done before. I'm tired of being raped!" In their first meeting, however, Tom is unable to comprehend Jeanne's sarcasm and mimicry as such and, in response to her mock romantic excesses, cries, "Magnifique! Coupez!"

Bertolucci obediently does, raising questions about the status of the film we are watching and its relation to the film we watch in the making. These questions are further emphasized by a curious portrayal of Paul in the next scene shot in the bathroom where Rosa's suicide has been effected. If Tom's role is to double Paul's erotic behavior with a camera, Paul seems to respond with a metacinematic double of his own, indeed on two levels. Filmed repeatedly behind the beveled and frosted glass of the bathroom, his face takes on, as I mentioned earlier, exactly the distortions of the Bacon paintings. Moreover, as the maid discusses her conversation with the police who had investigated the death, she repeats the salient features of Paul's biography: He was a boxer, had been a revolutionary in South America, had gone to Tahiti, and was later a journalist in Japan, ending up married to a rich woman in Paris. As Beverle Houston and Marsha Kinder have pointed out, each of these elements corresponds to a role Marlon Brando had played in earlier films: a boxer in *On the Waterfront*, a revolutionary in *Viva Zapata*, a sea captain in *Mutiny on the Bounty*, concluding with his roles in *Teahouse of the August Moon* and *Sayonara*.[26] That Paul's biography is in fact Brando's film biography suggests two different levels of interpretation: As actor, Brando's filmography would also have to include, if implicitly, his role as Val in the film version of Tennessee Williams's *Orpheus Descending*. Paul's bongos must then also certainly constitute another cinematic reference: to *Black Orpheus*. Secondly, this heightened consciousness of Brando as film actor further accentuates the spectator's sense of *Last Tango* as a *film* and emphasizes Paul's doubling of Tom as film director.[27] That doubling is conducted with extraordinary complexity throughout the entire film.

Each of Paul's interdictions against turning to the past is countered by Tom's enthusiastic insistence on capturing the woman and her past, but only on celluloid. Following Paul's manifesto, "No names here! . . . It's beautiful without knowing anything about your past," Bertolucci jump-cuts to Jeanne's country house where Tom's camera makes its symbolic but impotent descent: "The camera is high. . . . It slowly descends toward you. And as you advance, it moves in on you. . . . It gets closer and closer to you." Here Tom parodies the mythical descent of his more carnal partner, as always displacing his sexual drives onto the camera. As if instinctively applying Paul's rule to this other space, Jeanne discourages Tom's probing with the warning, "It's melancholy to look behind you." But Tom will not understand and shouts, "It's marvellous. . . . It's your childhood—everything I want. . . . I'm opening all the doors. . . . Reverse gear !!! Close your eyes. Back up, keep going, find your childhood again ! You are 15, 14, 13, 12, 11, 10, 9." Jeanne repeats the warning, holding up a portrait of her cousin *Paul, his eyes closed*, but Tom is oblivious. Significantly, he films her through glass in this scene, emphasizing the distance separating them. Exasperated by his single-mindedness and perhaps recalling Paul's reminiscences of cowshit, Jeanne reads a childhood composition about how the cow is entirely "clothed in leather," and instead of Paul's list of slang equivalents for the male member she offers dictionary definitions of menstruation and penis. Tom's exploration of surface and words have replaced Paul's hunger for carnal satisfaction.

Bertolucci presses this doubling throughout the film. For example, soon after we see Paul and Jeanne on the "good ship *Lollipop*" in the apartment, Bertolucci cuts to a scene of Tom and Jeanne on the *Atalante* in the canal. Not only do they replace physical presence with cameras and cinematic equipment, but they end up situated on a cinematic allusion to Jean Vigo. Everything Tom does or thinks seems "contaminated" by cinema. And whereas Paul and Jeanne have just discovered their Orphic names in a series of animalistic grunts and crows, Tom and Jeanne produce an empty parody of this language with a series of childlike yeses and nos. When Tom finally enters the Jules Verne apartment, he proposes his own form of intimacy: "I want to film you every day. In the morning when you wake up, then when you fall asleep. When you smile."

Significantly, Tom's obsession with capturing only the image of his lover places him in a focal position at the intersection of film director and film viewer. As a double of Bertolucci himself, he seems content to let Paul occupy the place of active lover while he assumes a more distant (and secure) position. Bertolucci said of this relationship, "Leaud is my past as a cinephile,"[28] and this is certainly borne out symbolically in such scenes as the gown fitting, where Tom is so ecstatic about comparing Jeanne to Rita Hayworth, Lauren Bacall, and the like that he loses sight of her altogether. But it is also true that Leaud is Bertolucci's past as cinéaste for, like the director of *Before the Revolution*, Leaud's camera frequently misses what it was intended to see. Twice during the interview with Jeanne at her house in the country the camera simply fails to keep up with the action. While Jeanne is reminiscing about her childhood, her faithful, racist maid interjects her own memories. Tom's crew wheels the hand-held camera to catch sight of the maid, but she disappears, leaving only closed doors or, in one case, a full-length portrait of de Gaulle. When they catch the children defecating in the family garden, Tom's crew rushes vainly after the kids, too late to catch what Bertolucci's camera has already captured. (In his ongoing and subtle doubling of Tom, Paul also evokes this earlier period of Bertolucci's when he recounts watching spittle on an old man's pipe. Always watching to see if it would fall off, like Bertolucci's camera on Agostino in *Prima*, Brando disappointedly admits, "I'd look around and it would be gone. I never saw it fall off.")

As a comment on his previous style, these scenes clearly mark Bertolucci's evolution from the earlier radical stylistic position of *Prima* toward a new exploration of the dynamics of the cinematic experience, less overtly radical but more determinedly aggressive.

In Tom's effort to restitute his sense of identity through a double displacement of his own desires onto the "legitimate" elements of filmmaking and through his projection of his own desires onto Jeanne, we may understand the underlying rationale for the filmmaker's and spectator's compulsion to watch the couple in the primal scene of the apartment. Earlier I cited Winnicott's reaction to the Bacon paintings that open the film. Winnicott suggests how these works relate to the frantic search for identity among the major characters of the film, but his thinking can also be applied to Bertolucci's long-standing issue of how "cinema looks at itself." Winnicott, in the passage already cited, convincingly relates Bacon to the issue of seeing and being seen: "When I look I am seen, so I exist. I can now afford to look and see. I now look creatively and what I apperceive I also perceive."[29] Nowhere is perceiving more "affordable" and ultimately more potentially creative (in an ontological sense) than in cinema. While Paul tries to be perceived in the expressionless face of Rosa and subsequently in the doubled and mirroring face and body of Jeanne, the film's spectator works unconsciously through voyeurism toward a similar need.

Indeed, the very essence of cinema involves a fundamental condensation and displacement of exactly the kind Brando acts out for us on the screen. For him, the issue is a narcissistic recuperation of identity; for us, potentially, no less so. As a psychic phenomenon, voyeurism is a desire based on the primal scene fantasy. As Leo Bersani has noted,

> desire is a movement in the sense of being a mental activity designed to reactivate a scene connected with the past with the experience of pleasure. It immediately moves away from the desired object in order to develop a desiring fantasy which already includes a certain satisfaction. It is fundamental to desire that it should constantly be detaching itself from its object and finding new representations. Repressed desires seek to be "ex-pressed" but in order to be pressed out they must, so to speak, become "ex-centric" to themselves and avoid censorship by moving about among "innocent" images. Displacement is one of the principal strategies of unconscious desire, for to desire is to move to other places. And those places are representations—which is to say the images of fantasy.[30]

The film viewer as voyeur recapitulates symbolically and unconsciously a pattern enacted symbolically and overtly by Paul in the Jules Verne apartment. Unlike Paul, but like (Peeping) Tom, the film viewer anonymously watches through the "keyhole" of the lens or screen, participant in yet always absent from the action. And the scene viewed is always potentially or symbolically a primal scene in the sense that it evokes the child's "total store of unconscious knowledge and personal mythology concerning the human sexual relation, particularly that of his parents."[31] The "inherently pornographic ontological conditions of film"[32] are thus symbolically redeployed in Paul's behavior with Jeanne. But the relation between the act of cinematic viewing and the primal scene goes well beyond a merely erotic tendency, toward issues of personal (rather than merely cinematic) ontology:

> The primal scene [argues Guy Rosolato] constitutes, among all the unconscious fantasies, a nucleus where origins are especially marked. First of all as an originating fantasy—genetic vis à vis the individual and even phylogenetic; secondly, as the nexus of curiosity about origins, birth, procreation, identity, filiation, and parenthood. . . . The primal scene can thus be considered as the most general yet concentrated of fantasies.[33]

Thus voyeurism itself, which initially seems merely a perversion of normal desire, is, by its connection to the primal scene fantasy, a potentially ontological phenomenon. As film viewers, we may be attracted to the images projected as an "innocent" form of what are thought to be merely perverse drives but which ultimately function as information about our own origins and the possibility of recuperation of those origins.

Last Tango in Paris, however, can be viewed as a cautionary meditation on what Winnicott calls "creative looking." In Paul's purely physical regression in search of earlier modes of identity, he encounters increasingly sadistic, vengeful, and morbid tendencies in himself. The discomfort of *Last Tango* for some viewers relates to a similar discovery in the voyeuristic mode. If Jeanne is understood to function merely as a mirror of Paul's regressive fantasies, she appears as a typical cinematic sexual object. But in fact Jeanne has a life of her own—and motives of her own. She is attracted to the Jules Verne apartment for reasons just as complex as those that bring Paul there.

Like her double Rosa, Jeanne also has two lovers, Tom and Paul. Like Rosa's Marcel, Tom ends up being merely an image—and less. He succeeds only in evoking and promising future images. Whereas Rosa commits suicide because she seems unable to do anything but proliferate series of identically dressed and housed lovers, Jeanne instinctively moves toward a space where she can put a stop to this proliferation of surfaces (the "pop" marriage) and reach some depth.

At yet another level we remember that in her father's apartment in Paris Jeanne comes across a photograph of a Berber servant woman, naked to the waist. Her mother carelessly dismisses this evidence of the colonel's relations with his maidservants, complaining only of the fact that "the race of Berbers were difficult to train as servants." Jeanne, however, recognizes the pictured woman as a sexual object of her father's and a subject of intense jealousy and pity. We, however, may recognize Jeanne herself in the photograph, both as Paul's sexual object (within the film narrative) and as *nude photograph* (as a cinema actress in *Last Tango in Paris!*).

Because her father is now dead, Jeanne's "return" to the apartment can be understood as a voyage of recuperation, much like Paul's. She wants to "get her father back" both in terms of the love and affirmation that she needs from the opposite-sex parent and in terms of punishing him for his infidelity (both to Mother and to herself) and for his racist and sexist exploitation of women. Paul presents her with a perfect object, for he seems both to satisfy her regressive-erotic urges and to set himself up as the object of her revenge. Like Paul's swings of mood, Jeanne moves from an immediate and aggressive sexual possession of Paul to more hostile and punitive moods, such as those where she traps him into breaking his own rules or causes him to shock him-

Figure 19. Paul dons the father's military cap. Courtesy National Film
Archive, London.

self with the faulty wiring of the phonograph. If her own identity, like
Paul's, is inextricably bound up with that of her parents, Jeanne manages to
act out much of her relationship with a father figure in Paul.

If these recuperative gestures are permissible within the privileged space
of the apartment, they are, like the fantasies of cinema itself, unacceptable in
the light of day. There she no longer reflects, she reacts. When Paul pursues
her, she leads him first to the dance hall where they reenact a burlesque of
their earlier relationship and where Jeanne ambivalently masturbates Paul
and then flees. In her father's apartment, Paul reduces to an aggressive,
sexist stranger, donning her father's military cap as a sign of his unambigu-
ous desires and a reaffirmation of his doubling of the father. Jeanne's pistol
shot fired at his genitals violently reaffirms the unacceptability of such
exploitation. Paul staggers to the balcony of her apartment and, as a reminder of his regression, childishly sticks a piece of gum onto the balcony
railing, curls into a fetal position, and dies. As the camera tracks back into the

apartment from the balcony, it catches, as if accidentally, the reflection of one of Bertolucci's camera crew in a pane of the French windows. Another viewer viewed!

Ultimately, the genius of this film is to have brought together in a single work several different levels of thinking: the mythic, the psychoanalytic, and the metacinematic. Jeanne may be said to be the nexus of these themes, for she represents at once the displaced object of Paul's Orphic quest, the projected image of Tom's artistic drive, and the distanced object of the viewer's voyeurism. In so interweaving these themes, the film does not merely contain a spectacle for the viewer but challenges his very status as viewer. The outraged, middle-aged dance hall judge shouts mindlessly to the mooning Paul, "Where's love fit in? Go to the movies to see love!" And so we have. The film achieved an extraordinary status because the critics assured us it was "the most powerfully erotic movie ever made."[34] While concentrating on Paul's obsession with penetrating Jeanne's body and Tom's frantic attempts to film it, Bertolucci has made his viewers conscious of their own role as voyeurs and ultimately of their own fascination with the primal scene.

Through the voyage enacted in this film, we may better understand the degree to which cinema itself is an Orphic experience: to descend into the darkness of a protected space in an effort to retrieve through images a lost origin.

If I go back and reread my working diary of *Novecento*, I realize that at
a certain point I developed diplopia . . . was seeing double. The more
I concentrated, the more I saw double. Appropriately it was in the ninth
month of shooting.

BERNARDO BERTOLUCCI

7 DOPPIA DELLA RIVOLUZIONE

Novecento and the Play of Repetitions as Revolution

It is difficult to imagine a more abrupt transition than that from *Last Tango
in Paris* to *Novecento*, or *1900* as it is known to American audiences. *Tango*
presents several days in the tortured and private lives of a bourgeois couple in
contemporary Paris. The only other characters besides Paul, Jeanne, and
Tom remain tangential to the intensity of their primarily sexual and explicitly ahistorical fantasy world of the apartment. Four years later, Bertolucci produced an epic film ostensibly about agrarian life in Italy's Emiliana
region, a film whose chronology spans this century. Bertolucci's candor
about the psychological "symptoms" that beset him during the filming of
1900 contrasts markedly with his conscious "intent" for the film:

> Everything that happens in this film on a personal level is relegated
> to have a larger, historical meaning. It's the story of a people, of the
> peasants of this area, a people developing their own creativity to
> build themselves a history. A history in the Marxist sense. Thus a
> film that set out to concern itself with what seemed to be the agony of
> peasant culture has been transformed by the peasants themselves
> who managed to pass from a pre-political moment in the beginning
> of the century to a political consciousness of much greater meaning.[1]

Despite this attempt to impose a Marxist interpretation on his work, Bertolucci betrays a surprising confusion about the film's purpose. For example, one would have expected him to say that "Everything that happens on a personal level is relegated to a position of lesser importance in favor of attention to historical concerns." But no, the personal is "relegated to have a larger, historical meaning." This "slip" reveals that the personal issues of the film have in fact interposed themselves between the spectator and the history that was to have been shown. Symptomatic of this distortion is the fact that this narrative of Italy's agrarian revolution is led by several of Europe's most popular actors, Gérard Dépardieu, Sterling Hayden, and Stefania Sandrelli, and not by a collective or anonymous hero. Moreover, Bertolucci argues that "a film that set out to concern itself with what seemed to be the agony of a peasant culture has been transformed by the peasants themselves who managed to pass from a pre-political moment in the beginning of the century to a political consciousness of much greater meaning." Now, Italian history between 1900 and 1930 may have produced the changes Bertolucci describes, but the peasants did not accomplish these changes *during the filming* of *Novecento* and therefore cannot be said to have transformed *the film*, as the director implies. This confusion between film and historical reality, coupled with the previous confusions about personal versus historical impact, constitutes a most fundamental "diplopia" about *1900*. Bertolucci betrays surprising confusions about the film's purpose in other statements as well. He termed this film "violently documentary," for example, and rather naively claimed that "the dialectic which in my film has always been that of son/father, now becomes the contest of peasant/landowner. Exploiter and exploited."[2] Experience of Bertolucci's films suggests that the earlier works hardly reduce to a son/father dialectic but rather spin off a myriad of metaphors that derive from that dialectic in very much the same way that such pairs as peasants (*contadini*)/landowner (*padrone*) do.

Though he argues that "The principal idea of *1900* that I tried to represent continually consisted principally in bending dramatic and narrative needs to the introduction of human, cultural, social—ultimately documentary materials: the materials of the world of the Emilian peasants," he subsequently reveals that he "tried to superimpose documentary and fiction, to achieve something that seemed to me very close to a representation of ideology, to an ideology expressed in poetic terms."[3] Elsewhere he notes that the film proceeds "through various episodes; the first and most important is the peasants' strike of 1908, a strike which united peasants from various levels: day laborers, tenant farmers, lessees, farmhands, and so on. These are historical moments which we have somewhat elaborated and manipulated."[4]

Indeed, the painting that serves as an introduction to the entire film, Pelizza's *Fourth Estate* (see fig. 20), placed as a background during the opening credits, serves also to introduce a highly ironic commentary on the duality of Bertolucci's intentions for his work. Painted between 1890 and 1900, *The Fourth Estate* was intended to be a major socialist statement. "I am attempting Social painting," Pelizza wrote; "a crowd of people, workers of the soil, who are intelligent, strong, robust, united, advance like a torrent, overthrowing every obstacle in its path, thirsty for justice."[5] The artist added, "Art must give the people a portrait of themselves, but embellished." Pelizza apparently intended the work to be exhibited at the Paris Exposition of 1900, but the unveiling was delayed until 1902 and the artist was bitterly disappointed by the critics' reception. Used to gruesomely realistic or pathetically sentimental depictions of the working classes, the public found this idealized version hard to accept. In addition, the political content and physical size of the work made it difficult to exhibit, and it never did reach or touch the large public for whom it was intended.

Clearly, there is an immediate irony signaled by Bertolucci's use of this canvas, for it points simultaneously to an ambiguous combination of realism and idealization in his own work as well as to an uncanny anticipation of the difficulties attendant on the distribution of the film. Pelizza's own rather cinematic idealization of his canvas is also ironic, for, rather than advancing "like a torrent, overthrowing every obstacle in its path," as Pelizza describes his peasant march, the people are portrayed as if choreographed for a curtain call: three "leading" figures several yards in front of the rest, as if advancing to be applauded. The people behind them appear oddly unintegrated with the three leaders in attitude, gesture, or positioning. They do not surge but form a massed backdrop.[6]

Pelizza's painting points up exactly the contradiction that occurs in Bertolucci's own vision of the masses. Not only is there a "manipulation," as Bertolucci would say, or an "embellishment," as Pelizza would put it, of the social scene, but in each case the masses tend to form a backdrop behind two or three stronger figures. Bertolucci's use of Sterling Hayden, Gérard Dépardieu, and Stefania Sandrelli significantly overshadows the "human, cultural, social—ultimately documentary materials of the world of the

Figure 20. G. Pellizza da Volpedo, *Il quarto stato*. Collection Galleria d'arte moderna, Milan.

Emilian peasants" who populate the backdrop and are ostensibly the subject of the film. Again, this duality of intents results in a film whose resonance moves uncomfortably between a history without a clear sense of dialectic and a story whose unconscious motifs vie constantly with the more "manifest" ones. These various (largely ironic) similarities between Pelizza's painting and Bertolucci's film also renew Bertolucci's meditation on the relationship of painting to cinema as *interpretations* of reality.

The intrusion of primarily aesthetic and personal considerations into what was presented as a Marxist endeavor seems to bring Bertolucci directly back to the concerns of *Prima*, but without the admirable political and aesthetic self-consciousness of that earlier film. On a less self-conscious level than in *Prima*, *1900* repeats, if in a different mode, the entire range of problematics of political cinema itself when conducted by a member of the bourgeoisie. "I am always making just one film," Bertolucci had said, and nowhere in his work does Bertolucci's "one film" so thoroughly, if implicitly, interfere with his expressed intentions.

The opening sequence of the film immediately reinforces the set of oppositions raised by the Pelizza canvass. From a lengthy pastoral long shot of a shepherd strolling across a green pasture with his sheep, the camera suddenly zooms to a close-up of the peasant's face as he perceives the danger in front of him. A uniformed man, hiding in the woods, sprays a burst of machine gun fire into the peasant's body, and the latter falls, his entrails streaming out of his stomach in a "violently documentary" manner. These close-ups contrast with the long shot in movement (both within the frame and in the use of the camera shot) and in tempo (the fixed long take vs. a series of hand-held short takes). The effect of these cinematic oppositions is to suggest a contrast between the pastoral and detachment on the one hand and, on the other, the violent and a closer look. On a general level one may already deduce from the cinematic effects of this sequence that scopophilia itself seems to be directly connected to forms of violence. In terms of *1900* as a film, the sequence presents a microstructure of the film's tendency to move rather rapidly from overviews of peasant or pastoral life to more passionate and often more violent close-ups of specifically heroic characters: Olmo (Dépardieu), Dalco (Hayden), and Anita (Sandrelli). There is, naturally, in this film as in all of Bertolucci's previous work, a predominance of interest in the psychological, almost always violent interrelationship of the principal characters rather than in the sociocultural or documentary statement. "Transforming Destiny into the Unconscious," Bertolucci argued, "also affects the rapport between sexuality and politics."[7] The phrase "violently documentary" thus serves as an encoding strategy for this dual structure.

The following scene introduces the other complementary set of oppositions suggested by Pelizza's *Fourth Estate*: realistic documentary versus a form of manipulation, embellishment, or poetic idealism. This sequence of women in the fields opens with a shot of a haystack from which several pitch- forks are pulled simultaneously—as if choreographed in an American musical comedy. The camera pans to the top of this haystack where a young girl stands surveying the countryside. She points *off* and cries: "I see so many things! I see a lot of blackshirts fleeing. . . . I see one of our people . . . running towards them without a gun. He's got only a stick in his hand. God what a beating he's giving them!" And the scenario indicates: "The woman has shouted toward an *imperceptible* part of the fields; toward the point where Anita's eyes *pretend to see the scene described. In reality* there is only a hut with an old man seated on the doorstep in the sun."[8]

Because nothing can be seen, according to the scenario, "one might as well invent" (*Novecento*, 7). Anita shouts again, "Hey! Look what I see! . . . I see someone on a white horse. You should see what a cloud of dust he's rais- ing! It looks like Olmo!" But the scenario again warns, "Despite her excited voice and fiery eyes and authentic emotion, the child has again made it all up. But suddenly Anita interrupts her fiction . . . and has returned to reality. 'But look who's running away! Attila and Regina!' " (*Novecento*, 7).

Bertolucci has thus drawn our attention to a subtle interplay between two kinds of seeing, the mythical visionary, which proposes to interpret the invisible—what Bertolucci might call "manipulation"—versus what Bertolucci would term the "documentary," which points more insistently to the visible. This single moment in which Anita "pretends to see" what is in fact imperceptible recapitulates both the relation of the oneiric to our waking state and the relation of the film experience itself to reality. What we see as well as why we look at films, dreams, and fantasies remain primary concerns of this motion picture, as has been the case throughout Bertolucci's work. By mixing the actual with the fantastic, the peasant girl exactly duplicates Bertolucci's own position as a filmmaker who "somewhat elaborates and manipulates" historical moments. And by interjecting the fantasy of Olmo on a white horse into the perceived reality of Attila and Regina, she "announces" the subsequent scene during which Olmo's return on Ada's white horse will embroil him as the accused in Attila and Regina's heinous murder and rape of the innocent child. Olmo will nightmarishly figure in their place as child-murderer. Because this event occurs both before (chronologically) *and* after (in the film sequence) its announcement, the vision becomes, like a dream, timeless. This tendency toward condensation is explicit in Bertolucci's plan for the dramatic structure of the film, which was intended to be:

> A day, the 25th of April, 1945, the Italian Day of Liberation and it includes the whole century. We took it as a sort of symbolic day on which is unleashed, on which flowers this peasants' utopia . . . and this day includes all the conditioning, all the needed facts.[9]

Once again, perhaps unconsciously, Bertolucci has "slipped." The twenty-fifth of April may indeed symbolize the entire century, but it cannot "include all the needed facts." This condensation of the metaphorical and "factual" levels of the work itself figuralizes Bertolucci's general filmic strategy.

These two structuring elements—the movement from the long-take pastoral sociocultural to the violence of individual psychology, and the movement from documentary to oneiric fantasies that reveal the condensation common to dreams—are closely connected, for the first commonly presents itself as the latent content of the second. Close analysis of this entire film reveals to how great an extent these two structures are essential to an understanding of the work. There is yet a third, also present in both Pelizza's painting and the opening scenes, which Bertolucci subtly but forcefully interweaves with the other two.

I noted that the arrangements of peasants in Pelizza's *Fourth Estate* give the impression of a dramatic presentation, almost a curtain call for the leading triumvirate, in which the woman's outstretched arm suggests acknowledgment of applause. Likewise, Bertolucci mixes an unusual degree of stylization or choreographed theatricality with an otherwise documentary-like film. It is as though Eisenstein has been superimposed on Dostoevsky; a sort of *General Line* where the stylization of a collective hero gradually evolves into a version of Jacob in *The Double* or Raskolnikov in *Crime and Punishment*.

Following a highly stylized opening sequence of the women grasping their pitchforks in a single dancelike motion, Bertolucci introduces, in a flashback, the scene of Alfredo's and Olmo's "twin" births. The sequence opens with a shot of Gobbo, the village "fool," dressed as a character from Verdi and running through the fields in what can only be understood as a parody of the immediately preceding pastoral scene, crying, "Verdi is dead!" while the music of *Rigoletto* gives a mock-tragic overtone to the scene. We hear the screams of a woman in labor, but instead of a shot of birthing Bertolucci gives us a group of children huddled in the stairwell of a peasant cottage burlesquing childbirth with a huge squash for a fetus. Bertolucci then abruptly cuts to a shot of the manor house, where the padrone (Burt Lancaster) repeats the birthing farce with Gobbo beneath the window of his daughter-in-law's labor room. As a finale to this farcical overture, the padrone, Alfredo, and Leo Dalco (Sterling Hayden), the patriarch of the Berlinghieri peasants, engage in a highly stylized debate—almost a dance. Alfredo invites Leo to toast the births with spumante. Leo is scything the field, and his sixteen farm hands participate in his refusal through a dance of imitation that could almost have been taken from *Oklahoma!* Each time that Alfredo offers the bottle, Leo sharpens his scythe blade and the camera pans to the sixteen men lined up in the field beyond, sharpening their blades in time with their foreman. When Leo scythes, they scythe, and when finally he accepts the toast, they imitate that gesture as well, always in perfect time with each other. This theatrical burlesque of a master–slave dialectic constitutes an allusion to the "stable theater" indigenous to the Emilia region of Italy.

Research on stable theater has uncovered a (now dying) form of spontaneous peasant drama that takes place during the coldest months of the year in the stable, the only space large enough and warm enough in which to congregate during the evenings. There the contadini act out with and for each other a play in which all the traditional roles are turned upside down: The padrone becomes a servant of the contadini. In the topsy-turvy world that follows, everything is undone; even the language suffers from playful distortions.[10] One might easily conclude that primary process thinking (the condensation and displacement of dreams) has taken over. A fantasized violence is committed against all the prescribed and enforced forms of social and psychological order. And yet this revolution against order traditionally remains disguised—hidden among the animals and hidden behind a farcical form that allows a cathexis of rebellious affect without perceivable effect. At its most revolutionary, stable theater both questions and guarantees the status quo. The staple of stable theater thus involves two motifs pertinent to *1900*: the compulsion to repeat over and over the same material and the ever-repeated (Oedipal) undoing of authority. The motive forces of that play are fundamentally ambivalent: The repetition compulsion is psychoanalytically linked to the death wish,[11] and the Oedipal conflict, deriving as it does from underlying sexual motives, is attributable to the deepest instinct for life. Such ambiguity is, as we shall see, endemic to the entire fabric of *1900*. The entire film is inscribed ambiguously in the genre "realistic opéra bouffe," a cross-fertilization of Olmi, Verdi, and Rodgers and Hammerstein.

Although the tone varies enormously from sequence to sequence, we are frequently reminded of the self-consciously theatrical quality of events. At virtually every major climax of the film, Bertolucci superimposes on his version of peasant history a thoroughly theatrical overlay.

At times this "overlay" takes the form of choreography, as in the scene in which Attila is pelted with grain by the contadini during his first imposition of a "tax" on the peasants' share. Such "staging" again colors the heroic scene of the peasants solidarity in the face of Orestes' eviction from his house. Here the peasants' choral response and ballet of passive resistance stylistically parallels the soldiers' orchestrated mounted charge. At the moment of contact, the horses turn in disarray, mimicking the earlier confusion of the peasant group before they have spontaneously organized. Bertolucci has already prepared his spectator for the pure theatricality of this gesture: In a previous scene, mounted police attack a Punch and Judy puppet theater in which the current political repression is parodied. In so doing, the

Figure 21. The staging of a heroic scene of resistance. Courtesy The
Museum of Modern Art/Film Stills Archive.

carabinieri both directly imitate the content of the puppet show they are
attacking and anticipate the later eviction scene.

Even in more solemn moments, the mise-en-scène adopts a curiously
theatrical and oneiric quality. During the funeral procession honoring the
four old men burned alive in the Fascist torching of the Casa del Popolo,
Olmo and Anita initially despair of finding any popular support for their
symbolic march. Standing alone, they peer in vain down an empty street. As
the camera zooms slowly toward the farthest point in view, an eerie sound of
band music greets the ear (reminiscent of the music preceding Agostino's
entry on his bike in *Prima*), and, mysteriously, a funeral cortege rounds the
corner and proceeds toward the waiting couple. The "curtain falls" on this
scene to end "atto primo" of *1900*, and it is never clear whether this procession belongs to the topos of the film's realism or to that announced by the
opening scenes when the young girl atop a haystack "invents" the scene she
so desperately wants (us) to see. Bertolucci seems quite content to allow,
even to promote, this confusion between oneiric and realistic levels of the

work. Indeed, this scene contrasts in a remarkably parallel fashion to the scene immediately preceding, in which Ada (Dominique Sanda) plays at being blind during a peasant dance in a barn. The major dialectic of the central moments of *1900* thus turns on the bourgeois pretense of failing to see what is versus the peasant illusion of seeing what might be. That "diplopic" opposition, so reminiscent of *Prima della rivoluzione*, dominates Bertolucci's treatment of both peasant and Fascist halves of his film.

The idealization of peasant life is achieved through a golden halo of light with which Vittorio Storaro bathes every peasant scene, through Ennio Morricone's unabashedly lyric musical accompaniment, and through Bertolucci's choreography. The total effect is a cumulative sense of the utter innocence and purity of the contadini's agrarian existence. These effects culminate in the rite of passage, filmed as a sort of Last Supper, in which Olmo, bathed in a golden haze, traverses the long supper table of the Dalco family to hear Leo pronounce the peasant creed and bestow his paternal blessing. Clearly none of these moments fits the genre of documentary or socialist realism. The "grande finale," in which the immense red banner becomes a tent housing Alfredo's "trial," is particularly operatic.[12]

(These "open-eyed," romanticized scenes contrast markedly with Bertolucci's handling of Alfredo's wedding, which inaugurates the reign of Fascist horror. If the contadini are filmed as if in a daydream, the wedding is a nightmarish affair, dark, menacing, haunted by Morricone's chilling musical theme and culminating in Attila's murder of the child Patrizio. This cinematic moment is so horrifying that both the rape and the murder are filmed as if by Ada—almost blind. Attila's spinning movement causing Patrizio's head to be crushed against the room's cement walls is filmed with the same blurred "inability to see" that had characterized Agostino's fall from the bike in *Prima*.)

This set of self-consciously theatrical peasant scenes is echoed by the highly staged quality of other moments in the film (e.g., the Molièresque falsification of Alfredo's will or the farcical scene of Alfredo [Burt Lancaster] and his youthful namesake [Paolo Pavesi] disrupting a formal dinner at the mansion).

Several scenes, although less staged, proclaim in subtler fashion their fidelity to the quiet revolution that occurs, in ritualized form, in the peasant stable theater. In particular, the sequence of old Alfredo's suicide faithfully reenacts the latent meaning and deeper structure of stable theater, for it begins with a beautifully choreographed peasant dance and then places the old padrone in a cow stall where he exchanges roles with the milking girl, taking her place beneath the cow. The scene includes obscene and utterly silly language: "Splish, splash . . . cows full of milk and shit. . . . Do you know what the real curse is? Milk and shit in the brain" (*Novecento*, 70). Alfredo ends this tragicomic moment with an exercise in autohumiliation (graphically revealing his impotence to the adolescent girl) and then commits suicide. His foreman, Leo, salutes the padrone's suicide with a sarcastic "Why did you have to go and untie all the cattle, eh? When a man does nothing all his life, he has too much time to think. And by thinking too much he becomes a child again" (*Novecento*, 75).

What is most significant about this scene is the way the padrone enters as if by incantation the realm and role assigned to him by stable theater. It is as though the dramatized ritual repeated incessantly, almost compulsively, had the power to control or evoke the reality it re-presents. Like Pelizza's *Fourth Estate*, like the puppet show, and like Anita's visions on the haystack, the sequence in the stable invites a meditation on the power of illusion: Fantasy seems to have the power of prescription for, if not direct prediction of, the film's "reality."

This "predictive" power is recognized implicitly in one of the final scenes of the film when Leonida (bearing the nom de guerre of Olmo) first shoots a portrait (representation) of Alfredo and then threatens to kill Alfredo's grandson Alfredo in exactly the same stall in which his grandfather and father had died. It is triply significant that (*a*) Leonida is merely playacting with Alfredo and ultimately leads him to a mock trial in which the padrone is "killed" but Alfredo is spared (another extension of stable theater—and *Spider*); (*b*) the Leonida scene both precedes (in the film sequence) and follows (chronologically) the "original" hanging in Bertolucci's narrative (like the white horse of the opening sequence, it is narratologically timeless); and (*c*) the two scenes exactly fulfill a compulsion to repeat a basically Oedipal configuration (of conflict with and ultimate outgrowing of the dependence on and need to destroy authority). As Freud noted, "Repetition of repressed material as contemporary experience . . . inevitably has to do with the Oedipus complex and its derivatives. What appears to be reality is in fact only a reflection of a forgotten past."[13]

Indeed, *1900* is replete with reflections of a not-quite-forgotten past rather than the progressive unfolding of a (Marxist) history. Such repetitions include the deaths of Leo and his "son" Olmo, both of whom die peacefully sitting against a tree, in an integrative and reintegrative moment. Each seems to be responding more to some unseen appeal of death, as the name of Olmo would imply.[14] These scenes also tend to accentuate the relationship between repetition (as a compulsion) and play (re-presentation, film itself).[15]

If the dialectic opposing contadini and padrone tends to be swallowed up in these series of repetitions, shifting the film's focus from the masses to individual patterns, so too does Bertolucci's treatment of fascism. It may be possible to conduct a political analysis of Attila's behavior that would produce a reasonable understanding of the role of fascism in prewar Italy, one that would suggest, for example, that the Fascists succeeded in interposing themselves politically between the dying caste of landowners and the restless class of the agrarian proletariat. To do so, however, would hardly do justice to the impact of Attila on the film. In fact, Attila enters the same pattern of repetition that includes the three generations of padrone: He dies in a pigpen in the stables. That Attila is also the name of Bertolucci's poet father evokes the ongoing struggle for/with author-ity so prominent in Bertolucci's earlier work. In Attila, however, we see less a representative of fascism than a configuration of what we may call the Laius complex. Attila's atrocious murder of an innocent child occurs at the chronological center of the film and is figured as a circle from which the child is brutally cast out.[16] The murder is prefigured by Attila's own bloody head in the Fascist épreuve of killing an innocent animal. In those two scenes the compulsion of atrocity tends to rob Attila of his political status and to focus on his psychoanalytic status as a Laius figure. That the children are exiled during the struggle between contadini and padrone also suggest the padrone's (father's) potential harm to the innocents. Nor is the name Orestes an innocent choice for one cast out of his home by the padrone.[17] All in all, there is a strong tendency to portray the Oedipal conflict as a protracted struggle with an essentially evil father who may starve, dismember, and otherwise brutalize his "children."[18]

That these Oedipal–Laius variations are repeated so insistently again suggests a repetition compulsion at work in the narrative purpose of Bertolucci's film. Nor is it surprising that Bertolucci suffered from diplopia during the filming of 1900, for all of these conflicts are oneirically condensed, projected, and displaced in the double configuration central to the entire film. This motif, operating as it does between and across the dialectical opposition of padrone and contadini, further tends to confuse and dissolve the power of historical dialectical analysis that the film might otherwise have proposed.

The role of doubling in Bertolucci's work is by this time well established. In *1900* Bertolucci introduces two boys born on the same summer day of explicitly ambiguous parentage: There is a strong implication that old Alfredo (Burt Lancaster) is the father of "the bastard" Olmo, because Leo capriciously names Olmo's father as one already long deceased and because old Alfredo clearly has no compunction about leading young peasant women into the stables for his sexual pleasure. It is not impossible that Alfredo is the father of *both* boys, given Giovanni's ineptitude. The "fool" Gobbo celebrates their births with a poem:

> Summer is here
> Whose heat is severe
> Two boys born today
> But a few meters away
> Destiny's design
> Seeks to intertwine
> The padrone's firstborn
> And peasant's bastard forlorn.[19]

"Lo scherzo del destino / Li volle unire insieme." Indeed, destiny unites these unequal twins as insistently as any other double configuration in Bertolucci's work. As grown men, Alfredo will boast, "We're twins. . . . We always do everything together. What's his is mine and what's mine is also mine."[20]

This awkward reminder of the class barrier that separates them barely masks the real dominance between these two. Alfredo may be the richer in possessions, but from the first Olmo claims a natural precedence: he is the firstborn and the initiator in all of their sexual games and competitions, which punctuate and upstage the film's entire peasant–landowner dialectic. At their first meeting, the young Olmo (Roberto Maccanti) intervenes between Alfredo and his girlfriend, Nina, and then shows his overly dressed companion how to "screw the earth." Bertolucci insists on the awkward parallelism of the two as Alfredo repeats, gesture for gesture, Olmo's mock combat and then mock sexual activity. Their mealtimes are likewise compared through parallel cutting, which contrasts the heartfelt camaraderie of the Dalco table and the icy hypocrisy of the Berlinghieris' formal dining room. Little Alfredo is force-fed the frog legs he had just seen dangling from hooks on Olmo's cap and vomits them up—one more example of Olmo's symbolic dominance of his landed friend. In the silkworm loft, Olmo

Figure 22. Destiny unites the "twins" Alfredo (Robert De Niro) and
Olmo (Gérard Dépardieu). Courtesy Paramount Films.

instructs Alfredo in the fine art of masturbation, as well as the "true meaning" of the phrase, "socialists with holes in their pockets," another sexual
metaphor. Later the two boys practice this art in the hayfields as Leo Dalco
sits dying nearby, protesting the soldiers protecting the padrone. As adults,
they evoke these earlier games when Olmo returns from the war to the same
loft and bestows an unmistakably sexual kiss on Alfredo. Much of the force
of the agrarian struggle against an unjust padrone is dissipated by the director's insistence on "translating" this struggle into childhood games of sexual
prowess.

As the film progresses, despite frequent allusions to historical developments, Olmo and Alfredo's relationship continues to function more like the
two sides of Giacobbe in *Partner* than as two opponents in a class struggle.
There always seems to be a woman at the fulcrum of their delicate balance,
as, for example, the epileptic laundry woman, who lies naked between them
and holds the penis of each, as if to measure them. This "game," like almost

all of their playful gestures, turns sour when Alfredo forces liquor on the woman and induces an epileptic seizure, which he refuses to stay to witness. Just as Olmo intervenes in the childhood play between Alfredo and Nina, he "captures" Ada like a bird in his hunting net on her wedding day, and thereafter she is never able to free herself completely from the fascination he holds for her. Later, Ada will flee the captivity of her alcoholism and her marriage to Alfredo in order to be with Olmo. As for the latter, he may rise to a position of leadership among the contadini and Alfredo may sink to an abdication of his place as padrone, but their particular relationship, so highlighted visually and thematically, never deviates from this more competitive and Oedipal level.

The most telling and remarkable of these mirroring repetitions frames the entire film, for Olmo had taught Alfredo what Freud might term a kind of "fort-da" game of lying within but parallel to the railroad tracks and letting the train sweep harmlessly by.[21] In the concluding sequence of the film, Alfredo and Olmo, now so old they can hardly walk, pursue their youthful tussles as if they were two adolescents. Alfredo repeats Olmo's game, this time lying crossways on the tracks, transforming the "play" into a potential murder-suicide reminiscent of his own grandfather's "stable theater" demise. The entire scene constitutes a visual repetition so striking as to provoke the realization that, due to psychological forces that far outweigh the purely political ones, everything is destined to be repeated without significant progression, always in a displaced or deviant form.

If there is any development within this play of repetitions in *1900*, it is not so much a dialectic but a simple displacement from tragic (the first strikes and the advent of fascism) to comic (the mock trial in which Alfredo is killed and spared simultaneously) to farcical (Olmo and Alfredo as old men reducing the "class struggle" to a tussle). Like Marx's analysis of Bonapartism, which Jeffrey Mehlman characterizes as a "ludicrous imitation of the tragic," the repetitions that are substituted for revolution in *1900* result in collapse of local history, thoroughly vitiating any strict sense of chronology.[22]

Rather than affirm a dialectical or historical process, the film undoes both dialectics and history. History is submerged not only in the repetition of events in the film and in the narrative circularity that brings the film uroborically back to its own beginnings but also repeatedly and consistently in the negation of any sense of the dialectical advance of such events as do "take place." By condemning the padrone and then setting him free and by giving

Figure 23. Olmo captures Ada (Dominique Sanda) on her wedding day.
Courtesy The Museum of Modern Art/Film Stills Archive.

up their arms to the first personification of authority that happens to drive through their barnyard, the peasants of *1900* return to the concept of *revolution* the repetitive connotation inherent in yet politically antithetical to it. Ultimately, Bertolucci is right when he terms their little republic a utopia, for it is categorically unlocatable in (or outside of) the film's narrative chronology.

Revolution may be defined either as "Orbital motion about a point" or a "sudden political overthrow brought about within a given system."[23] "Orbital motion about a point" may itself describe, variously, (a) the Oedipus–Laius configuration of Attila's child-murder (recalling both the winding scene of *Spider* and the dance scene of *The Conformist*); (b) the political progress portrayed in the film, which moves more through dramatic repetition than through dialectics; (c) the structure of the film itself, which ends where it began; and (d) the movement of the film strip as it winds or unwinds from reel to reel and of the eye as it follows the events on the cinematic screen. It is the conglomerate of these meanings, taken together, that forms the latent, unconscious perhaps, but more significant meaning of the film. In this sense, *1900* stands for cinema itself in its insistence on the shift of focus away from the history of events narrated to a "destiny" always already "written" in relationships, much like our own ongoing desire to reexperience the primal scene in the voyeuristic place of the darkened movie theater. The film's very title repeats the condensation of the above structures. The Italian allows a single term to stand for the year that initiates the film (and summarizes it) and the entire evolution of the film's "history." It announces and denounces the very concept of chronological or historical evolution, focusing instead on this uncanny repetitive structure.

Like Marx's vision of Bonapartism, Bertolucci's vision of agrarian "revolution" seems to generate a kind of circulation of terms no longer categorizable within a dialectic arrangement.[24] Terms in *1900* (whether political or psychological) are no longer opposed symmetrically but repeated in a specular (diplopic) assimilation. So many elements of this film become doubled either synchronically or diachronically that virtually any sequence may come to occupy the position of the repetitive structure.[25] Ultimately, in this insistence on repetition, which seems at each isolated moment potentially to involve a dialectical movement of history, there is only a return, apparently—ideologically, at least—the very opposite of revolution.[26] This phantasmal circulation of terms, the presence of the uncanny, condensation, doubling, and a compulsion to repeat all indicate that at one level the film itself *represents* what Freud termed the "urge inherent in organic life to restore an earlier state of things which the living entity has been obliged to abandon under the pressure of external disturbing forces . . . the expression of the inertia inherent in organic life."[27] If the repetitive structures in *1900* suggest a "death wish,"[28] it is in the sense that we most frequently encounter in dreams in the form of a structure in which affect is so repeatedly displaced that its original stimulus can no longer be recovered or serve as a source of new affect.[29]

Indeed, the entire structure of *1900*, like so much of Bertolucci's previous work, is, like a dream, an open structure in which primary process thinking predominates. Three years into the filming of *1900* Bertolucci said,

> We haven't written the ending yet. In any case the ending remains fairly open. We have a variety of ideas for it, but . . . films always take a different road than one plans for them . . . especially a film

> like this. They are like ships in the night, like a galleon that departs.
> One makes it depart but then it takes its own direction. So we left the
> end open for the time being.[30]

Aside from the obvious parallels with dream structure in these comments
(cf. "films always take a different road than one plans for them" and Freud's
"royal road to the unconscious"; "ships *in the night*"; "it takes its own
direction"), there is a remarkable allusion to his own film latent in Bertolucci's thoughts. The terms "ships in the night," "galleon that departs . . .
in its own direction," also evoke a scene and a character, both of which are
"spectacular" and remain otherwise difficult to analyze within the terms of
"intent" established at the outset for the film.

Bertolucci introduces Uncle Ottavio (Werner Bruhns) through the toy
galleon that he holds suspended over little Alfredo's sickbed. Significantly,
we first see the shadow of the galleon in the wavelike scroll of the wallpaper.
Ottavio is the "director" of this "movie," which so delights his nephew and
which is reminiscent of the play of shadows so central to *The Conformist*.[31]
Alfredo, capped in exotic turban, immediately speaks of escaping from his
situation. Ottavio thus situates the locus of and serves as the agent of escape:
through absence, shadows, opium, sexual otherness, the white horse—and
cinema itself. He not only designs shadow plays for Alfredo but voyeuristically peeps at nude boys and refers to this activity as "my secret . . .
photography." When Ada learns of his secret, she demands to be photo-
graphed as well, and Ottavio obliges, calling, "Hold it!" as the camera
freeze-frames the naked actress, making Ottavio's obsession momentarily
coincide with our own.

Like the film director or viewer, Ottavio virtually never participates
directly in any of the political action of the drama, preferring instead
observation, voyeurism, photography, and ultimately opium dreams. When
things become too grim, Ottavio withdraws, changes scenes, one might say.
His entire behavior evokes the problematics of desire (or absence), which are
fundamental to photography as a structure.[32]

Ottavio's voyeurism is frequently imitated by Bertolucci's camera, which
selects by preference windows or doors to "catch" a scene. The camera follows old Alfredo Berlinghieri through the closed doors of the barn as he
attempts a final seduction of a milking girl. It slips into the bedroom where
old Alfredo lies dead so that we may watch young Alfredo watching his

father take his grandfather's place in bed. We obtain a privileged view of Alfredo and Ada naked in the hay, and another of Olmo, Alfredo, and the laundry woman naked in bed. We are even permitted to see the grotesque disporting of Attila and Regina, which includes the rape and murder of a child. As in *Last Tango* and *The Conformist*, Bertolucci's camera begins with a kind of seductive, passive voyeurism and subtly substitutes a form of complicity with violence, which the spectator must confront as a natural extension of voyeurism itself.

The open-endedness of *1900* did not eventually include Ottavio, and he remains an absent presence at the end of the film, like the temptation to film/dream that he so clearly represents. His elusive presence suggests, however, that Bertolucci's title may signify yet a third meaning. In addition to coinciding with Verdi's death opening a new century and the century itself, like a screen memory, the title dates without naming the most significant psychological study of the century: Freud's *Interpretation of Dreams*, first published in 1900. Seductive and *traum*atic as it is, replete with repetitions of crucial moments, full of condensation and displacements, Bertolucci's film "subordinates its discourse only sporadically and superficially to logical imperatives; it constitutes a mode of thought that is free (in the sense of free associations), is undertaken 'in order to see' and implies a series of 'about faces,' acts of virtual repentance and denial."[33]

Although, in the spirit of irony, I have borrowed this passage from Laplanche's critique of Freud's *Beyond the Pleasure Principle*, its applicability to *1900* coupled with the film's use of dream structures clearly suggests a nexus of "artistic play" where, just as in dreams, seductive pleasure and traumatic pain are insistently mingled.[34]

As a film that aspires to give to the personal level a larger historical meaning, it can be thought of as a "screen memory" that groups together seemingly insignificant and unconsciously valuable elements in a structure that masks yet preserves what the psyche cannot afford to lose.[35] It is, at all levels, profoundly *conservative* while at the same time it allows the appearance of progressive movement. This "screen memory" is a locus of projection (in what it reveals of the filmmaker's and film viewers' emotions) as well as protection (in what it hides—albeit badly). Like a dream, *1900* fluctuates between its status as transitional object (a potential space allowing the constitution of the self through [metaphoric] experience) and as fetish (the petrified space of a phantasmal scenario, the repeated negation of self, a psychic pseudoreality).[36] The position of mediation between these two is clearly held by author as dreamer, personified by Ottavio, who represents a version of cinema itself. The illusions actively induced by Ottavio are congruent with those produced by Bertolucci. They constitute the necessary, if highly self-conscious, attempt to link interior reality and the exterior world in order to achieve intersubjective recognition.[37] For Bertolucci in particular, these binary oppositions, whether interior/exterior, illusion/reality, or poetry/documentary, ultimately refer to his most single-minded of projects.

If 1900 contains the illusion of agrarian revolution, it also contains the seeds for a revolution in our understanding of the mechanics of illusion itself, which like 1900 is both vital to intersubjective growth and based on disillusionment and the power of figuring absence. It is the genius of this film to have focused our consciousness at so many different levels on the relationships among politics, psychology, and the nature of cinema as an experience. If Uncle Ottavio disappears from the end of 1900, it is only temporary, for the opium dream he offers returns (like the repressed) in Luna where Bertolucci will experiment with the dream dreamed for the sake of dreaming itself.

While filming *Luna*, I found myself shooting in exactly the same places
that Gina traverses in *Prima* when she decides to leave. Searching for the
right frame in the viewfinder, I lost my equilibrium and fell, . . . as
though in returning to Parma and in bringing the mother back there I had
dared too much and found myself in the middle of an unbearable situation.

BERNARDO BERTOLUCCI

8 "... PERFORCE TO DREAM"

Oneiric Projection and Protection in *Luna*

"When I'd finished *1900*," Bertolucci recalls, "I began to have a recurrent
dream linked to the first memory of my life: my mother was transporting me
on her bicycle and I saw her face, still young, next to the ancient face of the
moon which bobbed along in the sky above hers."[1] The "text" of this dream
was to be transposed directly into one of the opening scenes of *Luna*, suggesting that Bertolucci had turned to his own memories and dreams as the
primary source for this film.

However, despite the fact that Bertolucci stressed that "the opening scene
derived from one of my earliest memories," elsewhere he denies vigorously
that the film is autobiographical.[2] This "attempt to discover something about
the mother and the son" is also "a search for the present and the past,
a therapy which, like psychoanalysis, allows me to be in harmony with
myself, to accept myself and to communicate with others . . . a type of very
wide mass communication."[3] One cannot fail to be struck by the very self-
contradictory nature of Bertolucci's ambitions for this film, expressed as if
they were a single idea: on the one hand, "a therapy which . . . allows me to
be in harmony with myself," and, conversely, "a type of very wide mass
communication." In the understanding of this apparent paradox lies the way
to comprehending the film itself and its place in Bertolucci's oeuvre.

Bertolucci had said of *The Conformist* that it was like "a memory of my own memory" and explained that what he meant by this phrase was the remembrance of cinema itself. Transposed to his experience with *Luna*, this phrase takes on an entirely new significance. What emerges in this film is a remarkable relationship to cinema, individually different from any of his other films yet somehow synthesizing all of them.

In one of the early sequences of the film, Joe Silveri (Matthew Barry) is standing with his (presumed) father, Douglas (Fred Gwynne), on a Brooklyn Heights balcony overlooking the East River. After Joe's challenge to his father to hit a tennis ball across the river, Bertolucci's camera follows the ball's trajectory over the nearby dockyards and catches the phrase "Pier 14" as the ball fades out of sight far from its goal. Pasolini's first name on a Brooklyn warehouse opens what is to become an intensely self-referential meditation on Bertolucci's relationship to authority and cinema.

In this single scene, two adoptive fathers are evoked: Douglas, whose claim to be able to hit the city is as empty as his promise to stay with Joe; and Pier Paolo Pasolini, who had died shortly before the shooting of *Luna*.[4]

Joe's relationship to Douglas is naively, indeed monstrously, Oedipal. Joe cajoles his mother into letting him accompany her to Italy with the utterly naive words, "I want to go to Italy with you. . . . I can do all the things Dad does. . . . I can do it better!"[5] Given the creative complexities generated by the theme of Oedipal rivalry in Bertolucci's earlier work—especially in *Spider* and *The Conformist*—the transparent, even simplistic Freudianism of this scene must come as a surprise and a disappointment. Gwynne, whose film career had been heretofore limited to playing a Frankenstein-like figure in the American television series "The Munsters," functions in his role as Douglas as a caricature of a father to be eliminated. Moments after Joe's assertion of his superiority to his father, Douglas obliges his "son" by dying, entombed in his white Mercedes in front of their Brooklyn Heights home. Douglas's death (recalling Pasolini's automotive murder) seems to concretize a sense of liberation: Both cinematic and contextual stepfathers are given a lip-service gesture of homage and then unceremoniously removed, apparently providing Bertolucci with a final "sense of liberation" from these "paternal figures."[6]

The inner complexity of such an otherwise innocuous scene should alert us to the latent intricacy of a film lambasted by the critics for its inauthenticity and overly simplistic symbolism.[7] Indeed, there is another element of this scene between father and son that we should not miss. The scene concludes with Douglas's discovery of a piece of chewing gum stuck to the underside of the balcony railing. "Jesus Christ," he mutters, "he leaves his gum all over the place." "He" is of course both Joe and Marlon Brando, who ended *Last Tango* by sticking his gum in an identical place as he assumed a fetal position to die. This moment constitutes the first of a series of carefully placed allusions to Bertolucci's earlier films.

Joe's desire to accompany his mother to Italy seems to coincide, in fact, with Bertolucci's desire to revisit the sites and situations of his earlier films. Even before they leave, this series of allusions begins. Aside from this first allusion to *Last Tango*, Douglas's death in the car constitutes an unmistakable visual allusion to Quadri's death scene, with the roles reversed. In *The Conformist*, it is the father figure, Quadri, who approaches the closed car and is unable to rouse an apparently dead figure slumped over the wheel. In *Luna*, Joe will repeat this gesture, moaning, "Dead, dead, dead." Seen in terms of Bertolucci's earlier work, this role reversal suggests an immediate assumption of the paternal persona for Joe himself, and the entire Italian experience will constitute a subtle shift of emphasis for Bertolucci, as we shall see.

Douglas's funeral opens another allusion to both *Before the Revolution* and *The Conformist*. As Joe and his mother sit in the back of the limousine awaiting departure, a series of mourners' faces appear at the windows of the car, sometimes pressed against the glass in an uncannily distorted fashion, recalling Anna's distorted and agonized face in the Quadri murder scene. Also, during Agostino's funeral, Fabrizio and Gina had occupied an identical position in the family sedan, in the first of their encounters alone, which become increasingly "incestuous." Bertolucci said of this "coincidence":

> *Prima della rivoluzione* told a story of incest, but very
> unconsciously and obliquely. Gina is Fabrizio's aunt. While I was
> making the film I was convinced that to recount a love story between
> an aunt and her nephew was only a way, not even very unusual, even
> fairly classic, of presenting the relationship where a man is younger,
> more immature, and less experienced than the woman. I had the
> sensation of referring to a neutral convention, full of literary
> precedents, and I told myself that Gina could well have been simply
> a friend of the family. I didn't realize that the mother's sister is

almost a mother. It is a fact that I obstinately hid from myself that I wanted to film the story of love between a mother and a son. . . . It took more than ten years of analysis for *Prima della rivoluzione* to become *La Luna* and the aunt to become the mother.[8]

Here Bertolucci credits his psychoanalytic experience with what amounts to a global rejection of the symbolic in favor of a frankly explicit rendition of mother–son incest. What we encounter, then, from the opening scenes of this film is a pattern of Oedipal wish fulfillment already "translated" by the director from the metaphoric to the metonymic. It is as though Charles Baudelaire had opted to become Emile Zola in order to "clarify" the concept of *correspondances*. As disappointing as this shift of register might at first seem, it has a fascinating corollary: The term "screen memory," also rendered literally, may lose in *Luna* some of its psychological depth in terms of the portrayal of character, but it nevertheless acquires new cinematic resonance. If the term "incest" no longer "hides and forever preserves" a maternal secret, its meaning has simply been displaced (in a movement quite common in psychoanalysis) to another level: that of film itself.

This degree of self-awareness in Bertolucci's comments about *Luna* is matched by a remarkable degree of self-conscious repetition in the film, as though Bertolucci had transposed the figure of repetition so insistently developed in *1900* to the level of his entire oeuvre. Once in Italy, the couple systematically retraces Bertolucci's own steps through the sets of all of his Italian films. In Rome, Joe traces and retraces paths already taken by Giacobbe in *Partner*. When Caterina escapes from the intensity of her struggles with her son, she heads for Parma, the set of *Prima*. It was here that Bertolucci experienced a "loss of equilibrium" because, as he tells it, he dared to bring the mother back to Parma and because of the unbearable situation thereby created. At Parma, Caterina visits Verdi's birthplace, and then she and Joe set out in her white Mercedes across the Emiliana countryside. Like psychoanalysis itself, theirs is a "voyage à deux, without maps on an uncertain road,"[9] during which they rediscover the courtyard so familiar to audiences of *1900*. "The past has to be crossed one way or another," Bertolucci explained, and added:

Caterina and Joe enter in an automobile a frame of *1900* and look at the courtyard in which the peasants celebrated the utopia of April 25th. When mother and son penetrate and pass through the

Figure 24. Joe (Matthew Barry) and Caterina (Jill Clayburgh) on their
"voyage à deux without maps on an uncertain road." Courtesy Twentieth
Century Fox.

Courtyard of the Piacentine, the soundtrack is silent for a few
seconds. Today as then Demessio Dalco is unloading hay. Then the
sound returns, the frame moves on, returns to the present, the
camera pans to Caterina and Joe, who are transformed from
spectators to actors again. [10]

This moment of silence, with which we ordinarily observe a memoriam to
the dead, would seem to be part of an attempt to "lay to rest" the all too vivid
images of Bertolucci's cinematic past. The gesture, however, recalls nothing
so much as Marlon Brando sitting beside Rosa's bier in *Last Tango*, moaning, "I might be able to comprehend the universe, but I'll never discover the
truth about you, never." I am suggesting that the maternal in this film has
been unconsciously displaced somewhere else and that Jill Clayburgh herself
is left to function as a screen memory for some other matrix. Her status as

an American movie actress is itself powerfully suggestive of this strategy of displacement.

When Caterina and Joe arrive at the roadside cafe where the scene of incest is to occur, who should appear out of Bertolucci's cinematic past, complete with a plate of sausages from his special store, but Gaibazzi (Pippo Campanini) of *Spider's Stratagem*, reminding the viewer that Draifa (Alida Valli) has already appeared in the "prologue" to the film as the companion to the "absent" father.

The scene of incest that follows in the back room of the cafe crystallizes the intimate relationship that exists between the narrative and metacinematic levels of Bertolucci's entire work. "Because of the theme that *La Luna* tells," Bertolucci argued, "it was inevitable ultimately to accept all the risks of a discourse on the past that was made *also* of the films of my past. A film about incestuous fantasies has to be traversed by this violently autoerotic and incestuous movement that is behind self-quotation."[11] There can be no doubt that for Bertolucci the anecdotal level (the story of heroin addiction, incest, and the search for a lost father) is inextricably linked to cinema and cinematic style. Thanks to his own interpretative intervention, *La luna* can be understood not only as the most insistently metacinematic but also as the most "violently" self-referential of all of Bertolucci's films. In *Luna* he has placed "quotations" from every one of his major films. The "incestuous" consequences of this latter trait are most significant for the position of *Luna* in Bertolucci's work.

Who is this "mother" who incites incestuous fantasies in her son? Bertolucci's earlier films and the movement of *Luna* itself provide several intriguing answers to this question. In *A Spider's Stratagem* there is a strong inference that the maternal represents the locus of dream and ultimately of cinema itself. In *Luna*, Bertolucci's astute montage contributes directly to this interpretation.

The film opens with a "prologue" in which Caterina is seen licking honey from her infant on the sun-drenched porch of a Mediterranean villa. Caterina's husband, Giuseppe (Tomas Milian) arrives to destroy this mother–son "honeymoon," creating what Bertolucci has called a "mielo-drama" for everyone involved.[12] Caterina and Giuseppe engage in a chaotic dance, Giuseppe waving a dead fish and a fisherman's knife as his body sways in the blinding Mediterranean sun—paraphernalia that cannot fail to have a devastating (even if symbolic) impact on the child. In fact, the child grows hysterical at the prospect of this dance, which Bertolucci terms "a barbaric war dance" and which is a thinly disguised version of the primal scene. Bertolucci called *Luna* a "dance of inconsistency, dance of incoherence, dance of confusion," which strongly suggests that the prologue's first tango embarrassment is a metaphor for the entire film as incest and primal scene.[13]

Said Bertolucci, "*Luna* represents the moment in which I found the courage to point the camera, as it were, *at* the primal scene." He added, in explanation, "Freud says that the child doesn't need to see the parents in coitus, it's enough and at the same time inevitable that he imagine it. Knowing the insane *pudeur* of my father, I think I had the experience of an imagined rather than real primal scene. My cinema was very much determined by this imagined memory. . . . The style of *Luna* is very revealing of the secret sides of my nature as a filmmaker."[14]

From this "violently incestuous movement" the scene shifts to Caterina on a bicycle fleeing the house one night as baby Joe sits before her transfixed by the two images of her face and the full moon overhead. This second experience of the "prologue" provides the other dominant theme of *Luna*. Joe seems never to recover from Caterina's moonlit image and the endless dream it engenders for her Endymion, who is, in classical mythology,

> a beautiful youth who, as he slept on Mt. Latmus, so moved the heart of the moon goddess that she came down and kissed him and lay at his side. *He woke to find her gone,* but the charms that she gave him were so strong and enthralling that he begged Zeus to give him immortality and allow him to *sleep perpetually.*[15]

To sleep, *perforce* to dream. For dreaming seems at every level of this film to be the primary object. Dreaming, for the sake of dreaming. Virtually all of the film's sequences seem to allude to the *unreal.* Bertolucci recently said, "If I don't see movies, I don't have any desire to make movies. Before making a movie, really, I go to see movies. Like somebody who dreams: when he's dreaming he desires to dream on."[16]

Bertolucci's equation of filming and dreaming is everywhere implicit in this work. The voyage from Brooklyn Heights to Rome is itself a dream trip because it is "begun" with Joe and Caterina "entombed" together in the large black funeral limousine (visually rejoining Douglas in his Mercedes "coffin") and completed through a jump cut to another large black limousine threading its way through the monuments of Rome. "At eleven," Bertolucci recalls, "I was sent to Rome, and it seemed to me like going to the Inferno." This version of Rome is indeed like "the far borders of the empire."[17]

In this labyrinthine city, Joe is initially guided by Arianna, who leads Joe to his first "formative" experience: the film *Niagara*, starring Marilyn Monroe. In a sense, Joe's presence in a movie theater does nothing more than recapitulate his first memories as voyeur of another primal scene. Like Marcello Clerici, Tom, and Ottavio before him, he doubles the position of the film spectator. But he creates a curious doubling of that role as well, for he sits in a darkened spot and carries on his own primal scene for *Luna's* spectators, thus becoming both subject and object of the primal scene experience, a curious cinematic rendition of symbolic autoeroticism. In keeping with his unusual degree of self-consciousness about *Luna*, Bertolucci mused, shortly after completing the film,

> Today, it seems that my entire cinema is, in a sense, contained in the primal scene observed by Marcello between Anna and Giulia in *The Conformist*, and when I was making *La Luna*, I opened the window on the possibility of this particular way of looking, in a sort of catalogue of possible primal scenes: at the movie theater when Joe and Arianna are watching Marilyn in *Niagara*; then, still from Joe's point of view, when the mother sings "Tacea la notte placida" and there is a vertical dolly movement (*in erezione*) together with Jill Clayburgh who is elevated simultaneously with our view of her. Not to mention the opening of the film.[18]

Joe repeats this position of primal voyeur yet another time when, like Tom in the bridal shop in *Last Tango*, he hides among the gowns in his mother's dressing room after the opera. Caterina, however, is destined to remain somewhat unreal and dreamlike for Joe, primarily because she spends most of the film in one unreal setting after another. She seems obsessed by movement and mythology, appearing either on the changing sets of various operas or in her apartment, a thoroughly unreal space, which Bertolucci described as "seen through the eyes of Joe . . . lost in the far borders of the empire."[19]

She seems unable to leave these unreal decors, moving about among the sets of Bertolucci's earlier films via a white Mercedes, much like the one Douglas had died in. The automobile seems to have much the same function it had in Cocteau's *Orphée*, linking the characters to the world of death (as in

Douglas's case) or to narcissistic dreams. Indeed, in their last ride together, Joe ends up asleep on Caterina's lap and wakes only on their arrival at their destination. Significantly, Bertolucci said, "I like to sleep in the car on the way to the set and try to have a dream."[20] When Caterina arrives at Verdi's birthplace she exclaims, "This is my family, it's like me, it's like my father, Verdi!"[21] Thus she centers her very genealogy in the operas in which she is, apparently at least, "only" an actress. "Verdi corresponds for me to the mythic dimension," Bertolucci had said while making *Spider*.[22] As an artist (a figurative double of Bertolucci himself), Caterina seems unable to locate her ontology in the real. Ultimately, the film becomes a hyperbole of Bertolucci's other work because, like Don Quixote in the second half of Cervantes' novel, it encounters its *own* mythology.[23]

As a spectator of his mother's mythology, Joe fares no better in his own ontology. As I noted earlier, Rome itself functions like a dreamscape with its labyrinth and mythological Arianna as guide. But Joe soon abandons Arianna and Caterina for his own "trip" into the dream world of heroin. As an infant Joe had found himself entangled in a ball of twine, connected to yet leading *away from* his mother. As an adolescent, he traverses a maze of Roman streets, marking his "progress" by a chalk line drawn along the walls of the street, another symbol of his nostalgia for the Ariadne/mother imago, yet leading away from her into a labyrinth of narcissism.

Caterina's gift of heroin when he needs a fix and her absence when he awakes suggest, much like Ottavio in *1900*, her complicity in a habit that invites a perpetual state of dream. When she finally draws him into the act of incest, we witness not only a primal scene but *the* primal scene of Bertolucci's autoerotic cinema: Joe the voyeur/dreamer is linked with a mother imago who personifies myth, dream, and the ontology of cinema itself. Because the nexus of these elements is so "violently" autoreferential, the union is bound to short-circuit and lead Joe back to the search for his real father.

When Joe ultimately finds the long absent father, Giuseppe too is lost in a drawing of a fictive universe; and Joe obliges by drawing a moon for this system rather than attempting to pull his father out. Their initial exchange is an exchange of shoes, symbol of movement and/or death. Joe's only communication with his father centers around the false news of his own death; that is, rather than awakening his father to his role, he portrays himself as dead, linking up once again with myth, dream, and the unreal.

Finally, the "reunification" of the family takes place in an ancient theater, literally an archaeological remnant, and is consecrated by a triumphant finale from *A Masked Ball* while mother, father, and son remain isolated physically from each other. This scene, too, is entirely immersed in a kind of self-reflective theatricality. Bertolucci explained:

> The Verdi opera in *Prima* separates Fabrizio from Gina and unites him to Clelia, who represents his bourgeois destiny. In *Luna* the finale of *A Masked Ball* separates Caterina from Joe and unites the kid with his father. The melodrama is immanent to the drama of the characters, but at a certain point it overflows from the stage onto the set and into the ruins of Caracalla. Invisible strings move the characters, draw them along, and make them falter. These strings are their looks: the exchanges of looks in the opera sequence in *Prima* trace a barely marked design. In *Luna* a fairly complex dynamic of looks is set in motion and ends up in a kind of game between objective framing and subjective point of view, following the musical scansions of *A Masked Ball*.[24]

Even the "resolution" of *Luna* is a nexus of autoquotation (of *Prima*), of operatic "overflow," and of puppetry. This film simply cannot escape from its own circumscribed pattern of reference. It remains encircled in the matrix of a dreamscape.

As a Bertolucci dream script, there are many examples of primary process thinking in the film: In terms of condensation, the film is particularly rich. Though it is true, as Bertolucci said, that "every character in this movie has two faces at least,"[25] it could also be argued that every two characters in this movie have one face. As Joe's guide to Italy, Caterina plays Ariadne doubled by Arianna; both offer their bodies to this lost adolescent, and each provides him with a "fix" on his birthday: Arianna at his party and Caterina at her party. In this sense, they each occupy the role previously held by Ottavio as *metteur en scène*.

On the male side, clearly each father doubles not only the other but also the son. Joe claims he can do everything that Dad does, assumes his dead father's place in the car. As a condensation of his Italian father, Joe exchanges shoes with him and then discovers that both father and son are in love with their mothers. The gay seducer in the bar where Joe does his Travolta imitation is not only a visual double of the Italian father but also one of Pasolini's actors and reputed lovers. This uncertainty about the parents' sexuality suggests condensations of father, the gay (Ottavio again), and Maria (as lesbian seductress of Caterina). Caterina's own search for a father figure (in her music and ultimately in Verdi) suggests a condensation of mother and son figures. Ultimately, the entire film can be read (oneirically) as a thinly masked ball in which any character can substitute for any other.

One of the reasons this becomes possible is the degree of projection operating throughout. If the film can be "read" from Joe's point of view, then much of the mother's and father's fantastic behavior can be seen as pure projection: Caterina's desire to find a father and the Italian father's attachment to his mother. From Caterina's point of view, Joe's incestuous feelings (the dinner, the seductions) read equally as mere projections of her desire.

The film also effects a remarkable series of displacements: The moon and heroin for Joe, opera and her own voice for Caterina, teaching and the creation of a fictive universe for Giuseppe are but a few striking examples of this phenomenon.

As a dream script, however, it differs from Bertolucci's earlier wish-fulfillment fantasies in its degree of overwhelming autoreferentiality. Unlike any of Bertolucci's earlier films, it seems to present itself almost uniquely as an *object for analysis or interpretation*, yet, like a dream, never totally accessible by the signs that point to it. As such it would belong to the class of dreams that are *dreamed for analysis*, which patients "have dreamt . . . directly as dreams, and dreamt . . . finally in order to tell them."[26] Bertolucci's outpouring of commentary on this film is so unusual as to corroborate this view. So much of *Luna* seems to be dedicated to making us conscious of its status as (an oneiric) film and especially as a part of a set of fantasies that, ultimately, it recalls the patients in analysis who produce dreams simply to defer the real object of analysis and end up in an elaborate system of self-deception![27]

Understanding the ulterior function of such dreamwork in this film re-evokes the degree to which the film itself and the dream process are originally linked to the mother imago. Understandably and perhaps somewhat unconsciously, Bertolucci said of *Luna*, "All my films are about father. In *Luna* I finally realized that this figure was a cover or screen for the mother whose importance is finally revealed."[28] Perhaps, but ironically not only—and not really—in the explicit fashion observable at the level of anecdote. If the dream is, as Freud proclaimed, a "misplaced maternal body," then dreaming (regardless of content) would always already constitute an attempt to continue an impossible union with the mother in a space outside of all temporal constraints.[29] We can, in this way, better understand the nostalgia for—and impossibility of—the union as constituting a single wish fulfillment! Both dream and film are projected onto a screen or at least suppose a space allowing representation. But this screen functions ironically in the dual modes implied by the two antithetical meanings of the word: as locus of projection and as means of protection. If the screen itself is (the) maternal (breast), as Lewin has suggested, then the dream (or film) points to the mother, indeed functions like the child's transitional object by connecting the dreamer with the mother *by making her absent*.[30] But it protects from the mother by more than assuring her absence. In dreams dreamed for analysis, according to J.-B. Pontalis, the dreamer valorizes an unusual aspect of oneiric activity:

> The dream . . . as a representation of an *elsewhere*, guarantor of a perpetual *double*, or a staging, a "private theatre" with its permutation of roles . . . allows one never to assume any of them. . . . One can find something useful in the functioning of the mechanisms [of the dream] much as a writer does in his methods of writing: The condensation, which collects in one image the impressions from multiple or contradictory registers, satisfies our desire to deny the radical difference; the compulsion to symbolize, . . . The wish to establish new links indefinitely, and in so doing to lose nothing. The displacement offers the possibility of never having to remain at a fixed point, but of assigning himself an elusive vanishing point. The subject identifies himself with the displacement itself, as though with a phallus, which is everywhere and nowhere, *nulliquité* more than ubiquity.[31]

The position of such a dreamer again displays an uncanny resemblance both to the content of *Luna* and to Bertolucci's relationship to the film and to cinema in general. The condensation of characters in *Luna* and the series of symbolic movements out of normal space toward a realm of fantasy or space before time both correspond to this particular type of dreamer's need to avoid a fixed point of reference. In discussing his ideal film, Bertolucci evoked *movement* as the very essence of the cinematic art: "All my pleasure is the camera, the movement is all my decision."[32] And elsewhere he exclaimed: "Where am I going? I don't know. . . . A movie is an adventure, really, of jumping on a boat and going with the wind that takes you nowhere."[33]

Bertolucci's "nowhere," his quest for mystery,[34] sounds remarkably like a dreamer who had identified with displacement or "nulliquité" itself.

In the light of *Luna*'s particular self-consciousness about incest coupled with an incestuous degree of autoreferentiality, virtually the entire set of Bertolucci's films can be understood as a structure of constant displacement, as an attraction/avoidance of the idealized, fantasized maternal object. *Prima della rivoluzione, The Spider's Stratagem, The Conformist, Last Tango, 1900,* and *Luna* all deal explicitly with a fundamental approach/avoidance position vis-à-vis a mother imago.

This dance of displacement ultimately functions as a screen, a protection against the *inside*, against the conceivable union with the mother imago that is implied by the dream screen as projection, but also with any conceivable cessation of movement.[35]

It is not surprising then, despite the consistent doubling of Caterina and Joe, that the central moment of *Luna* represents an attempted incestuous seduction by the mother (the dream screen as maternal object), which is thwarted and displaced by the son (the screen as protective projection). Joe leaves his mother's devouring and inert body to practice a game of self-penetration with the addict's needle—in order to return to dream. The scene is indeed emblematic of the thoroughly (and in this case morbidly) narcissistic tendency of the dream experience.[36]

In discussions of *The Spider's Stratagem* and *Last Tango in Paris*, Bertolucci has at least three times returned to the analogy of spiders, in which "the female devours the male." The dance of the male spider in this analogy, this "minimal approach" to the devouring female, recalls both Bertolucci's definition of *Luna* as a "dance of inconsistency, dance of incoherence, dance of confusion"[37] and the identification with displacement itself just discussed. Indeed, this play of perversity, coupled with the self-conscious perversion of the use of dreams in *Luna*, presents remarkable analogies to the structure of perversion itself.[38] Sexual perversion is often the result of the child's idealization of the mother in the absence of a meaningful father imago. Generally this leads to the projection of the destructive aspects of the same-sex parent onto the opposite sex, resulting in an overweening sense of guilt. Aberrant sexual configurations are compulsive, always involve game playing, and seem to require an anonymous spectator. The construction of essential illusions, which must not be tampered with, raises questions about what is real in much the same way dreaming does.[39]

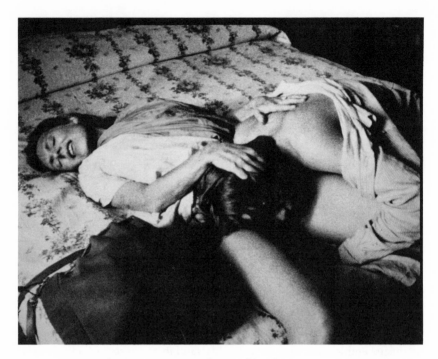

Figure 25. Caterina's incestuous seduction of Joe. Courtesy
Jerry Ohlinger.

By its "perversion" of the "normal" function of dream, by its tendency
toward a repetition compulsion of both fundamental themes and specific
elements of Bertolucci's other films, *Luna* emphasizes its own "play"ful-
ness. As such it functions as a sort of coda for Bertolucci's entire oeuvre up to
Luna. The intensely personal level of the content and structure of this film,
coupled with its self-consciousness as film and the ultimate identification
with displacement itself, suggests that the element of "perversion" within
Bertolucci's directorial stance may in fact be a hyperbole for cinema in
general. The experience of films in general and the set of Bertolucci's films in
particular would be the *matrix* (in the maternal sense of this term) of an
absent presence lying at the center of his and our desire for cinema—a desire
to be present yet absent (from) ourselves.

Bertolucci's almost voyeuristic manipulation of his actors—"Sometimes you have to cheat them. Sometimes you have to provoke them. Sometimes you have to rape them, in a way"[40]—his need for a specifically *anonymous* spectator, and his insistence on playfulness and perverse sexual themes both seduce the spectator into an identificatory role (as double or dreamer) and hold the audience at a distance. In enacting this desire "to be loved and rejected at the same time," Bertolucci recapitulates with his public the essential dynamics of the dream-for-analysis, of perversion, and finally of the cinematic experience itself. We unwittingly become both doubles and parental imagoes in what is finally and perhaps inevitably an "incestuous" film experience—identifying constantly with Joe *and* Caterina (who double and deny each other). Little wonder, then, that Bertolucci saw a relationship between the incestuous fantasies that punctuate *Luna* at the anecdotal level and the "autoerotic and incestuous" nature of self-quotation. And he is quite right in insisting that "my cinema was very much determined by the imagined memory of the primal scene, and is, in a sense, contained in the primal scene."[41]

In his desire to eradicate differences, Bertolucci seems to have entered cinema in order to insist on his own and his spectator's position of permanent displacement. Perhaps this is another reason why the automobile is so ubiquitous in *Luna*. For Bertolucci, the perpetual dream-filled sleep of Endymion, like Joe's nap nestled in his mother's lap in the back seat of their car, himself imitating his director's sleep in order to dream on the way to the set, recapitulates a primal and unconscious *mobilisation* of fantasy fundamental to the cinematic enterprise.

When I think of cinema, I see a very long film whose sequences are taken
from many directors in a complex play of references, quotes, influences,
remakes and variations. But I also think of a circle, of a wheel of continuity.
BERNARDO BERTOLUCCI

9 IN LIEU OF A CONCLUSION

One does not easily "close the book" on a filmmaker whose work is ongoing
and whose image of his work is so thoroughly engaged in a sense of continuity as to form its very fabric. Indeed, the wheels and circles in Bertolucci's
greater vision of cinema form "a pattern of familiar lines," for the same
image recurs repeatedly in his films, whether in the form of Agostino's rotations on his bike, Draifa's winding of Athos into an imprisoning web, the
whirling dance encompassing Clerici, the circular walls of the Jules Verne
apartment, or the horrifying rotations of the dying child in *1900*, so many
figurations of the act of filming itself. But these "wheels of continuity" may
also symbolize those of the automobiles of *Luna*, which rotate Joe and
Caterina through a review of Bertolucci's own work and into a pattern of
almost incestuous autoreferentiality. As Bertolucci himself noted, *Luna*
brought him "full circle," to what can be termed the end of a cycle of films.[1]
Luna can best be appreciated, then, not only as a coda of the themes that
permeate Bertolucci's work from 1963 to 1979 but also as an index of the way
in which, from displacement to displacement, autoreferentiality becomes the
very subject of that work, repeatedly centering on an understanding of the
dynamics of cinema itself.

André Bazin once argued that Delannoy's use of snow in *La Symphonie
pastorale* constituted a visual or cinematic "translation" of Gide's use of the
French past definite in the novel.[2] Although Bazin is to be congratulated for
the originality of this interpretation, his notion of cinematic style seems
remarkably unevolved in the light of Bertolucci's long-standing obsession

with creating "a cinema that speaks about cinema" in order to "teach people how to read film, because there is such widespread illiteracy about films."[3] It is Bertolucci's genius to have centered his own struggle with the authority of the paternal text on the question of adapting literary texts in an entirely original cinematic language that "posed moral problems in the style." Each of his major films from *Prima della rivoluzione* to *Luna* represents an advance in understanding the specificity of cinematic language and, by implication, the particular nature of the spectator's relationship to the film text. His career as a whole constitutes an extended and remarkably deep and varied meditation on the interrelationship of psycho-, literary, and cinematic analyses.

With *Tragedy of a Ridiculous Man*, Bertolucci seems to have begun a fresh cycle, moving into a new area of cinematic research without, however, altogether abandoning many of the concerns that characterize his previous work. All of his films before *Ridiculous Man* are actively engaged in elaborating a personal style, a cinematic rendition of his earliest poetic "search of mystery." *Ridiculous Man* seems to set off in a new direction, "abandoning itself," as Enzo Ungari phrases it, "to the reality of today's Italy, liberated from the weight of Bertolucci's earlier obsession with style."[4] One might even compare the latest film with Camus's *Stranger* as a sort of "zero degree of cinematic writing." Bertolucci himself noted that he no longer felt that cinema should "vampirize reality in order to represent it, but that in fact reality now vampirized cinema."[5]

Many of the old themes continue and will continue in Bertolucci's work after *Luna*. *Ridiculous Man* studies the complex relationship between father and son in a modern Italian economy. The film begins with yet another scene of voyeurism, but this one is significantly displaced, more a homage to Hitchcock's *Rear Window* than a continuation of *Luna*'s autoreferentiality. As Bertolucci explains it, "In *Ridiculous Man* I am no longer the one watching the primal scene in the first person, as I had done in *Luna*. This time it is my ridiculous hero."[6] This new emotional distance sets out both a fresh set of dynamics and a different style of film language for Bertolucci while ironically further developing the thematics of displacement so central to his work.

As this book goes to press, Bertolucci is at work on a film tentatively entitled *The Last Emperor of China*. It will revolve around another primal experience, that of a gardener in the former imperial gardens in Beijing

Figure 26. Primo (Ugo Tognazzi) as voyeur in *Tragedy of a Ridiculous Man*. Courtesy Warner Brothers.

whose first memory is of standing at age four before thousands upon thousands of people bowing down to him. The parents of the primal scene have become the people of China. Perhaps here we will find the synthesis so desired in *Luna:* "a search for the present and the past" coupled with "a type of very wide mass communication."[7]

For those who may see in Bertolucci's cinematic evolution a regrettable loss of political and specifically Marxist orientation, Bertolucci himself would answer that politics cannot be separated from psychology. He once rephrased Malraux's famous dictum, saying,

> Transforming Destiny into the *un*conscious, affects the rapport between sexuality and politics. I think the most important discovery I made after the events of May, 1968, was that I wanted the revolution not to help the poor, but for myself. I wanted the world to change for me. I discovered the individual level in political revolution. My slogan is "Serve myself," because only by serving

myself am I able to serve the people—that is, to be a part of the
people, not serve them.[8]

Both of his explicitly "political" films, *Prima* and its subsequent double,
1900, are testimony to the truth of this assertion.

As for the "evolution" of Bertolucci's meditation on the relationship
between politics and cinematic language, the director recently mused that

> Twenty years ago, *Breathless* revolutionized the language of
> cinema, the grammatical and syntactical rules of the cinema that was
> being done then. Times have changed, including the period in which
> I felt the need to effect a complete internal upheaval of the very idea
> of communication, the need to modify the cinema's relationship with
> the public, the *need to search for and discover a very deep bond with
> the spectator*. Roland Barthes writes in *The Pleasure of the Text* that
> the text says, "Desire me just as I desire you." Today I am for a
> cinema and a public that are not afraid of emotions, and *the spectator
> I am looking for is one capable of abandoning himself to the
> unconscious work of the film*, of participating in it.[9]

This new "unconscious" and "participatory" relationship with his spectator nevertheless has a familiar ring to it. Ironically, the "complete internal
upheaval of the very idea of communication" of those earlier films succeeded, as I have demonstrated in this study, in offering the spectator the
means of liberation from the manipulative illusions endemic to the cinematic
act itself. Curiously, the "need to search for and discover a very deep bond
with the spectator" of those years has now been artfully *displaced* by Bertolucci onto the screen itself.

If the screen is, as has been amply theorized here, a specular matrix (a
reminiscence of the mirror in which, at our most formative stage, we see
ourselves as other in the maternal look), then Bertolucci and his spectator
will continue to trade and displace their deepest fantasies on this dream
screen. If Bertolucci's films seem to constitute a "dance of incoherence" and
reel through perpetually mobile topoi of images of doubles, reassembled
decors, and dreamscapes in which history, genealogy, paternity give way to
a collapse of differences, it is because they figure, without ever identifying,
the matrix of cinema itself as the subject and object of desire. That matrix
may be rendered self-consciously, as in the "first cycle" of films described in

this study, or unconsciously, as Bertolucci now proposes, but it cannot fail to challenge the viewer's assumptions about cinema itself by reinvestigating the very ontology of the seventh art.

"Today," Bertolucci mused, "it seems my entire cinema is, in a sense, contained in the primal scene and has opened the possibility of this particular way of looking, in a sort of catalogue of possible primal scenes."[10] If so, we must remember that the primal scene is also the primary scene in the sense that it constitutes, against the modernist tendencies of Bertolucci's work, a nucleus of origins, filiation, and identity, yet is itself constituted by an imaginary scene that is always already a displacement, an unconscious fantasy that is both visual and *the* "truth" discovered and rediscovered through a seemingly endless series of repetitions and variations.

Ultimately we may reparaphrase the Bible one more time by stating (provisionally): "In the beginning was the look."[11] This look, in Bertolucci's vision of cinema, enters a chamber of mirrors in which it is displaced and replicated into "a stratification so mysterious that I could never separate politics from psychoanalysis, from language . . . etc. It seems to me that everything is mixed together and that my films are a means of seeking the way out of this labyrinth in this chaos of politics and psychoanalysis."[12] Constituted by an almost endless expansion of psychological, political, and aesthetic identities repeatedly refracted through a single lens, Bertolucci's cinema repeatedly proposes and obscures interpretation. As maker and guide to the mysteries of this labyrinth, Bertolucci reaches the ultimate double configuration, at one but never quite united with the maternal, Ariachne. Whatever the future holds, Bertolucci assures us that, "Despite the passage of years, to make a film has always meant for me an investigation into the nature of cinema, a long reflection without respite and with a thousand answers."[13] As Bertolucci himself and the myriad interpretations of his cinema "take no respite," there is, quite simply, no way to "conclude."

FILMOGRAPHY

MAJOR FILMS DIRECTED BY BERNARDO BERTOLUCCI

The Grim Reaper (La commare secca) 1962

PRODUCER:	Antonio Cervi
SCREENPLAY:	Bernardo Bertolucci and Sergio Citti
PHOTOGRAPHY:	Gianni Narzisi
EDITING:	Nino Baragli
MUSIC:	Carlo Rustichelli and Piero Piccioni
CAST:	

Canticchia:	Francesco Ruiu
Nino:	Vincenzo Ciccora
Bruna:	Marisa Solinas
Teodoro:	Allen Midgette
Francolicchio:	Alvaro D'Ercole
Pipito:	Romano Labate
Esperia:	Gabrielle Giorgelli
Domenica:	Emy Rocci
Milly:	Lorenza Benedetti
Mariella:	Erina Torelli

Before the Revolution (Prima della rivoluzione) 1964

PRODUCER:	Iride Cinematografica
SCREENPLAY:	Bernardo Bertolucci, Gianni Amico
PHOTOGRAPHY:	Also Scavarda
EDITING:	Roberto Perpignani
MUSIC:	Gino, Paoli, Ennio Morricone
CAST:	

Fabrizio:	Francesco Barilli
Gina:	Adriana Asti
Clelia:	Cristina Pariset
Cesare:	Morando Morandini
Agostino:	Allen Midgette

Puck:	Cecrope Barilli
Enore:	Guido Fanti
Friend:	Gianni Amico
Evalina:	Evalina Alpi

Agonia   1967

PRODUCER:	Carlo Lizzani
SCREENPLAY:	Bernardo Bertolucci
PHOTOGRAPHY:	Ugo Piccone
EDITING:	Roberto Perpignani
MUSIC:	Giovanni Fusco
CAST:	

Julian Beck and members of The Living Theatre.

Partner   1968

PRODUCER:	Giovanni Bertolucci
SCREENPLAY:	Bernardo Bertolucci and Gianni Amico
PHOTOGRAPHY:	Ugo Piccone
EDITING:	Roberto Perpignani
MUSIC:	Ennio Morricone
CAST:	
Giaccobe:	Pierre Clementi
Clara:	Stefania Sandrelli
Petrushka:	Sergio Tofano
Father:	Romano Costa
Soap girl:	Tina Aumont

The Spider's Stratagem (*La strategia del ragno*)   1970

PRODUCER:	Giovanni Bertolucci
SCREENPLAY:	Bernardo Bertolucci, Marilu Parolini, Edoardo De Gregorio
PHOTOGRAPHY:	Vittorio Storaro
EDITING:	Roberto Perpignani
MUSIC:	Excerpts from Schonberg and Verdi
CAST:	
Athos Magnani(s):	Giulio Brogi
Draifa:	Alida Valli
Costa:	Tino Scotti
Rasori:	Franco Giovannelli
Gaibazzi:	Pippo Campanini
Sailor:	Allen Midgette

The Conformist (Il conformista)   1970

PRODUCER:	Maurizio Lodi-Fé
SCREENPLAY:	Bernardo Bertolucci
PHOTOGRAPHY:	Vittorio Storaro
EDITING:	Franco Arcalli
MUSIC:	Georges Delerue
CAST:	
Marcello Clerici:	Jean-Louis Trintignant
Giulia:	Stefania Sandrelli
Quadri:	Enzo Tarascio
Anna Quadri:	Dominique Sanda
Lino Semirana:	Pierre Clementi
Manganiello:	Gastone Moschin
Italo:	José Quaglio
Raoul:	Christian Alegny
Clerici's mother:	Milly
Clerici's father:	Giuseppe Addobbati
Clerici as child:	Pasquale Fortunato
Giulia's mother:	Yvonne Sanson

Last Tango in Paris (L'ultimo tango a Parigi)   1972

PRODUCER:	Alberto Grimaldi
SCREENPLAY:	Bernardo Bertolucci, Franco Arcalli
PHOTOGRAPHY:	Vittorio Storaro
EDITING:	Franco Arcalli
MUSIC:	Gato Barbieri
CAST:	
Paul:	Marlon Brando
Jeanne:	Maria Schneider
Tom:	Jean-Pierre Léaud
Rosa's mother:	Maria Michi
Marcel:	Massimo Girotti
Jeanne's mother:	Gitt Magrini
Concierge:	Darling Legitimus
Rosa:	Veronica Lazare

1900 (Novecento)   1976

PRODUCER:	Alberto Grimaldi
SCREENPLAY:	Bernardo Bertolucci, Giuseppe Bertolucci, and Franco Arcalli

PHOTOGRAPHY:	Vittorio Storaro
EDITING:	Franco Arcalli
MUSIC:	Ennio Morricone
CAST:	
Olmo Dalco:	Gérard Depardieu
Alfredo Berlinghieri:	Robert De Niro
Leo Dalco:	Sterling Hayden
Alfredo Berlinghieri, Sr.:	Burt Lancaster
Attila:	Donald Sutherland
Regina:	Laura Betti
Ada:	Dominique Sanda
Anita:	Stefania Sandrelli
Ottavio:	Werner Bruhns
Signora Pioppi:	Alida Valli
Rigoletto:	Giacomo Rizzo
Giovanni Berlinghieri:	Romolo Valli
Rosina Dalco:	Maria Monti
Olmo as child:	Roberto Maccanti
Alfredo as child:	Paolo Pavesi
Regina as child:	Tiziana Senatore
Laundry woman:	Stefania Cassini

Luna (La luna)   1979

PRODUCER:	Giovanni Bertolucci
SCREENPLAY:	Giuseppe Bertolucci, Bernardo Bertolucci, Clare Peploe
PHOTOGRAPHY:	Vittorio Storaro
EDITING:	Gabriella Cristiani
MUSIC:	Excerpts from Mozart and Verdi
CAST:	
Caterina:	Jill Clayburgh
Joe:	Matthew Barry
Douglas:	Fred Gwynne
Giuseppe:	Tomas Milian
Giuseppe's mother:	Alida Valli
Marina:	Veronica Lazare
Arianna:	Elisabetta Campeti
Mustafa:	Stephane Barat
Man in car:	Renato Salvatori
Restauranteur:	Pippo Campanini
Mario:	Franco Citti

The Tragedy of a Ridiculous Man (La tragedia di un uomo ridicolo)   1981

PRODUCER:	Giovanni Bertolucci
SCREENPLAY:	Bernardo Bertolucci
PHOTOGRAPHY:	Carlo Di Palma
EDITING:	Gariella Cristiani
MUSIC:	Ennio Morricone
CAST:	
Primo Spaggiari:	Ugo Tognazzi
Barbara:	Anouk Aimée
Laura:	Laura Morante
Giovanni:	Riccardo Salvatori
Adelfo:	Victor Cavallo
Signora Romola:	Olympia Carlisi
Marshal Angrisani:	Vittorio Caprioli
Colonel:	Renato Salvatori

NOTES

Chapter 1 Bertolucci and the Specificities of Cinema

1 Pauline Kael, "Last Tango in Paris," *The New Yorker* 47, no. 10 (October 1972): 130–33.

2 Cited in Joseph Gelmis, "Bernardo Bertolucci," in *The Film Director as Superstar* (Garden City, N.Y.: Doubleday, 1970), p. 117.

3 Bernardo Bertolucci, *In ricerca del mistero* (Milan: Longanesi, 1962), p. 19.

4 D. W. Winnicott has much to say about this maternal process and how the child gains an early identity from the mother's look. See below, Chapter 6.

5 Enzo Ungari, *Scena madri* (Milan: Ubulibri, 1982), p. 195.

6 Francesco Casetti, *Bertolucci*, vol. 24 in *Il castoro cinema* (Florence: La Nuova Italia, 1975), p. 2. Cf. "From the day I began work with Pasolini, I stopped writing poetry. Poetry was only a means of expressing myself until I could find the real way—making movies. That's why each film I make is . . . a kind of poem, or at least an attempt at one." Charles Michener, "Tango: The Hottest Movie," *Newsweek*, February 12, 1973, p. 37.

7 Casetti, *Bertolucci*, p. 30; translation mine.

8 Cited in ibid., p. 3.

9 John Bragin, "A Conversation with Bernardo Bertolucci," *Film Quarterly* 20, no. 1 (Fall 1966): 43.

10 Cited in Jean Gili, *Le Cinéma italien* (Paris: Union Général d'Editions, 1978), p. 58; translation mine.

11 Cited in ibid., p. 59.

12 Stanley Cavell notes that, "In viewing films, the sense of invisibility is an expression of modern privacy or anonymity." *The World Viewed* (Cambridge: Harvard University Press, 1979), p. 40.

13 Jean-Louis Baudry, "Le Dispositif: approches métapsychologiques de l'impression de réalité," in *Psychanalyse et cinéma: Communications* 23 (February 1975): 59; translation mine. The place represented in these images is, according to Baudry, "the mother's uterus, the womb to which we aspire to return."

14 "It may well be that there was not an inaugural invention of the cinema. Before being the end result of technical advances and a certain social organization (necessary for its realization and its completion), the cinema would first of all be the object of a desire . . . a form of satisfaction lost which cinema's technology would strive to recover one way or another." Ibid., p. 63.

15   Barthes, "En sortant du cinéma," *Psychanalyse et cinéma: Communications* 23 (February 1975): 104–5; translation mine. Cf. Iouri Lotman, *Esthétique et sémiotique du cinéma* (Paris: Editions Sociales, 1977), pp. 27 ff.

16   Freud, *The Interpretation of Dreams, The Standard Edition* 4 (London: Hogarth Press, 1974).

17   J.-B. Pontalis, *Entre le rêve et la douleur* (Paris: Gallimard, 1977), p. 241.

18   Cited in Gili, *Le Cinéma italien*, p. 43.

19   Pontalis, *Entre le rêve et la douleur*, p. 241. See also Pontalis, *Après Freud* (Paris: Gallimard/Idées, 1968), pp. 47–48.

20   See, e.g., Tzvetan Todorov, *Introduction à la littérature fantastique* (Paris: Seuil/Points, 1970), p. 103.

21   Georges Poulet, for example, writes in the preface to *Littérature et sensation*: "Somewhere in the depths of consciousness, beyond the region where everything has become thought, at a point opposite the one where we have entered, there was, and still is light, objects and even eyes to perceive them. Criticism cannot be content with thinking a thought. It must work its way back across that thought from image to image all the way to sensation." Cited in Todorov, *Introduction*, p. 102. And J. P. Richard adds, "The fundamental intention, . . . at its most elementary level . . . is the level of pure sensation, of brute feeling or of the birthing image." Cited in Todorov, p. 102. Jean Dubois pursues a similar argument in *Grammaire structurale du français* where he argues, "The conditions for the graphic transcription of a message are the consequent serious loss of information" (p. 15). Cited in Guy Rosolato, *Essais sur le symbolique* (Paris: Gallimard, 1969), p. 288.

22   Susan Sontag, *On Photography* (New York: Dell, 1973), p. 4.

23   Peter Wollen, "The English Cine-Structuralists," *Film Comment* 9, no. 3 (May/June 1973): 47.

24   Peter Wollen, *Signs and Meaning in the Cinema* (Bloomington: Indiana University Press, 1972), pp. 167–68.

25   See Janine Chasseguet-Smirgel, *Pour une psychanalyse de l'art et de la créativité* (Paris: Payot, 1971), pp. 82 ff.

26   See Peter Wollen, "Eisenstein's Aesthetics," in *Signs and Meaning*, pp. 19–73.

27   Cited in Barthemy Amengual, "Portrait de l'artiste in jeune homme avant la trentaine," in *Bernardo Bertolucci*, ed. Michele Esteve (Paris: Minard, 1979), p. 33 (my translation).

28   Christian Metz, *Le Signifiant imaginaire* (Paris: Union Générale d'Editions, 1977), p. 270.

29   Ibid., p. 280.

30   See ibid., pp. 281, 324.

31   Cavell, *The World Viewed*, p. 41. For a discussion of the relationship between

displacement and desire itself, see Leo Bersani, *Baudelaire and Freud* (Berkeley: University of California Press, 1977), pp. 60–61.

32   Sandor Ferenczi commented on the relation between scopophilia and eroticism as follows: "One is told of nocturnal pollutions with orgasm whose psychic accompaniments were simply beautiful landscapes. . . . In these cases it is as though the whole gamut of possible genital sensations was transposed into the optic-aesthetic sphere . . . a synaesthesia. Optic sensation in and for itself is not free from erotic admixtures, and . . . scopophilia plays an important part in sexual excitement." *The Theory and Practice of Psychoanalysis* (London: Hogarth Press, 1926, 1950), p. 300.

33   Bersani, *Baudelaire and Freud*, p. 129. J.-L. Baudry has noted the close connection between psychological and cinematic projection: "The dream, said Freud, is a projection, and, in the context in which he uses it, the term projection evokes both its analytic usage as a defense mechanism consisting in attributing to the outside representations and affects which the subject refuses to recognize as his own; and also a use which can be cinematographic since it is a matter of images which, once projected, return to the subject as a reality perceived as exterior." "Dispositif," p. 66.

34   Pontalis notes that projection can be equivocal: "Sometimes the term designates the fact that perceptions are more or less deformed by subjective fears and desires, at other times in a differently radical way, an operation which constitutes both subject and object, a split of outside and inside, an operation which gives reality rather than presupposing it." *Après Freud*, p. 201. In this sense, the projection involved in art may initiate a process located in fantasy and leading to a more therapeutic sense of reality. This would apply particularly to a filmmaker like Bertolucci, who is able to use his creative work as a kind of analysis.

35   See Chasseguet-Smirgel, *Psychanalyse de l'art*, p. 83; Roland Barthes, *Camera Lucida*, trans. Richard Howard (New York: Hill and Wang, 1981), p. 40; Rosolato, *Essais*, p. 221; and Nick Browne, "The Spectator-in-the-Text: The Rhetoric of *Stagecoach*," *Film Quarterly* 29, no. 2 (Winter 1975/76): 36.

36   B. D. Lewin, "Sleep, Mouth, and the Dream Screen," *Psychoanalytic Quarterly* 15 (1934): 420.

37   Joyce McDougall, *Théâtres du je* (Paris: Gallimard, 1982), pp. 162–63; translation mine. Baudry seconds these conclusions of McDougall ("Dispositif," pp. 67–69) and theorizes that our total envelopment in the screen is a continuation of the oral phase.

38   Cited in Buadry, "Dispositif," p. 71.

39   Bragin, "Conversation," p. 42.

40   "We are fascinated, without seeing it directly, by this brilliant, immobile yet dancing space," writes Roland Barthes of the cinematic experience. "Everything happens as though a long shaft of light illuminated a keyhole which we are all watching, spellbound by this hole. . . . I must be in the story . . . but I must also be else-

where; a somewhat ungrounded imaginary space, and, like a scrupulous, conscious, and organized fetishist, that is what I demand of a film." "En sortant du cinéma," pp. 105–6.

41 Joyce McDougall, "Primal Scene and Sexual Perversion," *International Journal of Psycho-analysis* 53 (1972): 372. McDougall insists on the fact that the primal scene does not necessarily designate (or rely on) a supposed actual occurrence of a child's witnessing his/her parents in coitus. It is rather a fantasy constructed from various fantasied and real components. For further corroboration of this relationship between the cinema and the primal scene, see Chasseguet-Smirgel, *Psychanalyse de l'art*, p. 86. Metz insists that, because the subject of the film is radically ignorant of the spectator's look, the film becomes a primal scene of a specifically Oedipal type. *Le Signifiant imaginaire*, p. 89, cf. pp. 117–19.

42 Sontag, *On Photography*, p. 10; see also pp. 12, 13, 23–24, 55.

43 Cavell, *The World Viewed*, p. 45.

44 Rosolato, *Essais*, pp. 204–6; translation mine.

45 See Bersani, *Baudelaire and Freud*, p. 57.

46 See Rosolato, *Essais*, pp. 206–9.

47 See Lotman, *Esthétique*, pp. 25–26.

48 Metz, *Le Signifiant imaginaire*, pp. 64, 80, 93; translation mine. Stanley Cavell writes of "that specific simultaneity of presence and absence which only the cinema will satisfy" (*The World Viewed*, p. 42); and Roland Barthes sees the *noeme* of photography as *reference* to "the necessarily real thing which has been placed before the lens . . . *the thing that has been there* . . . and yet immediately separated; it has been absolutely irrefutably *present*, yet already *deferred*." *Camera Lucida*, pp. 76–77; cf. Sontag, *On Photography*, p. 16.

49 See Bersani, *Baudelaire and Freud*, pp. 37–38.

50 See Pontalis, *Après Freud*, p. 186.

51 D. W. Winnicott, *The Maturational Processes and the Facilitating Environment* (London: Hogarth Press, 1965). Developmentally, this is the stage in which the infant transfers its attention from primary objects (the mother) to secondary objects. Joyce McDougall sees it in particularly cinematic terms as the space "where all the cultural sets are laid out; a sort of space-time where the essential human forces are at play." *Théâtres du je*, p. 13. Elsewhere she calls it a "theater of transition" with a "stage director" and "roles" given to other parts of the ego (p. 14).

52 Rosolato, *Essais*, p. 354.

Chapter 2   The Absent Presence

1 *Prima della rivoluzione. L'Avant-scène* 82 (June 1968): 12; hereafter cited as *Prima* plus page number. Translations are mine.

2 "L'Ambiguité et l'incertitude au miroir," *L'Avant-scène* 82 (June 1968): 7. Translations are mine.

3 Marsha Kinder points out that although this allusion to Hawks's *Red River* "on the surface appears to be a glib remark that avoids Agostino's emotional pain concerning his Oedipal conflict, the particular film that Fabrizio (or rather Bertolucci) chooses to mention actually addresses that same Oedipal issue and in a style, though different from Bertolucci's, that was revolutionary in its own way. Thus while this remark seems callous and glib on the surface (like most popular cinema), it is actually . . . quite resonant and complicated and actually profound (the very qualities that Bertolucci was claiming for his anti-Bazinian cinema). This mode of treating a cinematic allusion is very similar to the way he handles the allusion to Godard's *A Woman Is a Woman*, and is of course analogous to (or perhaps a microcosm for) the way he handles the complex relation to the Stendhal novel." Personal communication.

4 Bragin, "Conversation," pp. 39, 40.

5 Ibid., pp. 42, 44.

6 See Brian Henderson, *A Critique of Film Theory* (New York: E. P. Dutton, 1980), pp. 16–61.

7 Ibid., pp. 22–23.

8 Collected in *Jean-Luc Godard par Jean-Luc Godard*, ed. Jean Narboni (Paris: Jean Belfond, 1968).

9 Cited in Henderson, *Critique*, p. 65.

10 Ibid., p. 89.

11 Naomi Greene, "Gramsci, Pasolini: The Role of the Intellectuals and the Organization of Culture," *Praxis* (an issue devoted to Gramsci), in press.

12 Ibid.

13 Ibid.

14 Ibid.

15 Beatrice Didier, "Postface," in Stendhal, *La Chartreuse de Parme* (Paris: Gallimard/Folio, 1972), p. 577; translation mine. Balzac adds, "Beyle a fait un livre où le sublime éclate de chapître en chapître" (p. 626).

16 J. L. Bory noted (*Le Nouvel Observateur*, January 17, 1968), "*Prima della rivoluzione* s'achève dans l'application morose, une sérénité amère, qui sont celles de l'Education sentimentale" (reprinted in *L'Avant-scène* 82 [June 1968]: 49). See also Roger Greenspun, "Before the Revolution," *Film Comment* 10, no. 3 (May/June 1974): 22–23.

17 Stendhal, *The Charterhouse of Parma*, trans. C. K. Scott Moncrief (London: Chatto and Windus, 1951), p. 95; hereafter cited as *CP* plus page number.

18 See John Thomas, "Before the Revolution," *Film Quarterly* 20, no. 1 (Fall 1966): 55.

19 Bragin, "Conversation," p. 42.

20 Brecht's presence in the film is rendered overtly through a shot of a poster announcing one of Brecht's plays, which Gina passes on her way to the train station, and implicitly in the several titles that break the realistic flow of the film, e.g., the Talleyrand quote that opens the film and such inserts as "Easter Sunday Morning: The sound of newly liberated bells flows over the city like butterflies. . . . They slept deeply"; or, "They continued to sleep: a real scandal, for everyone else in the house was already preparing for Mass." *Prima*, 8, 22, 23.

21 Henderson, *Critique*, pp. 22–23.

22 Caution is advisable, of course, when interpreting names in any text, yet the friend is played by Gianni Amico, who is listed in the credits as a collaborator on the film, and without question he voices the director's own theories of and attitudes toward film. Interestingly enough, the term reappears at a very charged moment in *Spider's Stratagem*, when the villagers of Tara repeat hauntingly, "Qui tutti sono amici." This can be interpreted as an expression of the condensation in which, in dreams, all characters represent at some level the dreamer himself. As for the name of the theater, Orfeo, it will reappear significantly in *Last Tango in Paris*; see below, Chapter 6.

23 Footnote to the scenario, *Prima*, 35.

24 See Sigmund Freud, *Jokes and Their Relation to the Unconscious, The Standard Edition* 8 (London: Hogarth Press, 1960).

25 Bragin, "Conversation," pp. 42, 44. Bertolucci continues, "The Italian films I love most are those of Rossellini. I like the French cinema as well—above all Godard. But Rossellini is the greatest of them all. It is one of the first cases of a truly open cinema. . . . The style of Rossellini is a profoundly moral style; a style with its own ethics."

26 Cf. Fabrice's statement, "I love you with the most devoted friendship, but my heart is not susceptible to love." *CP*, 219.

27 See Georges Poulet, "Stendhal and Time," *Revue international de philosophie* 16 (1962): 395–412.

28 Stendhal later compares Fabrice to Clelia's birds (*CP*, 381–82), and, significantly, Fabrizio compares himself to "one of those pigeons on the square pecking around under the status of Garibaldi. My Garibaldi is Cesare." *Prima*, 18.

29 Pontalis, *Entre le rêve et la douleur*, pp. 76–77; translation mine.

30 See n. 22.

31 Pontalis, *Entre le rêve et la douleur*, pp. 197–99, 213; translation mine.

32 For a discussion of literature as a "transitional object," see Murray Schwartz, "Critic, Define Thyself," in *Psychoanalysis and the Question of the Text*, ed. Geoffrey Hartman (Baltimore: Johns Hopkins University Press, 1978).

33 M. Blanchot, "Faux pas," cited in Pontalis, *Après Freud*, p. 284; translation mine.

34   M. Blanchot, *Le Livre à venir*, cited in Barthes, *Camera Lucida*, p. 106.

35   Cavell, *The World Viewed*, p. 42.

36   Sontag, *On Photography*, pp. 10–13. Cf. Cavell, "The ontological conditions of the motion picture reveal it as inherently pornographic" (*The World Viewed*, p. 45). See also Metz, *Le Signifiant imaginaire*, pp. 113–20.

37   Linda Williams, "Stendhal and Bertolucci: The Sweetness of Life before the Revolution," *Literature/Film Quarterly* 4, no. 3 (1976): 218. Williams's essay is a perceptive and illuminating treatment of visual styles in *Prima*, yet her conclusions seem to me to fall short of some of the larger implications of the film.

38   Cited in Gelmis, "Bernardo Bertolucci," p. 120.

39   Cited in Bragin, "Conversation," p. 42.

40   Ibid., p. 44.

41   Williams, "Stendhal and Bertolucci," pp. 217–18.

42   Incest as a theme was to reappear in Bertolucci's work in *A Spider's Stratagem*, *Last Tango in Paris*, and especially *La Luna*.

43   Roland Barthes has written of photography: "In Photography I can never deny that the thing has been there. There is a superimposition here of reality and of the past. And since this constraint exists only for Photography, we must consider it . . . as the very essence, the *noeme* of Photography. What I intentionalize in a photograph is Reference, which is the founding order of Photography. The name of Photography's *noeme* will therefore be 'that-has-been.' What I see . . . has been absolutely irrefutably present yet already deferred." *Camera Lucida*, pp. 76–77.

44   Cf. the following observation by Susan Sontag: "A photograph is both a pseudopresence and a token of absence. . . . Photographs are a way of imprisoning reality; understood as recalcitrant, inaccessible. . . . Photographs give people an imaginary possession of a past that is unreal and help to take possession of a space in which they are insecure. . . . A way of certifying existence, taking photographs is also a way of refusing it—by converting experience into an image, a souvenir." *On Photography*, pp. 9, 16, 163.

45   Barthes, *Camera Lucida*, p. 12.

46   Jacques Lacan, "Le Stade du miroir," *Revue française de psychanalyse* 13 (1949): 449–55.

47   Roland Barthes notes of such photographs, "Looking at such photographs it is as if I were certain of having been there or of going there. Now Freud says of the maternal body that 'there is no other place of which one can say with so much certainty that one has already been there.' Such would be the essence of [those photographs] (chosen by desire): *heimlich*, awakening in me the Mother (and never disturbing the Mother)." *Camera Lucida*, p. 40.

48   See below, Chapter 6.

49   Freud, *Interpretation of Dreams*, pp. 277 ff.

50   In a scene cut from the final version, the specifically Oedipal theme is emphasized. Fabrizio momentarily loses Gina in a crowd and shouts, "Where are you? I can't hear you anymore!" He repeats, "Where are you?" and the scenario indicates that Fabrizio emits a piercing, hoarse, and childlike cry, "Mommmmmmmy!"

51   Inexplicable visual elements permeate the entire film; e.g., in the scene of Gina's breakdown (following her encounter with Evalina), Fabrizio's hand is shown three different times closing on his aunt's approaching shoulder. Each shot is a different one, yet each must occupy an identical chronological moment in the "realism" of the logical narrative. In the earlier scene at the dinner table during his eulogy of Agostino, Fabrizio is four times dissolved and replaced by a slightly different take. Neither of these examples of editing (or others that could be mentioned) can be ascribed to any recognizable "realism" other than an oneiric or cinematically self-conscious mode.

52   Freud, *Interpretation of Dreams, chap.* 6. See also Edward Said, *Beginnings* (New York: Basic Books, 1975), pp. 168–69: "This is the dream's navel, the spot where it reaches down into the unknown. . . . The tangle ultimately refers to the Oedipus complex which is an upsetting of normal family sequence because of incest. . . . What had been a family romance becomes in Freud's interpretation of the Greek tragedy, an almost unbearably complex tangling of opposites."

53   Pontalis, *Entre le rêve et la douleur*, pp. 76–77.

54   Among the many allusions to Pavese are Cesare's quote, "Ripeness is all," from *La luna e i falo* (*Prima*, 29); the several allusions to suicide (Agostino, Marilyn Monroe); and Pavese's translation of *Moby Dick*, which Cesare reads in the penultimate sequence of the film.

55   Even as he figuralizes Pavese, Bertolucci alludes to Stendhal, for Fabrizio's image of birds is taken from *La Chartreuse*; see n. 28. The consequences of Fabrizio's worshipful attitude will be played out in *The Conformist* by Marcello and Quadri.

56   Interestingly enough, as a further link between novel and film, Leo Bersani saw in *La Chartreuse* Stendhal's desire to be his own father. "Stendhalian Prisons and Salons," in *Balzac to Beckett* (New York: Oxford University Press, 1970), pp. 102–3.

57   Freud, "A Special Type of Object Choice Made by Men," in *Contributions to the Psychology of Love, The Standard Edition* 11 (London: Hogarth Press, 1957): 173.

58   Bertolucci, "L'Ambiguité," p. 7.

59   Cited in Greene, "Gramsci, Pasolini," p. 18.

60   Ibid.

61   Bertolucci, "L'Ambiguité," p. 7.

62   Rosolato, *Essais*, p. 173.

Chapter 3   Doubling *The Double*

1   Cited in Ungari, *Scena madri*, p. 36. All citations from this text are my own translations.

2   Ibid., p. 51.

3   Ibid., pp. 45, 239.

4   Ibid., p. 51.

5   Ibid., p. 43.

6   Ibid., pp. 43–44.

7   Ibid., p. 44. Other parallels with the never-to-be-realized project: Giacobbe's unsuccessful militancy, his allusion to the priest who died in a urinal because he had too many buttons, and the film's implicit homage to Pasolini.

8   Ungari, *Scena madri*, pp. 51, 52.

9   Ibid., p. 52.

10   Fyodor Dostoevsky, *The Double*, in *Great Short Works of Fyodor Dostoevsky*, trans. George Bird (New York: Harper and Row, 1968), p. 3. All references are to this edition; hereafter cited in text by page number.

11   This confusion is repeated later by the narrator: "Andrey Filippovich at this moment of triumph does not look at all like a collegiate counsellor and head of a section in a certain department. No, indeed. . . . In some way he is different, but certainly he is unlike a collegiate counsellor. He is more exalted. And finally . . . Oh why do I not possess the secret of elevated forceful style—of an exultant style. . . . I will say nothing, but will point out to you in silence—for this will be better than eloquence. . . . I will say nothing, although I cannot help observing. . . . I shall not describe" (p. 28).

12   Recent film theory has made much of the place of the spectator in the film act. See Browne, "Spectator-in-the-Text," p. 36.

13   Gordon Gow, "Partner," *Films and Filming* 17, no. 4 (1971): 53. Cf. Geoffrey Norvell-Smith, "Partner," *Sight and Sound* 37, no. 1 (Winter 1968/69): 34.

14   In his *Introduction à la littérature fantastique*, Todorov suggests why this moment should be so powerful: "The fantastic implies an integration of the reader into the world of the characters; it is defined by the reader's ambiguous perception of the recounted events" (pp. 35–36; translation mine).

15   Todorov notes that the fantastic always involves uncertainty over the boundaries between matter and spirit and always engenders certain themes that include "multiplication of personality; the breakdown of the limits between subject and object, and finally the transformation of time and space." Ibid., p. 126.

16   Cf. Todorov, who notes, "These themes can be characterized as essentially concerning the structuring between man and the world; we are, in Freudian terms, in the perception-consciousness system. . . . We could designate all of these themes as

'themes of looking.' . . . Glasses and mirrors in particular allow us to enter the universe of the fantastic. . . . Reason pronounces itself against mirrors which offer not the world but only an image of the world, a dematerialized matter, in short, a contradiction with regard to the law of noncontradiction. . . . Pure and simple vision reveals to us a world which is flat and without mystery. Indirect vision is the only road to the marvelous. But this overstepping of normal vision, this transgression of the look, are they not its very symbol and, as it were, its highest praise ? Glasses and mirrors become the image of a look which is no longer purely functional, transparent, and transitive. These objects are, in some way, in their relation to the materialized or opaque look, the quintessence of the look." Ibid., pp. 127–29.

17   This ambivalence operates, in this case, on the level of anecdote as well, where there is a limited degree of fidelity, e.g., Yakov's meeting with his double and his visit to Klara Olsufyevna's house, and at least an equal degree of rejection, for Giacobbe's adventures extend far beyond his Russian model's.

18   When asked if he subscribed to Aristotle's theory of a beginning, a middle, and an end, Godard replied, "Yes, but not necessarily in that order !"

19   Artaud was to be resuscitated by the radical movement of 1968.

20   Antonin Artaud, *Le Théâtre et son double* (Paris: Gallimard, 1964), p. 78; trans. M. C. Richards (New York: Grove Press, 1958), p. 3; hereafter cited in text.

21   Ungari, *Scena madri*, p. 196.

22   Ibid., pp. 215–16.

23   Bertolucci noted that the Living Theatre was a major influence on his film. See ibid., pp. 44, 51.

24   Dostoevsky, *Dream of a Ridiculous Man*, in *Great Short Works*, pp. 724, 726. Elsewhere in the same text, Dostoevsky adds, "While understanding the words, I could never entirely fathom their meaning. It remained somehow beyond the grasp of my reason, and yet it sank unconsciously deeper and deeper into my heart" (p. 732).

25   C. G. Jung, *Dreams* (Princeton: Princeton University Press, 1974), p. 52.

26   According to Erwin Rohde, in Homeric times this doubling process of dreams was considered to be their explicit function: "According to Homeric conception, in the living human being, completely filled with his soul, there dwells, like an alien guest, a weaker double, his self other than his psyche, whose realm is the world of dreams. When the other self is asleep, unconscious of itself, the double is awake and active." Cited in Otto Rank, *The Double*, trans. Harry Tucker, Jr. (New York: New American Library, 1979), p. 60.

27   Jung, *Dreams*, pp. 38, 60–61, 101.

28   Charles Rycroft, *The Innocence of Dreams* (New York: Pantheon, 1979), p. 45. Freud notes, "a dreamer in relation to his wishes can only be compared to an amalgamation of two separate people who are linked by some strong element in common" (cited in Rycroft, p. 107). See also B. D. Lewin, *Dreams and the Uses of*

Regression (New York: International University Press, 1958), pp. 19–20, and Leon L. Altman, *The Dream in Psychoanalysis* (New York: International University Press, 1969), p. 31.

29   Havelock Ellis, *The World of Dreams* (Boston: Houghton Mifflin, 1911), pp. 20–21.

30   Rycroft, *Innocence*, p. 165.

31   Dostoevsky, *Dream of a Ridiculous Man*, p. 733.

32   Michel Tournier, *The Ogre*, trans. B. Bray from the French, *Le roi des aulnes* (New York: Dell, 1973), p. 303.

33   Rank, *The Double*, p. 86.

34   Ungari, *Scena madri*, p. 222.

35   The pun will be forgiven when the reader recalls that Bertolucci called *Luna* a "mielodrama." See below, Chapter 8.

36   Casetti, *Bertolucci*, p. 3.

37   Ungari, *Scena madri*, p. 52.

38   Ibid.

39   Ibid.

40   Ibid.

41   Ibid.

42   Jacques Derrida, *La Dissémination* (Paris: Editions du Seuil, 1972), p. 234.

Chapter 4   The Villa Borges

1   Ungari, *Scena madri*, p. 52.

2   Cited in Amengual, "Portrait de l'artiste en jeune homme."

3   Cited in Aldo Tassone, *Le Cinéma italien parle* (Paris: Edilig, 1982), p. 51; translation mine.

4   This is not a gratuitous reference, because the Borges story on which the film is based also alludes to an Irish-Italian parallel.

5   The actual town is Sabbionetta. For excellent discussions of the cinematic reconstruction of Sabbionetta, see Amengual, "Portrait," p. 37; Joel Magny, "Dimension politique de l'oeuvre de Bernardo Bertolucci de *Prima della rivoluzione* à *Novecento*," in *Bernardo Bertolucci*, special issue of *Etudes cinématographiques*, nos. 122–26 (1979), p. 61.

6   Roud's otherwise perspicacious essay on the Oedipal conflict in *Spider* suffers, it seems to me, from his failure to appreciate the dreamlike quality of the film and the resulting distortions and condensations that characterize the work of dreams. Richard Roud, "Bertolucci's *Spider's Stratagem*," *Sight and Sound* 40, no. 2 (Spring 1971): 61–64.

7   Nick Browne, "Rhétorique du texte spéculaire," *Psychanalyse et cinéma: Communications* 23 (1975): 208.

8   Cited in Ungari, *Scena madri*, p. 117; see also p. 63, and Jonathan Cott, "A Conversation with Bernardo Bertolucci," *Rolling Stone*, June 21, 1973, p. 46.

9   André Breton, *Manifestoes of Surrealism*, trans. Richard Seaver and Helen Lane (Ann Arbor: University of Michigan Press, 1969), pp. 26, 123. There are specific confusions in this film as to the living and the dead; e.g., during Draifa's first conversation with Athos Magnani, he asks her if Gaibazzi and the others are dead and she answers, "Yes," then catches herself and exclaims, "No!" Of Beccarria she says during the same conversation, "He does not live, he reigns."

10   Cott, "Conversation with Bertolucci," p. 44; also, remarks made at "A Weekend with Bertolucci," The New School, June 15–16, 1985.

11   Andrew Sarris argued that "Bertolucci throws up his hands at the prospect of restoring the past in period costume terms, not making the slightest effort at flashback illusionism. . . . The past is simply all those cantankerous old people in our midst who cling to life like castoffs from a Samuel Beckett ceremony of survival." "Films in Focus," *Village Voice*, October 8, 1970, p. 53. What Sarris failed to appreciate is the decision to mix images of the past with the present on an equal basis—a frequent characteristic of dreams.

12   Freud, *Moses and Monotheism, The Standard Edition* 23 (London: Hogarth Press, 1964), 43.

13   Norman O. Brown, *Love's Body* (New York: Random House, 1966), pp. 42–43. Brown goes on, in terms that will be particularly pertinent to *Last Tango in Paris*: "The woman penetrated is labyrinth. You emerge into another world inside the woman. The penis is the bridge; the passage to another world is coitus; the other world is womb-cave. Cave man still drags cave woman to his cave; all coitus is fornication [*fornix*, an underground arched vault]. And the cave in which coitus takes place is the grave; a cathonic fertility rite. . . . Death is coitus and coitus is death. Death is genitalized as a return to the womb, incestuous coitus . . . Life and death, equated" (p. 48; see also p. 41).

14   I am indebted to J. Hillis Miller for his excellent discussion of this Shakespearean character (she appears in *Troilus and Cressida*, 5.2). See "Ariachne's Broken Woof," *Georgia Review* 31, no. 1 (Spring 1977): 44–60.

15   Cited in Gideon Bachmann, "Every Sexual Relationship Is Condemned: An Interview with Bernardo Bertolucci," *Film Quarterly* 26 (Spring 1973): 3–4. As for the aspect of "embobinage," cf. Tom Conley's qualification of "debobinage" as "the shards of all representation, fragments and tatters which lead us to capture over and over again our primal and forever visual grasp of the world we touch." "Reading Ordinary Viewing," *Diacritics*, Spring 1985, p. 8.

16   Christian Metz notes that "The drive to perceive, contrary to other sexual drives, concretely establishes the absence of its object by the distance where it is maintained, which distance participates in its very definition. . . . The voyeur carefully maintains a gap, an empty space, between the object and the eye, the object and

the body; his look fixes the object at a proper distance, like spectators in the cinema who take care to be neither too near nor too far away from the screen. In this interrupting space, the voyeur stages the scene of his own dissatisfaction, which is just what he needs as voyeur, and therefore also his 'satisfaction' inasmuch as it is properly voyeuristic. To fill in this distance is to risk fulfilling the subject as well, to risk consummation of the object with the resultant elimination of purely voyeuristic pleasure." "Le Signifiant imaginaire," p. 42; translation mine.

17   Robert Chapetta, "The Meaning Is Not the Message," *Film Quarterly* 25, no. 4 (Summer 1972): 17.

18   Cited by Marilyn Goldin, "Bertolucci on *The Conformist*," *Sight and Sound* 40, no. 2 (Spring 1971): 65.

19   Jorge Luis Borges, "The Theme of the Traitor and the Hero," in *Labyrinths* (New York: New Directions, 1962), p. 73.

20   Ibid., pp. 73–74.

21   As Edward Said notes, "The tangle at the nexus of the dream ultimately refers to the oedipus complex which is an upsetting of normal family sequence because of incest. . . . The subsequent 'tangle' of roles resists ordinary sequential understanding, for the original author of the family line, the father is murdered and his place usurped by the son. What overwhelms Oedipus is the burden of plural identities incapable of existing within one person. In such a case the image of a man conceals behind its facade multiple meanings and multiple determinations. What had been a family romance becomes in Freud's interpretation of the Greek tragedy, an almost unbearably complex tangling of opposites." *Beginnings*, p. 163.

22   See Chapter 2, n. 46.

23   Said, *Beginnings*, p. 66. Said uses the figure of genealogy as a metaphor for narrative in a way that is most illuminating for this film. "The chief aim of the narrative's developing consciousness is to wed inaugural promise to time—to be, in other words, the course of such a marriage, the issue of which is discovery, explanation, genealogy. The narrative represents the *generative* process—literally in its mimetic representation of men and women in time, metaphorically in that by itself it generates succession and multiplication of events *after the manner of human procreation;* yet the history of the nineteenth century novel documents the increasing awareness of a gap between the representations of fictional narrative and the fruitful, generative principle of human life. These are divergent paths that eventually become completely irrelevant to one another" (p. 146).

24   Michel Foucault, *This Is Not a Pipe* (Berkeley: University of California Press, 1983), p. 44.

25   See Browne, "Rhétorique."

26   Borges, "The Wall and the Books," in *Labyrinths*, p. 188.

27   For a discussion of the implications of this "tangle," see Said, *Beginnings*, pp. 168 ff.

28   John W. Perry, *Lord of the Four Quarters* (New York: Braziller, 1966), pp. 16, 21–22.

Chapter 5   The Unconforming *Conformist*

1   Cited in Ungari, *Scena madri*, p. 71.

2   Alberto Moravia, *The Conformist*, trans. Angus Davidson (London: Secker and Warburg, 1953); all references in the text will be to this edition. (Original edition: Milano: Bompiani, 1951.)

3   Amos Vogel, "Bernardo Bertolucci: An Interview," *Film Comment* 7, no. 3 (Fall 1971): 26; Bernardo Bertolucci, "Seminar," *Dialogue on Film* 3, no. 15 (April 1974): 14, 16.

4   Cited in Roud, "Bertolucci's *Spider's Stratagem*," *Sight and Sound* 40, no. 2 (Spring 1971): 61.

5   Plato, *The Republic*, in *Collected Dialogues*, ed. E. Hamilton and H. Cairns, trans. Lane Cooper (New York: Pantheon, 1961), book 7, p. 747.

6   It is perhaps coincidental that *quadri* means "diamonds" in Italian, for what is difficult for Moravia's Marcello is the combination of political purity and ruthless hardness in the older man. But Bertolucci did not keep all of the original names in his film, and if he did so here it may have been because *quadri* not only means "diamonds" but sounds like *quadra* (a quadrant), from which the expression in Italian *dare la quadra a qualcuno*, meaning to hold someone up to ridicule; like *quadro*, meaning "square" or "sensible," "paintings," or "outline"; but also like *quadraiao*, a picture seller!

7   Baudry, "Dispositif," pp. 56–72.

8   Joyce McDougall, *Plaidoyer pour une certaine anormalité* (Paris: Gallimard, 1978), pp. 220–21.

9   Baudry, "Dispositif," p. 58; translation mine. Baudry further theorizes on the relation between the movie screen and the "dream screen," so convinced is he of the close relationship between film and dream: "Il est évident que l'écran du rêve est un résidu des traces mnésiques les plus archaïques. Mais on pourrait supposer en outre, ce qui est au moins aussi important, qu'il ouvre à la compréhension de ce qu'on pourrait appeler le dispositif formateur et la 'scène primitive' du rêve qui s'établit en pleine phase orale."

10   "Bernardo Bertolucci Seminar," p. 21.

11   Goldin, "Bertolucci on *The Conformist*," p. 66.

12   See above, Chapter 4.

13   "Bernardo Bertolucci Seminar," p. 16.

14   Ungari, *Scena madri*, p. 71.

15   Tassone, *Le Cinéma italien parle*, p. 54.

16   Ungari, *Scena madri*, p. 72.

17   McDougall, *Plaidoyer*, p. 221.

18   Ungari, *Scena madri*, p. 73.

19   Ibid.

20   Cf. the following observation of Edward Said: "Each text pushes aside ordinary discourse in order to place before the world a textual composition whose authority derives from two sources: the ancient originals whose style is being copied and the present text's appearance in the form of a preserved duration. To put pen to a text is to begin the movement away from the original; it is to enter the world of the text-as-beginning as copy and as parricide. The Oedipal motif lurking beneath many discussions of the text . . . makes more sense if we regard the text-copy as totem and the making of such a text as the beginning parricidal deed that Freud spoke of in *Totem and Taboo*." *Beginnings*, p. 209.

Chapter 6   "A Turbid, Unreal Past, in Certain Measure True"

Both title and epigram are taken from Borges's poem, "The Tango," in *A Personal Anthology* (New York: Grove Press, 1967), pp. 158–60.

1   Ferenczi (*Theory and Practice*, pp. 356–57) has explained the analytic implications of the bridge as follows: (1) as the male member that unites the parents during sexual intercourse; (2) as an important vehicle between the "beyond"—the condition of the unborn and the womb—and the "here"—life; (3) as a return to the womb, to water, to Mother Earth, where the bridge is also the symbol of the pathway to death; and finally, as a formal representation of transitions in general. Ferenczi's analysis of this symbol unites the themes of sexuality, regression, and death, each of which will play an important role in *Last Tango*.

2   The concierge also serves as a visual link between the Jules Verne apartment and the brothel, which houses a community of Caribbean-looking blacks who play hot music all day—undoubtedly an allusion to Camus's *Orpheu negro*.

3   Robert Alley, *Last Tango in Paris* (New York: Dell, 1973), pp. 13–14.

4   Bertolucci himself referred to the apartment as "a privileged space." Colette Godard, "Bernardo Bertolucci: On s'exprime toujours par ses défenses," *Le Monde*, December 11–12, 1972, p. 14.

5   Marcel's room holds a prominently displayed photo portrait of Albert Camus, whose essays centering on suicide and the absurd constitute a philosophical decor for the film. But behind this obvious allusion lies another: the visual pun "Marcel/Camus" calls to mind the director of *Orpheu negro* as well.

6   In the film version of *Orpheus Descending*, Brando's character is castrated by a blow torch.

7   Freud, "Creative Writers and Daydreaming," *The Standard Edition* 9 (London: Hogarth Press, 1959): 152.

8   Michel Serres, *Jouvences sur Jules Verne* (Paris: Editions de Minuit, 1974).

9   Winnicott, "Mirror-Role of Mother and Family in Child Development," in *The Predicament of the Family*, ed. P. Lomas (London: Hogarth Press, 1967), p. 27.

10   Ibid., p. 29.

11   Ibid., p. 31.

12   Ibid., p. 29. It is also noteworthy that Bertolucci said of Brando's role, "Brando feels, in a way, that he is as much the son of his wife as he is the father of the girl." Bachmann, "Every Sexual Relationship," p. 5.

13   Remarks at "A Weekend with Bertolucci," June 15, 1985.

14   Freud, "A Special Type of Object Choice," p. 173.

15   Bachmann, "Every Sexual Relationship," p. 6.

16   See Freud, "A Special Type of Object Choice."

17   Freud, "Creative Writers and Daydreaming"; also, *The Libido Theory and Narcissism*, *The Standard Edition* 18 (London: Hogarth Press, 1964), p. 255.

18   Freud, *The Libido Theory*, pp. 138–39.

19   Jean Normand, "Le Poète, image de l'étranger: l'Orphée de Tennessee Williams," *French American Review* 4, no. 2 (Fall 1980): 76–77; translation mine.

20   Bertolucci's comments on this scene are particularly useful here: "At the beginning of the film he is supervirile . . . but slowly he loses his virility. At a certain point he makes the girl sodomize him: going backwards, he has arrived at the anal stage. Let's say the sadico-anal stage. Then he goes back even further and arrives in the womb of Paris, dying with mother-Paris all around him. . . . There is a clear arrival in death. When we were planning the film, all this was only in my subconscious. My camera research clarified it for me. The irrational becomes lucid." Bachmann, "Every Sexual Relationship," p. 7.

21   Bachmann, ibid., pp. 4, 7.

22   Jean Matter notes, "Narcissus in love with himself can only be in love with death, for the contemplation of the self is fatally linked to the thought of Death. The mirror is an inevitable pathway to death. If Orpheus refuses to retreat in the face of Death, it is because Death attracts him and he loves her. He loves Death like a mother whose fate is bound up with his own. Narcissism usually flows from a fixation. The young man loves in himself the object of his mother's love. Orpheus is, literally, full of himself. That is why he listens to no one other than Death. . . . Death is beautiful, all-powerful and inaccessible . . . attributes of the mother in the child's eyes." "Le Mythe de Narcisse dans *L'Orphée* de Jean Cocteau," *Psyché* 6 (1951): 251. See also Freud, *The Libido Theory*, p. 430. Lacan ("Le Stade du miroir," p. 454) saw narcissism related to "instincts of destruction, even of death," and noted "the evident relation of the narcissistic libido to the alienating function of the I."

23   Godard, "Bernardo Bertolucci."

24   John Rothenstein, *Francis Bacon: Catalogue raisonné* (London: Thames and Hudson, 1964), p. 15.

25   Winnicott, "Mirror-Role of Mother and Family," p. 29.

26   Marsha Kinder and Beverle Houston, "Bertolucci and the Dance of Danger," *Sight and Sound* 42, no. 4 (Autumn 1973): 189.

27   It is interesting to note once again the degree of allusion to Orpheus in this film: Jean-Pierre Leaud played in Cocteau's *Testament d'Orphée.*

28   Ungari, *Scena madri*, p. 90.

29   Winnicott, "Mirror-Role of Mother and Family," p. 29.

30   Bersani, *Baudelaire and Freud*, pp. 37–38.

31   McDougall, "Primal Scene and Sexual Perversion," p. 372.

32   Cavell, *The World Viewed*, p. 45.

33   Rosolato, *Essais*, pp. 79–80.

34   Kael, "Last Tango in Paris," p. 130.

Chapter 7   Doppia della rivoluzione

1   Gideon Bachman, "Films Are Animal Events: Bernardo Bertolucci Talks about His New Film, *1900*," *Film Quarterly* 26, no. 3 (Spring 1975): 13.

2   Ibid.

3   Ungari, *Scena madri*, p. 180.

4   Ibid.

5   Cited in *Post-Impressionism: Cross-Currents in European Painting* (London: Weidenfeld and Nicolson, 1979), p. 132.

6   Significantly, the reviewer of the painting wrote, "Forced back into the distance by the enormous size of the painting the observer no longer finds the brushstrokes individually perceptible." Ibid.

7   Vogel, "Bernardo Bertolucci: An Interview," p. 26.

8   Bertolucci, *Novecento, atto primo* (Torino: Einaudi, 1976), p. 6; hereafter cited in parentheses in the text as *Novecento* plus page number. Translations are mine.

9   Bachman, "Films Are Animal Events," p. 12.

10   In an unpublished manuscript Paolo Braghieri discusses stable theater.

11   In Sigmund Freud, *Beyond the Pleasure Principle* (New York: Bantam Books, 1959).

12   See Pauline Kael, "Hail Folly," *The New Yorker* 52, no. 10 (October 31, 1971), pp. 148 ff.

13   Freud, *Beyond the Pleasure Principle*, p. 39.

14   See Goethe's "The Erl King."

15   See Freud, *Beyond the Pleasure Principle*, p. 37.

16   Cf. *A Spider's Stratagem*, in which there is a 360-degree "struggle" with the rotating statue of the father. Athos fils prefigures the child swung in a murderous circle.

17   And if Olmo refers to the Erl King legend, he too is terrified to death.

18   Cf. the scene of a peasant cutting off his ear to satisfy the padrone's greed—needless to say, a figuration of autocastration.

19   *Novecento*, 31.

20   *Novecento*, 142; cf. p. 51.

21   See Freud, *Beyond the Pleasure Principle*, on the "fort-da" experience and repetition compulsion.

22   See Jeffrey Mehlman, *Repetition and Revolution* (Berkeley: University of California Press, 1977), pp. 11–12.

23   *The American Heritage Dictionary*.

24   See Mehlman, *Repetition and Revolution*, p. 13. As if writing of Bertolucci's film rather than Marx's analysis, Mehlman adds, "The history of a *grotesque repetition* thus comes to be marked by the repetitive insistence of a specific structure: a specular—or reversible—relation is exceeded by a heterogeneous, negatively charged instance whose situation is one of *deviation* or *displacement* in relation to one of the poles of the initial opposition . . . giving way to farce" (p. 14; italics mine).

25   Ibid., p. 33.

26   In this sense, the film can also be understood as a "heterogeneous movement which would endlessly emancipate an *unheimlich* dimension indifferent to the distinctions truth/error, suppression/suppressed." Ibid., pp. 40–41.

27   Freud, *Beyond the Pleasure Principle*, pp. 67–68.

28   Ibid., p. 70.

29   Cf. "Whatever the biological fantasia accompanying the hypothesis of a death instinct, what the absolute discharge of tensions originally referred to was the total evacuation of affect from ideational representative to ideational representative in *dreams* and hysterical symptoms: that is, the fact of unconscious displacement as 'primary process thinking,' " Mehlman, *Repetition and Revolution*, p. 32.

30   Bachmann, "Films Are Animal Events," p. 12.

31   See Chapter 5.

32   Cf. "A Photograph is both a pseudo-presence and a token of absence . . . an incitement to reverie. The sense of the unattainable that can be evoked by photographs feeds directly into the erotic feelings of those for whom desirability is enhanced by distance." Sontag, *On Photography*, p. 16.

33   Jean Laplanche, *Life and Death in Psychoanalysis*, trans. Jeffrey Mehlman (Baltimore: Johns Hopkins University Press, 1976), p. 107.

34   As Laplanche reminds us, "The artistic play and artistic imitation carried out by adults which, unlike children's, are aimed at an audience, do not spare the spectators (for instance, in tragedy) the most painful experiences and yet can be felt by them as highly enjoyable. This is convincing proof that, even under the dominance of the pleasure principle, there are ways and means enough of making what is in itself unpleasurable into a subject to be recollected and worked over in the mind." Ibid.

35   See Pontalis, *Entre le rêve et la douleur*, p. 84.

36   See ibid., pp. 49–51.

37   See ibid., p. 98.

Chapter 8   ". . . Perforce to Dream"

1   Ungari, *Scena madri*, p. 127.

2   Lee Tsiantis, "Bertolucci's *Luna*," *Chairman's Choice* 4, no. 1 (Winter 1980): 12.

3   Ibid. Piera Fogliani, "Bertolucci: La Faccia nascosta della *Luna*," *Grazia*, October 21, 1979, p. 67.

4   Bertolucci elaborates on this connection in an interview with Jean Gili, "A propos de *La Luna*: Entretien avec Bernardo Bertolucci," *Bernardo Bertolucci*, special issue of *Etudes cinématographiques*, nos. 122–26 (1979), pp. 18–19.

5   George Malko, *Luna* (London: Pan Books, 1980), p. 14.

6   Casetti, *Bertolucci*, p. 28; translation mine.

7   Vincent Canby, "Bertolucci's *Luna*," *New York Times*, October 7, 1979, sec. 7, p. 1.

8   Ungari, *Scena madri*, pp. 35–36.

9   Joyce McDougall's description of psychoanalysis itself, in *Théâtres du je*, p. 19.

10   Ungari, *Scena madri*, p. 191.

11   Ibid.

12   Ibid., p. 192. In fact, the film is more operatic than melodramatic; yet, when Bertolucci's insistence on the term "melodrama" was questioned, he invented the term "new dramaturgy," whose "ambition is to be loved and to be rejected at the same time." Cited in Rob Baker, "Bernardo Bertolucci: In Defense of *Luna*," *Soho Weekly News* 7, no. 2 (October 17–19, 1979): 67.

13   Baker, "Bernardo Bertolucci," p. 8.

14   Ungari, *Scena madri*, pp. 191, 193.

15   "Endymion," *The Reader's Encyclopedia*, ed. William Rose Benét (New York: Crowell, 1965), pp. 314–15.

16   Bertolucci, in "Dialogue on Film: Bernardo Bertolucci," *American Film*, January–February 1980, p. 36.

17   Ibid., p. 42.

18   Ungari, *Scena madri*, p. 192.

19   "Dialogue on Film," p. 113.

20   "A Weekend with Bertolucci," June 15–16, 1985.

21   Malko, *Luna*, p. 113.

22   Cited in Goldin, "Bertolucci on *The Conformist*," p. 65.

23   See "Don Quichotte," in Michel Foucault, *Les Mots et les choses* (Paris: Gallimard, 1966), pp. 66 ff.

24 Ungari, *Scena madri*, p. 36.

25 "Dialogue on Film," p. 38.

26 J.-B. Pontalis, "Dream as Object," *International Review of Psychoanalysis* 1 (1973): 130.

27 Pontalis cites "patients who will bring *dream after dream*, and relentlessly manipulate images and words. The dream will incessantly move him further away from self-recognition, while he claims to look for it by auto-interpretation. . . . He steals his own dreams from himself." Ibid.

28 Cited in Tassone, *Le Cinéma italien parle*, p. 52.

29 "Dreaming ," Pontalis argued, "is above all an effort to maintain the impossible union with the mother, to preserve an undivided totality, to move in a space prior to time." "Dream as Object," p. 127.

30 Ibid., p. 128.

31 Ibid., p. 132.

32 "Dialogue on Film," p. 41.

33 Ibid., p. 38.

34 Cf. Bertolucci, *In ricerca del mistero*.

35 See Pontalis, who describes this protection as serving "against incest consummated with the mother, incest which combines joy and terror, penetration and the *act of devouring*, the nascent body and the petrified body." "Dream as Object," p. 132.

36 As Pontalis would put it, "In the end, the dream process (of the dream-for-analysis) is diverted from its major function—to produce wish-fulfillments, or make it rise to the surface—to being taken as an aim in itself. The dreamer attaches himself to his dreams so as not to be cast adrift." Ibid., p. 135.

37 Baker, "Bernardo Bertolucci," p. 8.

38 I am generally indebted to Joyce McDougall's discussion of perversion in "Primal Scene and Sexual Perversion," pp. 371–84.

39 "In many ways," notes McDougall, "the perverse play is comparable to a dream . . . and resembles a stage play in which some verbal links are missing. . . . It is in a manifest content, making use of primary thinking, reversal, displacements and symbolic equivalents." She adds, "The pervert has created a sexual mythology whose true meaning he no longer recognizes, like a text from which important pieces have been removed. . . . The illusion must be acted out endlessly, and this helps to avoid the danger of recuperation through delusion." ibid., pp. 377, 379.

40 "Dialogue on Film," p. 38.

41 Ungari, *Scena madri*, p. 192.

Chapter 9   In Lieu of a Conclusion

1   Ungari, *Scena madri*, p. 195.

2   André Bazin, *What Is Cinema?*, trans. Hugh Gray (Berkeley: University of California Press, 1968), pp. 66–68.

3   Cited in Gili, *Le Cinéma italien*, p. 47.

4   Ungari, *Scena madri*, p. 216.

5   Ibid.

6   Ibid., p. 219.

7   Cited by Tsiantis in "Bertolucci's *Luna*," p. 12.

8   Vogel, "Bernardo Bertolucci," p. 26.

9   Ungari, *Scena madri*, p. 177.

10   Ibid., p. 192.

11   See Rosolato, *Essais*, p. 346.

12   Cited in Gili, *Le Cinéma italien*, p. 57.

13   Ungari, *Scena madri*, p. 196.

SELECTED BIBLIOGRAPHY

Works by Bernardo Bertolucci

"L'Ambiguité et l'incertitude au miroir." *L'Avant-scène* 82 (June 1968): 7.
"Dialogue on Film." *American Film,* January–February 1980, pp. 35–43.
In ricerca del mistero. Milan: Longanesi, 1962.
Novecento, atto primo. Torino: Einaudi, 1976.
Novecento, atto secundo. Torino: Einaudi, 1976.
Prima della rivoluzione. L'Avant-scène 82 (June 1968): 12.
"Seminar." *Dialogue on Film* 3, no. 15 (April 1974): 14–28.

Works on Bertolucci

Amengual, Berthélmy. "Portrait de l'artiste en jeune homme d'avant la trentaine." *Bernardo Bertolucci,* special issue of *Etudes cinématographiques,* nos. 122–26.
Bachmann, Gideon. "Every Sexual Relationship Is Condemned: An Interview with Bernardo Bertolucci." *Film Quarterly* 26 (Spring 1973): 2–9.
———. "Films Are Animal Events: Bernardo Bertolucci Talks about His New Film, *1900." Film Quarterly* 28 (Spring 1975): 11–19.
Baker, Rob. "Bernardo Bertolucci: In Defense of *Luna." Soho Weekly News* 7, no. 2 (October 11–17, 1979): 8–9.
Bragin, John. "A Conversation with Bernardo Bertolucci." *Film Quarterly* 20, no. 1 (Fall 1966): 39–44.
Bory, J. L. *"Prima della rivoluzione." Le Nouvel Observateur,* 17 January 1968. Reprinted in *L'Avant-scène* 82 (June 1968): 60.
Canby, Vincent. "Bertolucci's *Luna." New York Times,* October 7, 1979, sec. 7, p. 1.
Casetti, Francesco. *Bertolucci.* Vol. 24 in *Il castoro cinema.* Florence: La Nuova Italia, 1975.
Cott, Jonathan. "A Conversation with Bernardo Bertolucci." *Rolling Stone,* June 21, 1973, pp. 44–46.
Fogliani, Piera. "La Faccia nascosta della *Luna." Grazia,* October 21, 1979, p. 67.
Gelmis, Joseph. "Bernardo Bertolucci." In *The Film Director as Superstar,* pp. 113–20. (Garden City, N.Y.: Doubleday, 1970).
Gili, Jean. "A propos de *Luna:* Entretien avec Bernardo Bertolucci," in *Bernardo Bertolucci,* special issue of *Etudes cinématographiques,* nos. 122–26 (1979): 2–26.
Godard, Colette. "Bernardo Bertolucci: on s'exprime toujours par ses défenses." *Le Monde,* December 11–12, 1972, p. 14.

Goldin, Marilyn. "Bertolucci on *The Conformist:* An Interview with Marilyn Goldin." *Sight and Sound* 40, no. 2 (Spring 1971): 64–66.

Gow, Gordon. "Partner." *Films and Filming* 17, no. 4 (1971): 53.

Greenspun, Roger. "Before the Revolution." *Film Content* 10, no. 3 (May/June 1974): 22–23.

Kael, Pauline. "Hail Folly." *The New Yorker* 52, no. 10 (October 31, 1977): 148–61.

———. "Last Tango in Paris." *The New Yorker* 47, no. 10 (October 1972): 130–33.

Kinder, Marsha, and Beverle Houston. "Bertolucci and the Dance of Danger." *Sight and Sound* 42, no. 4 (Autumn 1973): 186–91.

Kline, T. J. "The Absent Presence: Stendhal in Bertolucci's *Prima della rivoluzione.*" *Cinema Journal* 23, no. 2 (Winter 1983): 4–28.

———. "Doubling *The Double.*" In *Fearful Symmetry: Doubles and Doubling in Literature and Film,* edited by Eugene Crook, pp. 65–83. Tallahassee: University Presses of Florida, 1981.

———. "Endymion's Wake: Oneiric Projection and Protection in Bertolucci's Cinema." *Dreamworks* 2, no. 1 (Fall 1981): 26–34.

———. "Father as Mirror: Bertolucci's Oedipal Quest and the Collapse of Paternity." *Psychocultural Review,* Spring 1979, pp. 91–109.

———. "Orpheus Transcending: Bertolucci's *Last Tango in Paris.*" *International Review of Psychoanalysis* 3 (Spring 1976): 85–95.

———. "The Unconformist." In *Modern European Filmmakers and the Art of Adaptation,* edited by A. S. Horton and J. Magretta, pp. 222–37. New York: Frederick Ungar, 1981.

Magny, Joel. "Dimension politique de l'oeuvre de Bernardo Bertolucci de *Prima della rivoluzione* à *Novecento.* In *Bernardo Bertolucci,* special issue of *Etudes cinématographiques,* nos. 122–26, pp. 49–76. Paris: Minard, 1979.

Malko, George. *Luna.* London: Pan Books, 1980.

Michener, Charles. "Tango: The Hottest Movie." *Newsweek,* February 12, 1973, p. 37.

Norvell-Smith, Geoffrey. "Partner." *Sight and Sound* 37, no. 1 (Winter 1968–69): 34.

Roud, Richard. "Bertolucci's *Spider's Stratagem.*" *Sight and Sound* 40, no. 2 (Spring 1971): 61–65.

Sarris, Andrew. "Films in Focus." *Village Voice,* October 8, 1970, p. 53.

Thomas, John. "Before the Revolution." *Film Quarterly* 20, no. 1 (Fall 1966): 52–58.

Tsiantis, Lee. "Bertolucci's *Luna.*" *Chairman's Choice* 4, no. 1 (Winter 1980): 12.

Ungari, Enzo. *Scena madri.* Milan: Ubulibri, 1982.

Vogel, Amos. "Bernardo Bertolucci: An Interview." *Film Comment* 7, no. 3 (Fall 1971): 25–29.

Williams, Linda. "Stendhal and Bertolucci: The Sweetness of Life before the Revolution." *Literature/Film Quarterly* 4, no. 3 (1976): 215–21.

Other works cited

Alley, Robert. *Last Tango in Paris*. New York: Dell, 1973.

Altman, Leon L. *The Dream in Psychoanalysis*. New York: International University Press, 1969.

Artaud, Antonin. *Le Théâtre et son double*. Paris: Gallimard, 1964.

Barthes, Roland. *Camera Lucida*. Translated by Richard Howard. New York: Hill and Wang, 1981.

———. "En sortant du cinéma." *Psychanalyse et cinéma: Communications* 23 (February 1975): 104–5.

Baudry, Jean-Louis. "Le Dispositif: approches métapsychologiques de l'impression de réalité." *Psychanalyse et cinéma: Communications* 23 (February 1975): 56–72.

Bazin, André. *What Is Cinema?* Translated by Hugh Gray. Berkeley: University of California Press, 1968.

Bersani, Leo. *Baudelaire and Freud*. Berkeley: University of California Press, 1977.

———. "Stendhalian Prisons and Salons." In *Balzac to Beckett*. New York: Oxford University Press, 1970.

Borges, Jorge Luis. "The Theme of the Traitor and the Hero." In *Labyrinths*. New York: New Directions, 1962.

———. "The Wall and the Books." In *Labyrinths*. New York: New Directions, 1962.

Breton, André. *Manifestoes of Surrealism*. Translated by Richard Seaver and Helen Lane. Ann Arbor: University of Michigan Press, 1969.

Brown, Norman O. *Love's Body*. New York: Random House, 1966.

Browne, Nick. "Rhétorique du texte spéculaire." *Psychanalyse et cinéma: Communications* 23 (1975).

———. "The Spectator-in-the-Text: The Rhetoric of *Stagecoach*." *Film Quarterly* 29, no. 2 (1975–76).

Cavell, Stanley. *The World Viewed*. Cambridge: Harvard University Press, 1979.

Chapetta, Robert. "The Meaning Is Not the Message." *Film Quarterly* 25, no. 4 (Summer 1972): 10–18.

Chasseguet-Smirgel, Janine. *Pour une psychanalyse de l'art et de la créativité*. Paris: Payot, 1971.

Conley, Tom. "Reading Ordinary Viewing." *Diacritics* (Spring 1985): 4–14.

Derrida, Jacques. *La Dissémination*. Paris: Editions du Seuil, 1972.

Didier, Beatrice. "Postface." In Stendhal, *La Chartreuse de Parme*. Paris: Gallimard, 1972.

Dostoevsky, Fyodor. *The Double*. Translated by George Bird. In *Great Short Works of Dostoevsky*. New York: Harper and Row, 1968.

———. *Dream of a Ridiculous Man*. Translated by George Bird. In *Great Short Works of Dostoevsky*. New York: Harper and Row, 1968.

Ellis, Havelock. *The World of Dreams*. Boston: Houghton Mifflin, 1911.

"Endymion." In *The Reader's Encyclopedia*. Edited by William Rose Benét, pp. 314–15. New York: Crowell, 1965.

Ferenczi, Sandor. *The Theory and Practice of Psychoanalysis*. London: Hogarth Press, 1926, 1950.

Foucault, Michel. *Les Mots et les choses*. Paris: Gallimard, 1966.

———. *This Is Not a Pipe*. Berkeley: University of California Press, 1983.

Freud, Sigmund. *Beyond the Pleasure Principle*. New York: Bantam Books, 1959.

———. "Creative Writers and Daydreaming." *The Standard Edition* 9 (London: Hogarth Press, 1959).

———. *The Interpretation of Dreams*. *The Standard Edition* 9 (London: Hogarth Press, 1974).

———. *Jokes and Their Relation to the Unconscious*. *The Standard Edition* 8 (London: Hogarth Press, 1960).

———. *The Libido Theory and Narcissism*. *The Standard Edition* 18 (London: Hogarth Press, 1964).

———. *Moses and Monotheism*. *The Standard Edition* 23 (London: Hogarth Press, 1964).

———. "A Special Type of Choice of Object Made by Men." In *Contributions to the Psychology of Love*. *The Standard Edition* 11 (London: Hogarth Press, 1957).

Gili, Jean. *Le Cinéma italien*. Paris: Union Générale d'Editions, 1978.

Girard, René. *La Violence et le sacré*. Paris: Grasset, 1972.

Godard, Jean-Luc. *Jean-Luc Godard par Jean-Luc Godard*. Edited by Jean Narboni. Paris: Jean Belfond, 1968.

Greene, Naomi. "Gramsci, Pasolini: The Role of the Intellectuals and the Organization of Culture." *Praxis*, in press.

Henderson, Brian. *A Critique of Film Theory*. New York: E. P. Dutton, 1980.

Jung, C. G. *Dreams*. Princeton, N.J.: Princeton University Press, 1974.

Lacan, Jacques. "Le Stade du miroir." *Revue française de psychanalyse* 13 (1949): 449–55.

Laplanche, Jean. *Life and Death in Psychoanalysis*. Translated by Jeffrey Mehlman. Baltimore: Johns Hopkins University Press, 1976.

Lewin, B. D. *Dreams and the Uses of Regression*. New York: International University Press, 1958.

———. "Sleep, Mouth and the Dream Screen." *Psychoanalytic Quarterly* 15 (1934): 416–25.

Lotman, Iouri. *Esthétique et sémiotique du cinéma*. Paris: Editions sociales, 1977.

Matter, Jean. "Le Mythe de Narcisse dans *L'Orphée* de Jean Cocteau." *Psyche* 6 (1951): 250–52.

McDougall, Joyce. *Plaidoyer pour une certaine anormalité*. Paris: Gallimard, 1978.

———. "Primal Scene and Sexual Perversion." *International Journal of Psycho-analysis* 53 (1972): 371–84.

———. *Théâtres de Je*. Paris: Gallimard, 1982.

Mehlman, Jeffrey. *Repetition and Revolution*. Berkeley: University of California Press, 1977.

Metz, Christian. *Le Signifiant imaginaire*. Paris: Union Générale d'Editions, 1977.

Miller, J. Hillis. "Ariachne's Broken Woof." *Georgia Review* 31, no. 1 (Spring 1977): 44–60.

Moravia, Alberto. *The Conformist*. Translated by Angus Davidson. London: Secker and Warburg, 1953.

Normand, Jean. "Le Poète, image de l'étranger: l'Orphée de Tennessee Williams." *French American Review* 4, no. 2 (Fall 1980): 72–79.

Perry, John W. *Lord of the Four Quarters*. New York: Braziller, 1966.

Plato, *The Republic*. In *Collected Dialogues*, trans. Lane Cooper, ed. E. Hamilton and H. Cairns. New York: Pantheon, 1961.

Pontalis, J.-B. *Après Freud*. Paris: Gallimard/Idées, 1968.

———. "Dream as Object." *International Review of Psychoanalysis* 1 (1973): 130.

———. *Entre le rêve et la douleur*. Paris: Gallimard, 1977.

Post-Impressionism: Cross Currents in European Painting. London: Weidenfeld and Nicolson, 1979.

Poulet, Georges. "Stendhal and Time." *Revue international de philosophie* 16 (1962): 395–412.

Rank, Otto. *The Double*. Translated by Harry Tucker, Jr. New York: New American Library, 1979.

Rosolato, Guy. *Essais sur le symbolique*. Paris: Gallimard, 1969.

Rothenstein, John. *Francis Bacon: Catalogue raisonné*. London: Thames and Hudson, 1964.

Rycroft, Charles. *The Innocence of Dreams*. New York: Pantheon, 1979.

Said, Edward. *Beginnings*. New York: Basic Books, 1975.

Schwartz, Murray. "Critic, Define Thyself." In *Psychoanalysis and the Question of the Text*, ed. Geoffry Hartman. Baltimore: Johns Hopkins University Press, 1978.

Serres, Michel. *Jouvences sur Jules Verne*. Paris: Editions de Minuit, 1974.

Sontag, Susan. *On Photography*. New York: Dell, 1973.

Stendhal. *The Charterhouse of Parma*. Translated by C. K. Scott Moncrief. London: Chatto and Windus, 1951.

Tassone, Aldo. *Le Cinéma italien parle*. Paris: Edilig, 1982.

Todorov, Tzvetan. *Introduction à la littérature fantastique*. Paris: Seuil/Points, 1970.

Winnicott, D. W. *The Maturational Processes and the Facilitating Environment*. London: Hogarth Press, 1965.

———. "Mirror-Role of Mother and Family in Child Development." In *The Predicament of the Family*, ed. P. Lomas. London: Hogarth Press, 1967.

Wollen, Peter. "Eisenstein's Aesthetics." In *Signs and Meaning in the Cinema*. Bloomington: Indiana University Press, 1972.

———. "The English Cine-Structuralists." *Film Comment* 9, no. 3 (May/June 1973).

INDEX

	DATE DUE		